HOW TO
PAINT
YOUR CAR

David H. Jacobs, Jr.

MBI Publishing
Company

First published in 1991 by MBI Publishing Company, PO Box 1, 729 Prospect Avenue, Osceola, WI 54020-0001 USA

The information in this book is true and complete to the best of our knowledge. All recommendations are made without any guarantee on the part of the author or Publisher, who also disclaim any liability incurred in connection with the use of this data or specific details.

We recognize that some words, model names and designations, for example, mentioned herein are the property of the trademark holder. We use them for identification purposes only. This is not an official publication.

MBI Publishing Company books are also available at discounts in bulk quantity for industrial or sales-promotional use. For details write to Special Sales Manager at Motorbooks International Wholesalers & Distributors, 729 Prospect Avenue, PO Box 1, Osceola, WI 54020-0001 USA.

Library of Congress Cataloging-in-Publication Data
Jacobs, David H.
    How to paint your car / David H. Jacobs, Jr.
        p. cm.
    ISBN 0-87938-523-5
    1. Automobiles—Painting. I. Title
TL154.J226   1991
629.26—dc20   91-9365

On the front cover: A beautiful 1956 Chevrolet Bel Air convertible owned by Danchuk Manufacturing, Inc., of Santa Ana, California. *Randy Leffingwell*

On the back cover: Terry Van Hee of Newlook Autobody in Kirkland, Washingon, carefully sprays paint under a taillight assembly. To the right, this diagram from PPG Industries, Inc., shows why spray paint nozzles must always remain perpendicular to the surfaces on which they are spraying.

Printed in the United States

Contents

Acknowledgments

Although their names will appear throughout this book, I would like to thank the following people for being so helpful and patient during interviews and photo sessions conducted while working to complete this project. Their enthusiastic attitudes and professional demeanor were most appreciated.

First, I want to thank Dan Mycon, owner of Newlook Autobody in Kirkland, Washington. Along with being a true professional, his avid interest in automobiles is refreshing. He spent a great deal of time explaining the ins and outs of auto painting and the chemistry involved. He took extra time to explain various trade secrets and never hesitated to help out whenever possible. He was also a terrific host during the numerous photo sessions conducted at his shop. I also want to thank Dan's wife Kathryn Mycon for her patience.

Terry Van Hee is a professional auto painter at Newlook. Like Mycon, he has amassed a great deal of technical auto paint knowledge over the years. It was easy to get him into conversations about any number of auto paint topics. I very much appreciate his expertise and the time he took to explain the intricacies of his trade.

Todd K. Shrewsbury is also a professional painter for Newlook. Just a few minutes with him will convince anybody that he likes painting cars. He was most helpful during photo sessions by posing for pictures and explaining work maneuvers under way. Jeff Lund, owner of Jeff's Quality Auto Glass in Bellevue, Washington, does a lot of work for Newlook Autobody, as well as several other professional bodyshops. He provided some interesting insights into the world of automotive window glass. I am grateful for his time and patience.

Jim Poluch and Christine Collins are advertising executives for The Eastwood Company, Malvern, Pennsylvania. They were very helpful and supportive by supplying auto paint tools and equipment, photos and valuable technical information regarding the operational use and maintenance of each item. I appreciate their spirit and enthusiasm.

Tim Murdock, manager of Wesco Autobody Supply in Kirkland, Washington, has been around the auto paint business for a long time. His experience proved quite valuable as he answered lots of questions while allowing photo sessions in his store. Gayl Smith and Colley Matheny, also from Wesco, provided many informative tips regarding color selection and paint system compatibility.

Dennis Laursen was an auto painter for twenty years before switching to the autobody paint and supply jobber arena as a representative for Bel-Tech Auto Paint of Bellevue, Washington. He provided some interesting observations from both painter and jobber perspectives. His deep concern for overall painter safety is admirable and acknowledged. I want to thank him and Brian Keck, manager of Bel-Tech, for letting me spend time at their store to take pictures.

Linda Toncray, advertising manager for the Automotive Products, Coatings and Resins division of PPG Industries, Inc., Strongsville, Ohio, provided a wealth of technical information pertaining to the chemistry and application techniques required for automotive painting. I very much appreciate her support. Likewise, I want to thank the following individuals and companies for supplying much-needed information: George P. Auel from BASF Corporation, Dearborn, Michigan; Thomas P. Speakman from E. I. DuPont De Nemours & Company, Wilmington, Delaware; Alan B. Abbott from Metalflake Corporation, Haverhill, Massachusetts; and Jon Kosmoski from the House of Kolor, Minneapolis, Minnesota.

Janna Jacobs was most helpful by providing a car that needed paint work after collision repairs were completed. She was also instrumental in helping to organize, label and sort hundreds of photographs with their captions, as well as hundreds of pages of text. Her support and encouragement are most appreciated.

Finally, I have to thank Tim Parker, Barbara Harold, Michael Dregni, Greg Field and Mary LaBarre of Motorbooks International for their continued support and editorial assistance. They make writing books worthwhile experiences.

Introduction

When automobiles made their debut into our mechanized and somewhat mobile world, they were so unique that their color was of least importance. Paint was applied to car bodies solely to help prevent rust and corrosion on sheet metal. If it were not for oxidation problems associated with bare steel, automotive paint may have never been developed.

As more and more auto makers began manufacturing cars and other motor vehicles, competition became keen. Different bodystyles were designed, performance features improved and various comfort options made available in hopes to entice customers to purchase one make or model over another.

In a relatively short time, inventive auto engineers and sales professionals realized that customers wanted more than just a means of transportation. In essence, they wanted their automobiles to be unique, different than the cars driven by their neighbors or friends. It was discovered that, although particular makes and models could be identical in design and accessory options, body color could make them appear uniquely different, at least from a visual perspective.

Before long, cars were rolling out of factories with all sorts of colors and color combinations. Two-tone designs came out with fenders one color and bodies another. Later, systems were worked out where two tones could be economically applied to actual car bodies, resulting in one predominant color flowing along specific body lines and another complementing the first with a more subtle tint filling in other spaces. The 1955 through 1957 Chevrolet models are excellent examples of two-tone designs where body trim along their sides serve as a breaking point between two distinct colors.

It would be unfair to ignore the paint developments of maverick auto enthusiasts throughout the years. Not satisfied with stock paint colors or designs provided by auto manufacturers, these people went out on their own to develop new auto paint colors and bold applications. Through their efforts, manufacturers realized the significance of automotive paint patterns and colors to customer satisfaction and eventually offered larger and larger varieties of color and custom paint options. Likewise, auto paint manufacturers steadily continue research to the point where over 50,000 different colors are now on file.

Along with the advent of so many different colors, the chemical makeup of automotive paint products has changed dramatically. Tim Murdock, manager of Wesco Autobody Paint and Supply, says that auto paint has changed more in the last two years than it has in the last twenty. New, high-tech paints have been developed which are fast drying, durable and more resistant to airborne pollutants and other hazards than any automotive paint ever used before. Dan Mycon, owner of Newlook Autobody, agrees. He goes a step further to say that these new paint products are easy to apply and just about bullet-proof when it comes to long-lasting shine and overall longevity.

However, these products are not without drawbacks. Hardening agents used to help them be so rugged and durable contain certain chemicals, like isocyanates, which are hazardous when inhaled or absorbed through the skin. Their use requires painters to wear positive-pressure respirators, rubber gloves, hoods and coveralls to ensure maximum personal safety and protection. In addition, improper paint, reducer and hardener mixtures could easily render blends grossly inadequate, possibly to the point where they will not spray uniformly or bond to surfaces securely. Users must follow paint product mixing instructions and application procedures closely to be sure that mixtures conform to manufacturers' implied standards and their own desired coverage expectations.

To say the least, a lot of automotive painting operations have changed in the last few years. Conscientious auto enthusiasts can still paint their cars with excellent results, but have to be aware of specific mixing and application processes. One-, two- and three-step paint systems provide beautiful paint finishes with deep, lustrous shines, but must be applied on top of surfaces that are properly prepared, according to explicit application instructions.

Pearl and metallic additives have become manufacturers' paint options on many newer cars. Quality touchup operations for minor body repairs or finish blemishes on these, though, could require entire car sides be repainted from headlight to taillight. Minor repair touchups for other paint products are generally much less complicated, although specific procedures must be followed to achieve quality results.

Professional autobody painters spend more time learning about specific paint systems than ever before. They have to be well-versed in a variety of different systems in order to accomplish quality paint work on all sorts of auto makes and models. On the other hand, nonprofessionals with just one or two cars needing paint work have only to concentrate on the prevalent characteristics of one paint system at a time to achieve professional results.

In addition, plenty of technical help is generally available from local autobody paint and supply store jobbers. Automotive paint products are their business, and conscientious jobbers generally pride themselves by staying up to date on the latest technological advances in the auto paint industry. If need be, one could even seek assistance from a professional autobody painter to help solve puzzling problems, even if a nominal fee was involved.

Repairing nicks and scratches, painting a panel or two and even effecting complete paint jobs should carry with them degrees of enjoyment and an overall sense of personal achievement and satisfaction. You must not expect to become a professional auto painter overnight, nor should you anticipate achieving perfect results the first time you pick up a spray paint gun. But, if you read and follow instructions, listen to advice and practice on an old hood or trunk lid, you should become proficient enough at autobody painting to be able to paint your car or truck with professional results and long-lasting quality.

1

Automotive Painting Defined

Paint may be applied to automobile bodies in more than one way, depending upon the job at hand. Initially, of course, paint is sprayed on car bodies at the factory. Later, after a car or truck has experienced some road miles, nicks are touched up with small brushes attached to caps on bottles of touch-up paint. Material from spray cans might be applied to blemishes on urethane bumper faces and even used to black out trim pieces or other small body items. Collision damage repair generally consists of panels or sections being repainted with conventional spray paint guns or High Volume Low Pressure (HVLP) units (more on those later).

The techniques and products used to apply automotive paint are determined by the type of coverage needed and the condition of existing surface material. To achieve a visually acceptable, compatible and durable paint job, whether it be a repair or complete repaint, you have to use prod-

Most automotive body repair work requires spray painting with production paint guns or High Volume Low Pressure (HVLP) systems. However, small items, like this Chevrolet emblem, can be satisfactorily touched up or repainted with quality paint from spray cans. Especially during cooler weather, warm cans of spray paint in a sink of lukewarm water before painting. This helps all of the material's ingredients to mix thoroughly and gives propellant its maximum power. Do not heat spray cans over their recommended safety temperatures, which are clearly indicated on labels.

Pete Noyes' 1941 Plymouth is flanked by Dan Mycon's 1939 Buick and 1948 Chevrolet. All three cars were originally spray painted at the factory in stock colors available during their era. Although in various stages of restoration and customization at this point, they will eventually be sprayed with newer high-tech paint products which requires they be stripped to bare metal so that all of the components in the paint system will be totally compatible.

Mycon is using a high-speed rotary sander and 36 grit sanding disc to remove accumulations of paint, rust and old plastic filler from Noyes' 1941 Plymouth. Painters spend more time preparing automobiles for paint than they do painting them. Especially with the newer types of paint undercoats and topcoats, it is important that all contaminants be removed from body surfaces before they are painted. Sander and face shield courtesy of The Eastwood Company.

ucts that are designed to be used over existing paint finishes or undercoat preparations.

Terry Van Hee, professional painter for New-look Autobody, estimates that 70 percent of his time is dedicated to preparation tasks, while only 30 percent is actually spent applying paint. With that in mind, it is important to understand that automobile painting entails much more than just spraying paint. It is a combination of surface preparation, undercoat applications, sanding and then, finally, a controlled method of spray paint application.

Determining the Type of Paint on Your Vehicle

Before the advent of high-tech urethane paint products, cars were painted with either enamel or lacquer products. Each had its own distinct characteristics. Enamels were quick and easy, generally covering in one or two coats and not requiring any clear coats or rubbing out. Lacquer, on the other hand, required multiple color coats and clear coats, but allowed imperfections to be easily rubbed out and quickly repainted because its fast drying time afforded painters the opportunity to fix blemishes almost immediately.

Although both paint products offer painters specific benefits, they cannot be used together on car bodies because they are not compatible. It would be all right, under proper conditions, to spray enamel over lacquer when surfaces are properly prepared, but lacquer applied over enamel will almost always result in wrinkling or other severe finish damage. This is because the solvent base for lacquer paint (lacquer thinner) is much too potent for the rather soft materials used in enamel products.

Product compatibility factors are also extremely important today. This is not confined to just enamel, lacquer or urethane bases. Every product in an entire paint system must be compatible with the surface material to which it will be applied, as well as with every other product used in the system. For example, using a PPG reducer with a BASF hardener in a DuPont paint product is asking for trouble. Because the individual products were not designed as parts of a single compatible paint system, the color, adhesion and surface flow of that combination could be adversely affected. More about paint chemistry and compatibility is covered in chapter 2.

Before arbitrarily purchasing paint for your car, you have to determine what type of material currently exists on the vehicle's surface: enamel, lacquer or urethane. For those cars still hosting factory paint jobs, specific paint codes are listed on their identification tags. In addition, autobody paint and supply store jobbers can determine the exact type of paint and color from the vehicle identification number (VIN). This makes material identification easy when planning to match existing paint.

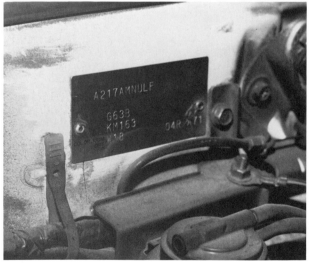

This is a typical vehicle identification (ID) plate. On this Mitsubishi coupe, it is located on the firewall. At the bottom left corner, you can see, "Color Trim Opt.—W18." That number designates the original factory paint code which indicates the type and color paint product used during production. Painters refer to numbers like this to determine which paint material and color to use when completely repainting the identical color or making spot repairs.

At the top of this Mazda pickup truck ID plate, just to the right of center, the paint code L3 is imprinted. Once again, it is found on a firewall. Each manufacturer locates ID plates in various locations. Some are found on radiator supports, others on driver's doorjambs. If an actual ID plate paint code has been destroyed, jobbers at autobody paint and supply stores can also decipher original paint codes from Vehicle Identification Numbers (VINs), as seen here on the center of the plate.

If your car or truck has been repainted with a paint type or color different from its original factory job, you will have to obtain paint code numbers from a paint can used during the repaint or from some other source, like the painter who completed the job. Hopefully, that person kept track of this information and will make it available to you.

Should you not be able to determine specific paint codes or information relating to the type of paint used on your car, you will have to test an inconspicuous spot on the vehicle body with lacquer thinner; you could also test a spot on an area already slated for repaint. Dab a clean, white cloth with lacquer thinner and rub a spot of paint. If color comes off immediately or the spot begins to wrinkle, the paint type is enamel. Should color wipe off onto the cloth after vigorous rubbing, lacquer paint is present. If nothing wipes off, the paint is probably a type of urethane.

To determine if finishes include coats of clear paint over their base color, sand an inconspicuous spot with 600 grit or finer sandpaper. White sanding residue indicates the existence of a clear coat finish, whereas a color residue denotes the lack of any clear to prove that the body was painted with a color material only.

Too much emphasis cannot be placed on determining the type of paint currently existing on the surface of your car before applying new coats of fresh paint. About the only exceptions would be those vehicle bodies that have been stripped to bare metal in preparation for complete new paint system applications. If you are still unsure about the type of paint on your car after this test, or if you have any other related questions or problems, consult a professional autobody paint and supply store jobber. Be up-front and attentive with that person in order to receive definitive answers and patient assistance.

Nick and Scratch Repair

Minor nicks and scratches can sometimes be polished or buffed out. They must be shallow and expose paint at their deepest point. Should damage have occurred to the extent that primer or bare metal is visible, new paint must be applied.

An easy and inexpensive way to repair nicks involves the use of touchup paint. Small bottles of stock factory colors are commonly available at autobody paint and supply stores and a number of auto parts houses. Mostly supplied for newer cars, you match the paint code on your vehicle's ID tag to that on touchup paint containers. Application is made by simply using a small brush attached to the bottle's cap or with an artist's fine paintbrush. For years, auto enthusiasts have successfully used the clean end of paper matchsticks to apply touchup paint. The choice is yours.

It is imperative to cover nicks as soon as possible, especially when bare metal is exposed. Oxi-

dation quickly attacks bare metal to begin a rust and corrosion process. Like a cancer, oxidation spreads undetected beneath paint until damage is so extensive that flakes of paint peel off at random. Before the advent of handy touchup paint bottles, auto enthusiasts applied dabs of clear fingernail polish to nicks in efforts to protect bare metal and stem the progress of oxidation, rust and corrosion.

Compared to tiny nicks, long, deep scratches may pose more serious problems. Although minor scratches may be touched up in basically the same fashion as nicks, long strokes with a touchup paintbrush may be too rough or noticeable. Depending on the color and type of paint finish, you may be best off to carefully sand scratches smooth and then feather in new layers of fresh paint with an aerosol can of touchup (available at some auto parts stores and autobody paint and supply outlets) or a regular spray paint device. These problems are covered more fully in chapter 7.

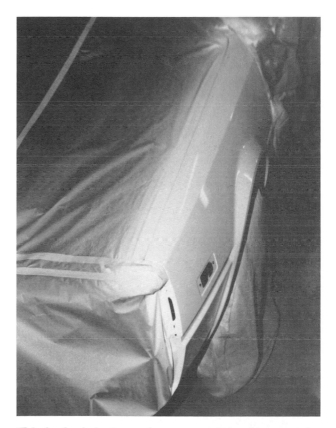

This fender is just one of many panels used to comprise an entire vehicle. For certain repair spot painting endeavors, manufacturers suggest that entire panels be sprayed in lieu of just repairing spots. The type of paint system used and the amount of repaint area involved determine whether or not entire panels require complete repainting. Note that the grille, bumper, headlight and side light were removed to facilitate preparation and paint work. Also, notice the amount of masking needed to provide optimum overspray protection for the rest of the car.

Panel Painting

With the possible exception of a few special automobiles, most vehicles are comprised of a number of separate sections welded or bolted together to make single motorized units. Professional autobody people generally refer to these sections as panels, for example, quarterpanels and rear body panels. In addition, cars and trucks have roofs, hoods, fenders, doors and so on.

In a lot of body collision or simple repaint situations, painters have to spray complete panels in lieu of spraying specific spots. The determination of whether to spot paint or cover entire panels depends upon the type and style of the existing paint finish, size of the repair area and the ability to blend new paint into the surrounding body paint area.

For example, spot painting a number of minor ding repairs scattered over an entire hood panel

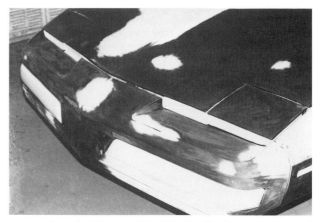

The paint finish on this Firebird's hood, nose and fenders was damaged by a vandal who scraped it with a key. Repairs are evident by the light shaded areas of primer-surfacer application and sanding work. The rest of the paint finish was scuffed with a fine Scotch-Brite pad. Repainting just the repaired spots would make the overall surface finish look blotchy. A complete repaint is required, therefore, to make the job look uniform and professional.

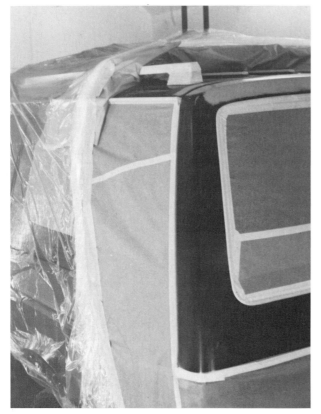

Body repairs were conducted on the top part of this minivan hatchback. The area around the repair was masked, and the rest of the van was covered with a sheet of plastic to guard against overspray. Because the paint system on this van incorporates a clear coat, spot painting will include clear coat coverage over existing painted areas adjacent to the repair in order to maximize blending efforts. As a result, repaint work will not exhibit noticeable edges to make the hatchback appear factory fresh, the goal of every painter.

Since damage was confined to the rear corner of this quarterpanel and because the paint system used on the car allows, repainting will be limited to color coats over the repair area extending only a little into the surrounding area, as opposed to completely repainting the vehicle's side and rear sections. However, clear paint must be sprayed over the entire quarterpanel, up the C-pillar and along the full bumper length to maximize overall blending efforts. With a different paint system, blending might only require paint be feathered out a few inches past a required area.

would probably turn out to look something like a spotted leopard. This work would be much easier and the finish look much more uniform and professional, if the entire hood was completely prepared and painted all at one time. The same holds true for other panels in need of more than just a spot or two of new paint.

Some situations allow for the painting of just parts of panels, as opposed to entire units. Such would be lower panel sections up to featured grooves, ridges or trim lines on doors, fenders and quarterpanels. Special graphics or vinyl stripes might also serve as perimeters to cordon off particular areas, allowing for partial panel repaints.

Color blending and uniform paint feathering is of utmost importance when painting panels. Your ultimate goal is to apply paint in such a way that no definitive edges are visible, making that area appear as if it had never been repaired or repainted. To accomplish this, some single-panel repaint jobs require that adjacent panels on either side be lightly sprayed with feather coats of paint. This is done to help a primary painted panel's bright new finish blend in with surrounding panels.

Complete Paint Jobs

When Van Hee mentioned that 70 percent of his work involved surface preparation and only 30 percent related to actual paint application, he was referring to partial repaints, like one or two panel jobs. For complete paint jobs, he estimates that 95 percent of his work is concentrated on surface preparation and masking, while only 5 percent is spent using a spray paint gun.

This may be an area of confusion to many people who do not understand that the condition of body surfaces prior to paint application can directly affect the outcome of paint jobs. In other words, every "nib" of dirt, sanding scratch, pinhole or other tiny blemish is magnified to a great extent after paint has been applied over it.

Complete paint jobs call for all exterior body trim to be removed. You should take off door handles, trim pieces, mirrors, emblems, badges, key locks, radio antennas and anything else attached to your car's body. This effort alleviates the need for intricate masking and will prevent accidental overspray onto them as a result of inadequate masking. Likewise, it allows paint to cover all vehicle body parts evenly and greatly reduces the chance of paint build-up or thin coat coverage on areas obstructed with handles, adornments and add-ons.

Removing body trim and accessories will require the use of hand tools to loosen nuts, bolts and screws. Other pieces held in place by adhesives or

The entire rear section was repainted a stock factory color after body repairs were completed. No noticeable signs of repainting are evident as blending techniques were carefully employed. The color coat was lightly feathered into forward sections of both quarterpanels by thinning the last few ounces of paint in the gun cup with three times the normal amount of required reducer. This softened up existing paint just enough to allow a hint of new color to penetrate and tint the surface for a perfect blend.

Auto enthusiast Art Wentworth's 1970 Buick GS 455 has just been completely repainted. Notice that all exterior accessories were removed before painting began. This greatly reduced the amount of intricate masking that would have been required, and allowed the painter to maintain excellent coverage without having to maneuver around masked obstacles. It also guarantees that exterior parts will not suffer the slightest hint of overspray anywhere on their surface. The roof will stay masked until all rubbing out and polishing work is complete.

Not all emblems, badges and trim are secured to body panels in the same fashion. Some are held on by clips, others with nuts or adhesive. Sometimes, you just have to pry on an edge and look behind them to determine how they are attached. Be very careful, as too much prying force will break plastic pieces or cause their mounting pins to snap off. This emblem is secured with adhesive. After it has been painted, old adhesive residue will be removed and new material applied.

As you can tell, the key vandal struck more than just the hood and front end on this Firebird. Mycon and Terry Van Hee spent considerable time preparing these surfaces for paint. In the paint booth, it is masked and ready for a coat of adhesion promoter. After the appropriate amount of time has passed, according to the adhesion promoter's label, paint will be sprayed. It is important to note that those body areas exhibiting otherwise good paint were scuffed to remove their shine and make for a much better paint bonding surface.

double-backed tape may require the use of an adhesive remover product. You must take your time and remove items in a controlled manner so that none of them are broken during dismantling.

Once you start taking parts off of your car you will probably be surprised at the amount collected. In addition to door handles, key locks and trim, you'll be removing light assemblies, reflectors, grille pieces, bumpers, license plates, mud guards and a lot more. Therefore, develop a systematic plan of organized parts storage before haphazardly tossing parts all over your garage or workshop.

Have plenty of sturdy boxes on hand to store related parts as they are taken off of specific body areas. Keep fender parts together in one box, door items in another and so forth. This way, when you start replacing them after paint work has been completed, you will be able to quickly and easily locate all necessary body and trim pieces, as well as their fastening nuts, bolts, screws, clips and so on.

Expect to spend plenty of time sanding every square inch of your car or truck's body surface before picking up a spray paint gun. All imperfec-

tions must be smoothed or repaired to give paint a blemish-free bonding base. By itself, paint is not thick enough to hide sand scratch swelling or pinholes. For those problems, products like primer-surfacer are used which also have to be sanded and smoothed to perfection if paint is expected to lay down evenly and be visually attractive.

Color Selection

Choosing the right color for blending in repaint areas on newer cars is easy. You simply go by the vehicle's ID tag color code or let an autobody paint and supply store jobber decipher that information from its VIN.

However, selecting a new color for the complete repaint of a vehicle might not be quite as easy. BASF Corporation already has 50,000 different automotive paint colors on file, and its engineers are kept busy using computer science and experience in graphic arts to develop new hues. Wesco Autobody Supply has the ability to mix any one of 29,000 different colors, including those stock blends used on vehicles dating back to 1929.

Tim Murdock, veteran auto painter and manager of Wesco Autobody Supply, says the days of walking into a store and simply asking for a quart of red paint are gone. Today, there are easily over 600 different shades of red, and customers have to be a lot more specific. They need to pick out a certain color chip from any number of color cata-

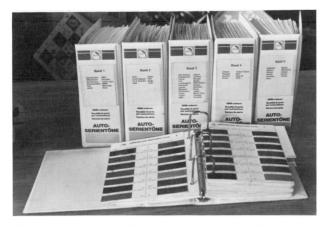

These are just a few of the color chip catalogs featured at most autobody paint and supply stores. As indicated by the logo at the top of each book, these are Glasurit manuals which list stock color chips and codes for just about every automobile make and model on the road. PPG, DuPont and other major paint manufacturers also provide paint and supply stores with similar catalogs. In addition to matching the stock color on your car, you could also pick out new colors for cars that will receive complete new paint jobs.

logs or have a particular paint code number available. Most other colors are equally as varied.

Dan Mycon, owner of Newlook Autobody, has recognized the evolution of customlike colors appearing on new cars as stock items from the factory. To help his customers decide on new paint colors, he suggests they visit local automobile dealerships.

When customers find a car or truck with a paint scheme that satisfies them, all they have to do is copy the vehicle's numerical paint code and bring it to Mycon. He uses the microfiche machine in his paint room to decipher the proper mixing solution for that color, or has an autobody supply store deliver it to him. In lieu of actual paint codes, proper paint mixing formulas may be located on microfiche or computer files with just the year, make and model of most any newer vehicle. Customers can confirm particular colors by comparing that information with corresponding color chips from paint color catalogs.

Along with color selection, you may want to investigate the option of special custom additives to the new paint that will be applied to your car. Metallics have improved since their heyday in the sixties. Now, instead of large, bold flakes loudly accenting a car body, you can add specific doses of tiny micro flakes to make an otherwise bland color light up to a magnificent and brilliant finish. A good number of newer cars are adorned with tiny metallics in their paint finish. You can see them firsthand on automobiles at almost any new car dealership or on color chips at your local autobody paint and supply store.

Although it displays years of use, the microfiche machine in Newlook Autobody's paint mixing room works just fine to light up disks displaying exact mixing procedures for all sorts of automotive paint colors. Specific paint codes are listed under vehicle year and model information numbers. From there, additional data lists specific units of paint weight, in as low as tenths of a gram, which must be mixed together to arrive at definite colors.

An entire series of PPG paint tints are located on a special rack which includes automatic stir mechanisms attached to the can lids. Each morning, Mycon turns on the stirring machine to keep paint in mixed condition. Likewise, painters allow the machine to operate for about fifteen minutes before using any paint in a blend mixture. Grams of these products are poured into base paints as prescribed by microfiche paint code data in order to reach specific color tints.

The addition of pearl additives is another means by which you can make a solid color look custom. In years past, fish scales were used to give stock colors a pearlescent appearance that made them look different shades when viewed from various angles. In essence, a vehicle that might appear white when viewed straight on, may offer a bright pink or blue shade when seen from a lower angle or looked upon from the front or back.

Today's pearls are made of plastic (Mylar). These tiny chips may be painted on one side while remaining clear on the other. Depending on the pearl color selected and the angle of light reflection from one's viewpoint, these paint jobs can offer truly unique perspectives. A definite drawback to pearl colors, however, may be that repaint efforts cannot be limited to just single spots or panels. Manufacturers frequently advise painters to completely repaint entire vehicle sides from headlight to taillight that suffer damaged pearl paint finishes. This is so each part of the full side will display identical tints from all directions and not cause clouds of varying degrees between panels or parts of panels.

Because there are so many different automotive paint colors to choose from, it may become confusing or downright frustrating trying to pick just one dynamic color for your car. Have patience. Look at issues of car and truck magazines to get ideas of the colors other enthusiasts are putting on their cars. Attend car shows and talk to fellow car buffs about how they arrived at certain color schemes used on their vehicles.

Many times, especially for older classic and vintage automobiles, certain color schemes prove more visually appealing than others. While a pink 1957 Thunderbird may be a head turner, an equally pink 1956 Oldsmobile might look a bit out of place. Car guys, like Mycon, have a knack for envisioning the outcome of cars painted specific colors. From their experience around bodyshops and car shows, and through reading hundreds and maybe thousands of auto magazines, they know which colors look best and are in style for most types of vehicles, from sports cars to pickups and late-model sedans to classic coupes.

True auto enthusiasts can be found in a variety of places. One of the best is through car clubs. Members have keen interests in automobiles—why else would they belong to such an organization? Many clubs specialize in certain types of vehicles, like 1955 through 1957 Chevrolets, 1960s vintage Corvettes, all Mustangs, particular Ford F-100s, MGs and so on. If yours is an older project car that is finally ready for paint and you find yourself in a quandary as to what color to paint it, locate a local car club whose members share an interest in the same make, model or general vintage. A few casual conversations with them should help you to at least narrow your color choices to a select few.

Talking with a Professional Auto Painter

Automobile owners with little or no knowledge of the autobody repair and paint business are frequently surprised at the cost for quality paint jobs. They have no idea of the amount of work involved during preparation stages before painting, nor of the cost for materials such as primers, sealers, reducers, hardeners and paint. Uninformed car owners have a difficult time understanding why some companies can paint cars for as little as $99.95, while other shops might charge as much as $3,500 for top-notch, complete paint jobs.

Should you decide to have a professional paint your car, remember that you get what you pay for. Outfits that specialize in cheap paint jobs cannot afford to spend a lot of time preparing or masking cars. Their business relies on volume. The more cars they paint, the more money they make. Therefore, sanding and masking work is normally minimal.

Close inspection of vehicles that have been repainted by inexpensive paint shops generally feature overspray on fenderwells, leaf springs, emblems, badges, window trim, spare tires under pickup truck beds and the like due to minimal masking. Rough surface spots may receive a quick pass or two with sandpaper, but extra time cannot

A good look at this Jeep Wagoneer fender indicates a lot of accessory features that must be accounted for in any repaint estimate. Depending upon the degree of repaint needs, by way of collision damage or vandalism, painters may have to plan for the removal and replacement of the fender flair, pinstripes, vinyl siding, trim borders, emblems, headlight, bumper and top grille piece. All of this takes time, and required replacement parts such as vinyl pinstripes and siding will figure into an overall parts and material package.

The amount of time and effort Mycon and Van Hee put into the preparation of this Firebird's body surface paid off with a smooth, uniform and good-looking paint job. Low-budget paint shops cannot afford to spend that much time on prep work and still be expected to keep customer costs down to just a few hundred dollars per job. Time is money and you get what you pay for. In this case, quality materials used on the job cost well over $400 and it took a full five days to complete the project, for an overall cost of $2,000. By the way, actual paint spraying took only about four hours, including the wait between flash times for each applied paint coat.

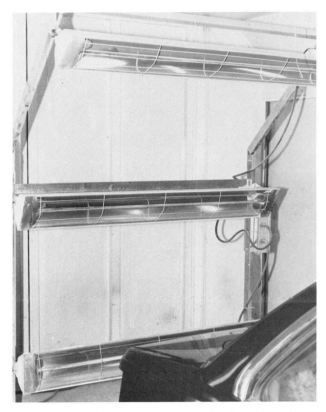

At Newlook Autobody, painters use this large heat lamp unit to help paint dry on cars faster to speed production time. The amount of electricity needed for its operation is staggering, while figured in as just a small part of the shop's total operating cost. Overhead factors like this have to be accounted for in professional painters' cost estimates. Do-it-yourself painters do not have to employ heat lamps for their projects, as overnight drying is sufficient for most paint systems.

be allotted for definitive sanding and feathering needs.

Now, should you want a much more thorough paint job than the one just described, and most people do, these shops can provide better quality service. This will, of course, cost you more. As far as paint is concerned, inexpensive paint shops are forced to use bulk supplies. Color choices are usually limited to the colors on hand in fifty-five gallon barrels. Frequently, shops like these will buy out paint manufacturers' supplies of discontinued colors at huge discounts. They pass this savings on to you. In many cases, enamel-based products are used because they cover in one or two coats and do not require rubbing out or polishing work afterward.

Auto paint shops that specialize in overall quality and customer satisfaction are vastly different than high-volume shops. You will have to pay more for their service, but your car or truck will be meticulously prepared and then painted with a high-quality, durable and long-lasting paint product. All exterior accessories will be removed, including bumpers and grille. Masking will be complete and work required after spray painting will be accomplished professionally.

Skeptics may still not completely understand the enormous difference between paint jobs that

cost only a few hundred dollars and those that may command up to $5,000. Simply put, professional paint technicians spend hours and hours sanding surfaces to perfection. Then they apply required coats of primer-surfacer to fill in tiny sand scratches and other minute blemishes. Those surfaces are also sanded to perfection.

Once the surface has been meticulously smoothed, coats of sealer are sprayed on to protect undercoats from absorbing potent solvents included in paint. Sufficient drying time must be allotted. Professionals often use high-intensity heat lamps to speed this process. These lamps use a tremendous amount of electricity which must be figured into estimates as part of overhead costs.

After that phase has been completed, color coats are applied and then cured with assistance from heat lamps. Depending upon the type of paint system used, clear coats might then be sprayed over the entire vehicle. Normally, three coats are enough. When clear has dried, painters carefully inspect car bodies for imperfections. Then 1000 to

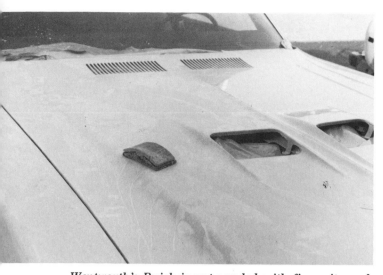

Wentworth's Buick is wet sanded with fine-grit sandpaper. This is a messy and time-consuming chore, but plenty worth the effort when end results are matched against those paint jobs where wet sanding or polishing is not carried out. Should a section require extensive wet sanding to smooth blemishes or remove imperfections, additional clear coats may have to be applied. Masking was taken off the windshield and side window so the painter could see while driving the car out of the paint booth to a sanding area.

1200 grit sandpaper is used to smooth blemishes, as needed, and additional coats of clear are applied.

Satisfied that their job has turned out correctly, painters buff entire vehicle bodies with fine polish and a soft buffing pad. After all of that has been done, parts still have to be replaced. Again, this takes time as gaskets and seals must be perfectly positioned in order to function as intended. Care must be taken so that parts are not bumped against newly painted finishes to cause nicks or scratches.

As if that were not enough, each vehicle is then detailed to perfection. I doubt many customers would pay their paint bill if glass, wheels, tires, weatherstripping and other parts of their car were dirty and covered with sanding dust when they arrived to pick it up at the shop. Like Mycon, most quality bodyshop owners insist their customers' cars be detailed before delivery. This way, not only do they get to enjoy a freshly painted car, they can relish the fact that it has been cleaned to perfection, to stand out, look crisp and be a pleasure to drive.

When shopping for a professional auto painter, be sure to ask if your car will be detailed before delivery. Ask if all exterior accessories will be removed for painting, and whether or not overspray to fenderwells and suspension assemblies will be removed or painted over. Be certain that

When shopping around for a quality auto paint facility, take notice of the business' location, tidiness and general appearance. Chances are, those places that take pride in their overall work environment also take pride in their work. You should be able to easily converse with estimators and get understandable answers to your questions. As indicated here, Mycon and his crew maintain a clean and pleasant store front and customer waiting area.

maximum attention will be given to masking, and that quality paint products will be used throughout the job.

Finding a professional auto paint shop with a reputable track record should not be too difficult. Word-of-mouth recommendations are generally reliable. If you know of friends or neighbors who have just had their car painted, ask them how they feel about the quality of service they received. You can talk to your auto insurance agent, fellow car enthusiasts, a local detailer or mechanic.

You might even ask the owner of a local specialty auto sales business. These folks are true auto enthusiasts, they have to be in order to stay up to date on the latest classic car trends and make the best deals when it comes to sales of classic and vintage automobiles. To them, a less than professional autobody shop is a nightmare. They expect to pay higher prices for quality work, but in return demand that work be of the highest caliber. Dealers in this business get a lot of money for the cars they sell. They know that quality $5,000 paint jobs can easily raise values of special automobiles by $6,000 or more.

Your telephone book's yellow pages are loaded with autobody repair and paint shop advertisements. Call a few of the shops to get a feel for their professionalism over the phone. As your list grows to three or four, take time to visit selected facilities to see firsthand what kind of operations they conduct. You should expect courteous and knowledgeable estimators and organized, well-lit, tidy work areas. Talk to estimators and ask direct questions. Get estimates from each shop before committing to one. At the end of the day, compare prices and select the shop that offered the best service for the most equitable price.

The Autobody Paint and Supply Store

Autobody paint and supply stores are in business to keep bodyshops adequately supplied in

To help autobody repair and paint shops determine estimates, many estimators rely on the Mitchell Collision Estimating Guide. *Subscribers receive updated versions of this manual every two months, or so. Inside, vehicles are displayed in segments, each with listed time frames that allot for the dismantling and replacement of body parts or assemblies. Based on this information, estimators can quickly tally the amount of time needed for specific repair or repaint jobs. This organized system also displays part replacement costs to help estimators calculate accurately.*

paint products, body repair materials and tools for both types of work. The jobbers who work in these stores are constantly updated with product information from manufacturers of paint and body repair supplies. Although some jobbers may never have actually painted cars, their technical knowledge of paint product usage is second to none.

Novice auto painters can learn a great deal from jobbers when both parties fully comprehend the paint project at hand. Be up-front and honest with the jobber. If possible, bring your car to the store's location so the jobber can see your project firsthand. This way, he or she can best recommend a proper paint system to use and supplies you will need to complete the job.

Now, don't expect jobbers to drop everything just to give you lessons in painting cars. Their primary job is to serve professional bodyshops, not teach auto painting. For the most part, Mondays and Fridays are their busiest days. Shop owners generally call in orders on Monday for supplies they will need for their week's work. On Fridays, shops may need special deliveries of materials needed to

Gayl Smith operates the paint computer at Wesco Autobody Supply. Information regarding paint codes keyed into the computer is quickly deciphered and then displayed on the monitor. Once Smith determines that the information shown is what's needed, she has it printed out. Printed copies include labels for paint cans describing exactly the kind of paint ordered, and a copy to be used by the person who mixes the paint blend. Over 29,000 different paint colors are included in the computer's memory banks.

complete jobs that customers expect to pick up that afternoon. So, plan to visit an autobody supply store during mid-week, when jobbers may have more time to converse with you.

In addition to stocking everything from paint guns to sandpaper, autobody paint and supply stores carry information sheets and application guides on almost all of the paint-related products they sell. This material is provided by paint manufacturers. You can get sheets on the use and application of primer-surfacers, sealers and three-step paint systems, as well as just about every other product you might ever put on your car's body. They are free, and you are advised to take one for every product you intend to use.

Autobody paint and supply stores can match almost any color of automotive paint. However, if you want a specific color that is not displayed in any color chart or paint chip catalog, realize that it will have to be made by hand using trial-and-error methods. Expect to pay a lot more for this service than for stock colors because of the added labor involved.

This situation arises when customers request a color match with a repainted car when there is no way to determine or they have no idea what color was used or who did the work. In those cases, jobbers simply ask customers to search through volumes of color chips until the closest match is found. Then, he or she works with specific tints until a suitable color is produced. Unless a paint chip can be found that perfectly matches the paint on that car, jobbers mix by hand until a match is

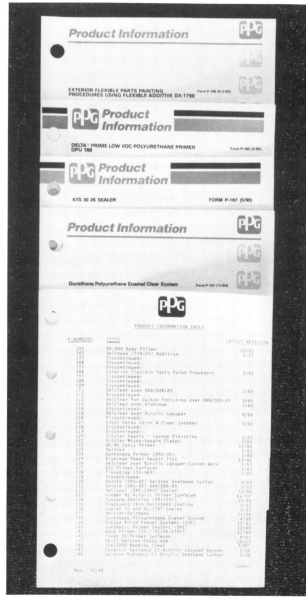

This is a very small sampling of the product information sheets provided to autobody paint and supply stores by PPG Industries with reference to just about every product they manufacture. Painters are able to obtain a great deal of information from these sheets and it is suggested you pick up material pertaining to every product you intend to use. Paint manufacturers like BASF, DuPont and Glasurit also provide stores with information sheets and application guides for all of their products. They are free for the asking and very helpful.

Colley Matheny, a branch manager for Wesco, mixes an order of paint according to color chip paint code information. Jobbers have to hand tint those special, non-stock orders by trial and error after specific blends are achieved through paint code instructions. This is done for customers who want to match the existing paint on their cars that have been repainted an unknown color. Customers select a color chip that matches best and then it is up to the jobber to fine-tune that blend to a perfect match. Special service like this costs more because of the amount of time the process requires.

accomplished, a process that may require hours and hours of work. This is why special, hand-matched colors cost a lot more than standard quantities of those colors whose formulas are stored in company computers.

Unless you have experience painting cars, you might ask your autobody paint and supply jobber how much sandpaper of which grit you'll need to properly prepare your car's finish for new paint. Sanding chores are different with each job, and fine-grit paper does not last as long as one might expect. Along with sandpaper, plenty of automotive paint masking tape and paper should be purchased. Two-inch tape works great for some chores, while ¾ in. and ⅛ in. works better for more detailed tasks.

By and large, your autobody paint and supply store jobber can be a fountain of information. Take advantage of this person's knowledge by being polite, courteous and asking intelligent questions. Be aware of the store's busiest hours and plan to visit during slack times.

Special Considerations

Automotive painting has surely become a high-tech business. Not only do painters have to be concerned about the finished product, they also must be keenly aware of personal safety hazards involved with potent chemicals used in paint bases and hardeners. Where filter masks proved to be health-conscious aids a few years ago, positive-pressure respirators are the state of the art now. Be aware of fire hazards, namely hot-water heater and home heating systems' pilot lights. Thinners and reducers are highly flammable, so be sure smoking and other sources of ignition are kept far away from your project.

Special paint systems utilizing metallics and pearls can be satisfactorily applied by novice painters if all label instructions and tips from application guides are followed. Take advantage of this wealth of information at your fingertips to make your paint job progress as expected.

Be sure to spend an adequate amount of time preparing your car or truck's surface for paint. Too many times, enthusiastic novice painters get ahead of themselves. They believe that a thick coat of paint will hide blemishes or flaws. Don't settle for that. Plan on spending a day or two just to prepare your car's body surface for paint. Be sure that the paint system you employ is compatible with surrounding paint. And, decide early on that you will practice on an old hood or trunk lid before starting work on your favorite automobile.

Metallic flakes are available in containers from which painters can add specific quantities to their special paint blends. Autobody paint and supply stores generally carry a variety of sizes and colors. Along with their purchase, users are advised to obtain information sheets or application guides that fully describe their mixing methods and spraying techniques. Do not touch metallic flakes with your hand, as skin oils can cause them to tarnish.

The hood and nose on this Firebird look great. Remember what it looked like just before painting with primer-surfacer patches and its scuffed finish? The only way you can expect your paint jobs to turn out this nice is to spend the required amount of time preparing body surfaces. Do not try to cut corners by haphazardly completing one phase and expecting the next procedure to cover up mistakes. Each job has its purpose and no other successive procedure can take its place.

Health & Safety Tips for PPG Products

GENERAL

PPG products are formulated to provide excellent quality and lasting beauty when properly applied. They are designed for application by professional, trained personnel who apply them using the proper equipment under controlled conditions in automotive, aircraft, and similar refinish operations. They are not intended for sale to the general public and should never be used on household items such as toys or furniture.

The best results will be obtained when the person applying these coatings is thoroughly familiar with the correct application procedures and techniques. Painters should also be familiar with and follow all applicable safety and health precautions. All chemicals may affect your health when you breathe their vapors, get them on your skin, or ingest them. The breathing of excessive amounts of volatile solvents or paint spray mists may produce effects such as drowsiness, lack of coordination, and irritation of the eyes, nose, and throat. Very heavy exposures may cause damage to the blood, lungs, liver, kidneys, and nervous system.

In addition, skin contact with thinners and spray mists may produce irritation, rashes, and allergic reactions.

Since the effect these chemicals may have on your body depends upon how they are used and how long you are exposed, safe handling of them is necessary and important for the prevention of these effects. Get specific details from your PPG salesman or jobber. Some general guidance in the safety and health area follows.

Material Safety Data Sheets — These forms detail product composition and precautionary information for all products which present a health or safety hazard. These and all other PPG technical bulletins are available through your sales representative.

Warning Labels — All PPG products carry warnings and precautionary information which must be read and understood by the user before application. Attention to all label precautions is essential to the proper use of the coating and for prevention of hazardous conditions.

CONTROL OF HAZARDS

Ventilation — Vapors and spray mists of PPG products should be controlled by local exhaust ventilation. Local exhaust systems, such as spray booths or spray rooms, remove these contaminants at their source before they can escape into the surrounding area where they could create safety and health hazards.

A spray booth is an enclosure with an open front or face and with mechanical exhaust designed to keep vapors and spray mist away from the painter. A spray room is an enclosed area equipped with a mechanical exhaust system. It is large enough to permit the painting of large objects such as cars and boats.

The mechanical exhaust system in a spray booth or a spray room draws the vapors and mists toward a collection system which may be wet (waterfall type) or dry (filter bank). Remember that to draw airborne contaminants away from the painter, the piece being sprayed must be placed between him and the exhaust grille. The painter should NEVER position himself between the workpiece and the exhaust, since this would draw the airborne vapors and mists into his face. The exhaust and collection system must be in operation during all spraying and drying operations, including the clean up of the spray area.

To be sure that the spray booth or room is functioning properly, it should be checked regularly for signs of clogging due to paint residue. The manufacturer should be able to provide an alarm which indicates that the airflow in the booth or room is too low. Consult the manufacturer for specific details in the proper operation of any ventilation system.

When sanding or using other abrasive methods while preparing surfaces for painting, local exhaust should be used to remove the dusts which are generated. If this is not possible, respiratory protective devices must be used to protect the lungs.

Respirators — As an added precaution, respirators can be used — and in cases where local exhaust ventilation is unavailable or inadequate, they *should* be used — to reduce the painter's exposure to thinner vapors and paint spray mists. Respirators act as a barrier between the painter's lungs and these airborne chemicals, filtering them out of the air before it is breathed. Thus, the painter does not breathe materials which might harm him.

Respirators are selected for their ability to protect against specific hazards. Some guidelines for choosing the correct respirator follow:

In outdoor or open areas, thinner vapors are diluted by natural air movement. Therefore, you should use NIOSH/MSHA* approved filter type respirators for removal of airborne mists generated during spraying. For restricted ventilation areas, where thinner vapors may accumulate, use NIOSH/MSHA approved paint spray respirators which are designed to purify the air by removing solid airborne particulates and organic vapors generated during spraying. When sandblasting or sanding for surface preparation, use NIOSH/MSHA approved respirators for protection against pneumoconiosis-producing (lung damaging) dusts. In confined areas where ventilation is inadequate, use NIOSH/MSHA approved pressure-demand or continuous flow-type atmosphere-supplying respirators or hoods. In all cases, read the respirator manufacturer's instructions and literature carefully. They provide important information: the types of contaminants against which the respirator is effective; how to properly fit and use the respirator; how to maintain it; and when to replace respirator parts, cartridges, and filters.

The National Institute for Occupational Safety and Health and the Mine Safety and Health Administration have joint responsibility for approval of all respiratory protection devices.

NOTE: Several PPG products, including, but not limited to, DELSTAR, DURETHANE, DELTRON and DURACRYL, may require the addition of isocyanate-containing additives before use. These additives, such as DELTHANE, require special handling and control. The isocyanates contained in these products are hazardous materials which may cause lung irritation and an allergic respiratory reaction. They should not be used by any person who has chronic (long-term) lung or breathing problems or who has ever had a reaction to isocyanates. These materials should be used only with adequate ventilation. Where overspray is present, a NIOSH/MSHA approved pressure-demand or continuous flow-type atmosphere (air) supplying respirator is recommended. Wear the respirator while spraying and until all vapors and mists are gone.

Other Personal Protective Equipment — Gloves, goggles, protective clothing, and other personal protective equipment function as physical barriers to protect the skin and eyes from contact with the product being used. Specific safety and health regulations regarding personal protective equipment are covered by the Occupational Safety and Health Act (29CFR1910 Subpart I).

Skin and eye protection must be selected on the basis of the hazards presented by the coating. For example, gloves of Viton® or butyl rubber will retard the penetration of most hydrocarbon solvents and should be used with products containing them. Similarly, chemical goggles, hoods, or both may be required to protect against hazardous materials that could get into the air by evaporation or spray, or could splash into the eyes.

The best source of information on personal protective equipment available in your area is the local safety supply company. Look under "Safety Equipment and Clothing" in the Business and Industrial Yellow Pages.

Safety Considerations — PPG products contain volatile solvents and, therefore, are flammable. Work areas must be properly designed for use and storage of flammable liquids and NO SMOKING is to be permitted. The quantity of flammable liquids stored in the spraying area should not exceed what is required for one day's use. Paint and solvent products should be kept away from all sources of ignition including heat, sparks, flame, motors, burners, heaters, pilot lights, and welding. Explosion-proof equipment is recommended in all areas where flammable liquids are handled. Static electricity generation by liquid transfer must be prevented by proper grounding of solvent containers. Clogged spray booth filters and paint-soaked rags present a hazard of spontaneous combustion. Filters should be changed when airflow becomes restricted; rags should be replaced frequently. Proper fire extinguishers and other fire extinguishing systems should be readily available when handling any flammable liquids. Facilities should be designed in accordance with the guidelines of the National Fire Protection Association and should meet the specifications of all applicable federal, state, and local fire codes. You should consult your insurance carrier for specific requirements in the area of fire protection.

Spraying equipment can be hazardous if used improperly. Spraying with airless or electrostatic methods may create a fire hazard since static electricity will be generated. Careful grounding and bending practices should be observed. The high pressures used in the airless spraying may inject coating into the skin causing serious injury requiring immediate medical treatment. Observe all precautionary safety measures recommended by the spray equipment manufacturer. When spraying coatings always wear approved eye protection.

Waste Disposal — All liquid (paints, thinners) and solid (spray booth filters, rags) wastes must be disposed of properly. Paints and thinners should be placed in containers suitable for storage of flammable liquids. Solid wastes may be placed into metal containers filled with water to reduce the chance of spontaneous combustion. In all cases, dispose of wastes in accordance with local, state, and federal regulations. **NEVER** pour combustible or flammable liquids into sinks or floor drains.

First Aid — In case of skin contact, flush with plenty of water. For eye contact, immediately flush with plenty of water for at least 15 minutes and get medical attention. If inhalation of vapor or spray mist occurs, remove to fresh air. If breathing difficulty persists or occurs later, consult a physician and have label directions available. If ingestion occurs, DO NOT induce vomiting — seek medical attention immediately. If coating is injected into the skin by high pressure spray equipment, seek medical attention immediately. In all instances, medical and product information can be obtained through PPG and the National Poison Center Network.

FOR EMERGENCY INFORMATION —
24 HOURS PER DAY
CALL (304) 843-1300

This is a page out of PPG's Full Line Catalog. *Automotive paint manufacturers take their work very seriously and insist all users heed their health and safety recommendations. Along with this, labels on paint products, information sheets and application guides carry user safety information. Although these paint materials work great on car surfaces, when applied correctly, they are not always compatible with your skin or respiratory system. Allot whatever time necessary to read warning labels, and then follow instructions.*

2

Auto Paint Chemistry

Automotive paint manufacturing is a highly technical and scientific business. Along with satisfying customers' needs with quality products, these companies must conform to increasing governmental, environmental and personal health safety standards and regulations. Should a new product be developed that could literally revolutionize the auto paint industry, it must meet all of the strict regulations related to personal user safety and overall environmental pollution criteria.

Just because a fantastic new product might be able to cover car bodies in one easy step, shine forever without wax or polish and resist oxidation and other debilitating factors, does not guarantee it would be safe to use. It may require a different kind of application procedure or special high-tech

---

DELTRON® Universal Basecoat (DBU)

This material is designed for application only by professional, trained personnel using proper equipment under controlled conditions, and is not intended for sale to the general public.

DELTRON Universal Basecoat (DBU) is specifically designed for spot and panel repair of original basecoat/clearcoat finishes and for use in overall painting. *True basecoat systems must always be clearcoated.*

PREPARATION: All normal preparation steps involving bare metal treatment, corrosion resistant primer, primer-surfacer and/or sealer are required. Spot repairing requires the use of BONDING CLEAR (DSX 1900). When overall painting is intended, all surfaces should be sanded with fine sandpaper. **For maximum adhesion and appearance or when using KONDAR® (DZ 3 or 7) or K 200 Primer Surfacers, DEL-SEAL® Acrylic Sealer (DAS 1980) or EPOXY PRIMER (DP 40/DP 401 reduced as a sealer) must be used prior to applying DBU.**

SPOT REPAIR: Following damaged area repair steps, compound the adjacent areas far enough to apply BONDING CLEAR so that the basecoat color and subsequent clearcoats can be applied within the BONDING CLEAR area. Clean entire area with ACRYLI-CLEAN™ Wax and Grease Remover (DX 330) and tack off. The use of STAT FREE™ Dirt Eliminator (DX 102) just before BONDING CLEAR will aid in assuring a clean finish.

PANEL AND OVERALL PAINTING: The same system as for spot repairing is used up to the compounding step. The entire surface(s) should be sanded and then sealed with 1 or 2 full wet coats of DAS 1980 or DP 40/DP 401 (reduced as a sealer).

COLOR MIXING: Reduce DELTRON Universal Basecoat in a ratio of 1 part DBU to 1½ to 2 parts DRR 1170 or DRR 1185 REACTIVE REDUCER (150%-200%). Mix thoroughly. Pot-life of mixed DBU is approximately 4 hours.

COLOR APPLICATION: Apply two light to medium coats or to hiding. Spot repair coats should slightly overlap. Recommended air pressure: 35-45 PSI at the gun. Do not attempt to spray the color to achieve gloss. Allow the final color coat to set-up 20-60 minutes before applying clearcoats. The basecoat color should be clearcoated within 24 hours.

CLEAR COATINGS: DELTRON Universal Basecoat may be clearcoated with either DELTRON Universal Basecoat Polyurethane Clear (DBU 88), DELTRON Universal Basecoat Acrylic Clear (DBU 60), DELGLO® Acrylic Urethane Clear (DAU 82) or NCT Clearcoat (DC 1100). Each possess different properties and should be chosen to match the specific need. Refer to respective clearcoat product label or Product Information Bulletin for proper application.

FLEXIBLE PARTS PAINTING: FULL PANEL REPAIR ONLY. Apply 2-3 coats of basecoat color. **Do not use FLEXATIVE® (DX 369) in color coats.** Allow the final color coat to set-up 20-60 minutes before applying clear coats. Refer to respective clearcoat product label or Product Information Bulletin for proper application.

NOTE: Excessive coats of color and/or clear will result in slow drying, extended film softness and cracking.

Clean up all equipment immediately after use with the reducer used for the specific product.

IMPORTANT: Spray equipment must be handled with due care and in accordance with manufacturer's recommendations. Spraying of any material can be hazardous. Wear respirator, eye protection and protective clothing.

PHOTOCHEMICALLY REACTIVE

WARNING! HARMFUL OR FATAL IF SWALLOWED. CONTAINS LEAD. DRIED FILM OF THIS PAINT MAY BE HARMFUL IF EATEN OR CHEWED. MAY CAUSE MODERATE SKIN IRRITATION, SEVERE EYE IRRITATION AND MAY BE ABSORBED THROUGH THE SKIN. PROLONGED OR REPEATED CONTACT MAY CAUSE AN ALLERGIC SKIN REACTION. VAPOR AND SPRAY MIST MAY BE HARMFUL IF INHALED. SANDING AND GRINDING DUST MAY BE HARMFUL IF INHALED.

FLAMMABLE. Keep away from heat, sparks and flame. Contact with flame or hot surfaces may produce toxic decomposition products.

CONTAINS: RESINS, PETROLEUM DISTILLATES, XYLENE, TOLUENE, ESTERS, KETONES, ALCOHOLS, HIGH BOILING AROMATICS, ADDITIVES, LEAD CHROMATE
Overexposure to lead may cause adverse effects on blood and blood forming tissues, kidneys, liver and the central nervous system. This product contains an insoluble form of a chromium (6-) compound. NTP and IARC have designated these materials as contributing to an increased risk of developing cancer. Recent studies indicate that insoluble chromium (6-) compounds are probably not carcinogenic in humans. Avoid contact with skin and eyes and avoid breathing of vapors and spray mist. Repeated exposure to high vapor concentrations may cause irritation of the respiratory system and permanent brain and nervous system damage. Eye watering, headaches, nausea, dizziness and loss of coordination are indications that solvent levels are too high. Intentional misuse by deliberately concentrating and inhaling the contents can be harmful or fatal. Do not apply on toys or other children's articles, furniture or interior surfaces of any dwelling or facility which may be occupied or used by children. Do not apply on those exterior surfaces of dwelling units, such as windowsills, porches, stairs or railings, to which children may be commonly exposed. Wash thoroughly before eating or smoking.
Wear chemical-type splash goggles or full face shield and protective clothing, including impermeable apron and gloves. USE WITH ADEQUATE VENTILATION. Overexposure to vapors may be prevented by ensuring ventilation controls, vapor exhaust or fresh air entry. NIOSH/MSHA-approved (TC-23C-) organic vapor respirators may also reduce exposure. In all cases, read the respirator manufacturer's instructions and literature carefully to determine the type of airborne contaminants against which the respirator is effective and how it is to be properly fitted.
FIRST AID: If swallowed, do not induce vomiting. In case of skin contact, remove promptly by wiping, followed by waterless hand cleaner and soap and water. In case of eye contact, flush eyes immediately with plenty of water for at least 15 minutes. If affected by inhalation of vapor or spray mist, remove to fresh air. Apply artificial respiration and other support measures as required. If any of the following occur during or following the use of this product, contact a POISON CONTROL CENTER, EMERGENCY ROOM OR PHYSICIAN IMMEDIATELY; have label information available. • INGESTION • EXCESSIVE EXPOSURE TO A CORROSIVE MATERIAL • PERSISTENT SKIN/EYE IRRITATION OR BREATHING DIFFICULTIES • OTHER SYMPTOMS

Close container after each use.
KEEP OUT OF THE REACH OF CHILDREN
Emergency Medical or Spill Control Information (304) 843-1300

PPG PPG INDUSTRIES, INC.   **DBU LABEL #2**
PPG FINISHES
P. O. BOX 3510   MADE IN USA
TROY, MICHIGAN 48007-3510   FORM 1033

This is the typical backside part of a label from a gallon can of PPG paint. It is loaded with information, including application recommendations and safety tips. PPG also lists its mailing address in the lower right-hand corner should users need to contact company representatives for any reason. The writing at the bottom left corner suggests users wear a respirator, some form of eye protection and proper painting attire. PPG Industries, Inc.

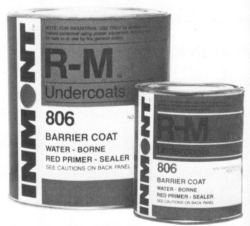

In an effort to reduce the amount of pollution caused by volatile organic compounds (VOCs) released by evaporating solvents, manufacturers like BASF have successfully developed waterborne paint materials. Along with providing a means to help reduce airborne pollution, this R-M brand Water-Borne Red Primer-Sealer is compatible with a number of different undercoat products. You must read all user instructions and cautions carefully to be certain it is applied as intended. BASF Corporation

22

filtering system to prevent deadly fumes from injuring users or poisoning the atmosphere. Therefore, an even balance has to be found for every paint product used which will not only serve its intended function, but also be safe for users and the environment.

The research required to develop quality paint products includes continuing studies by paint manufacturers through their teams of scientists and engineers. In addition to the development of new vibrant colors, researchers in this field conduct tests to determine the amount of hazardous materials created by various paint products and their application techniques. Through their efforts, and those from scientists in related fields of study, some water-based automotive paint products have

been invented and are currently offered; they are mostly undercoat materials.

Along with that, a new system of paint application has been successfully developed which incorporates a high-volume spray with very low pressure. This system, referred to as High Volume Low Pressure (HVLP), allows more paint to adhere on vehicle bodies with far less overspray than encountered with conventional spray paint systems. In essence, since more material sticks to properly prepared sheet-metal surfaces, much less is lost to the atmosphere through clouds of overspray that ricochet off body panels into the air.

Through increased safety awareness and continued research, manufacturers are determined to eventually develop environmentally safe paint ma-

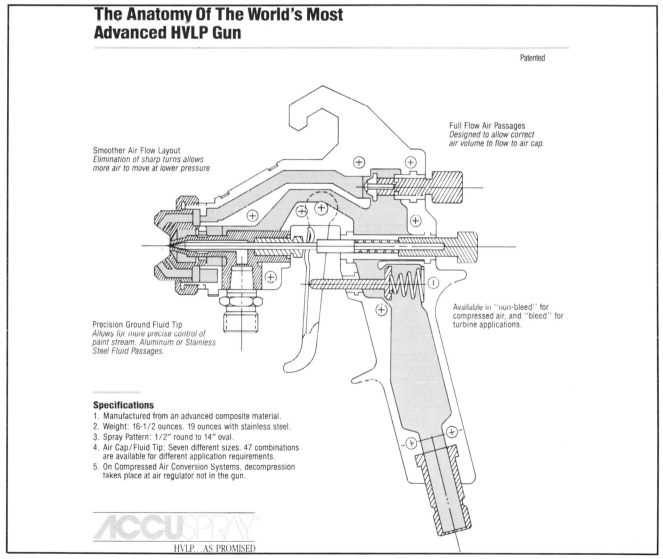

The Anatomy Of The World's Most Advanced HVLP Gun

Patented

Smoother Air Flow Layout
Elimination of sharp turns allows more air to move at lower pressure

Full Flow Air Passages
Designed to allow correct air volume to flow to air cap.

Precision Ground Fluid Tip
Allows for more precise control of paint stream. Aluminum or Stainless Steel Fluid Passages.

Available in "non-bleed" for compressed air, and "bleed" for turbine applications.

Specifications
1. Manufactured from an advanced composite material.
2. Weight: 16-1/2 ounces. 19 ounces with stainless steel.
3. Spray Pattern: 1/2" round to 14" oval.
4. Air Cap/Fluid Tip: Seven different sizes. 47 combinations are available for different application requirements.
5. On Compressed Air Conversion Systems, decompression takes place at air regulator not in the gun.

ACCUSPRAY
HVLP...AS PROMISED

This is the Accuspray high-volume, low-pressure spray paint system available through Eastwood. The handy unit supplies dry, heated air at low pressure and is designed to put more paint on a car's surface and less in

the form of overspray. As stricter controls regulate the use of high-pressure spray paint systems to reduce over-spray pollutants, use of HVLP systems is likely to increase. The Eastwood Company

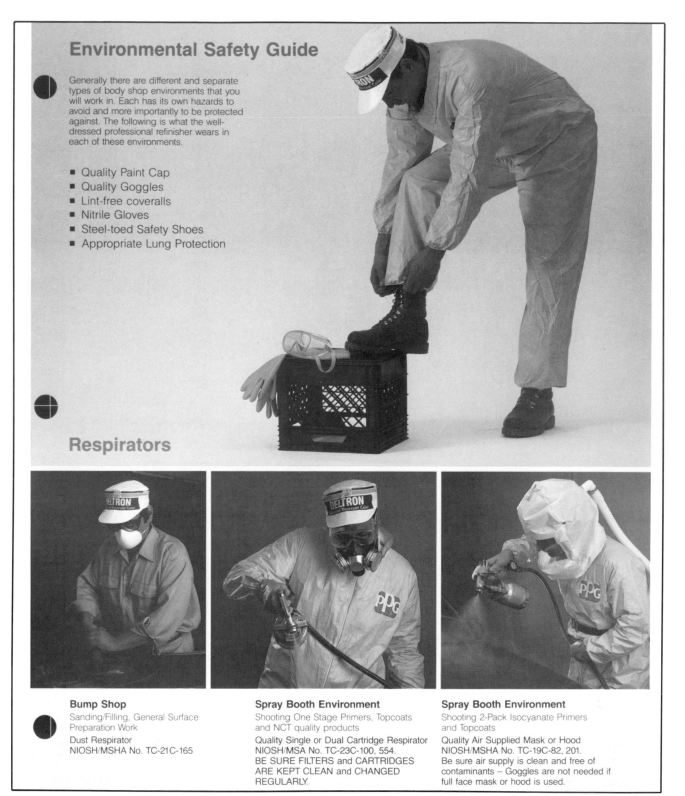

Environmental Safety Guide

Generally there are different and separate types of body shop environments that you will work in. Each has its own hazards to avoid and more importantly to be protected against. The following is what the well-dressed professional refinisher wears in each of these environments.

- Quality Paint Cap
- Quality Goggles
- Lint-free coveralls
- Nitrile Gloves
- Steel-toed Safety Shoes
- Appropriate Lung Protection

Respirators

Bump Shop
Sanding/Filling, General Surface Preparation Work
Dust Respirator
NIOSH/MSHA No. TC-21C-165

Spray Booth Environment
Shooting One Stage Primers, Topcoats and NCT quality products
Quality Single or Dual Cartridge Respirator
NIOSH/MSA No. TC-23C-100, 554.
BE SURE FILTERS and CARTRIDGES ARE KEPT CLEAN and CHANGED REGULARLY.

Spray Booth Environment
Shooting 2-Pack Isocyanate Primers and Topcoats
Quality Air Supplied Mask or Hood
NIOSH/MSHA No. TC-19C-82, 201.
Be sure air supply is clean and free of contaminants – Goggles are not needed if full face mask or hood is used.

A page from PPG's "Safety First" brochure displays some of the personal safety equipment available to auto painters. Respiratory protection is of utmost importance, as noted by the NIOSH/MSHA designations. A dust filter is suitable while sanding some filler materials while a regular cartridge-type mask is better suited for the spraying of certain paint products, like undercoats. The full-face and head fresh-air respirator on the bottom right is just one design of available fresh-air respirator systems. The painters coveralls not only protect against paint exposure, they are also lint-free, a great feature for auto painting work. PPG Industries, Inc.

terials that can be satisfactorily applied by a means that will almost completely eliminate overspray and hopefully reduce pollution to practically nothing. This effort will take time to design, develop and implement. Meanwhile, automotive painters must be especially aware of potential user hazards and take advantage of all recommended safety procedures and equipment. This includes the use of positive-pressure full-face respirators, protective hoods, quality rubber gloves and painters' coveralls.

The chemistry surrounding automotive paint materials is quite complex. You can certainly learn a lot more, should you want to, about the molecular structures, atomic weights and other chemical compositions of these products through voluminous tomes at a library. Although that information may be of interest to certain scientific folks, it really won't be of much help to those who simply want to learn how to effectively paint their car or truck. But, you should understand some automotive paint properties in order to wisely choose the proper products needed to achieve a professional looking and long-lasting paint finish on your vehicle.

Basic Ingredients

Auto paint is made up of pigments, binders and solvents. Pigments give paint material its color. Binders are used to hold pigment materials together and keep them in a state which remains solidly attached to vehicle bodies. Solvents are those liquid media (thinners and reducers) which transform solid pigment and binder materials into sprayable liquids. Solvents are, for the most part, the materials that evaporate into the atmosphere to cause pollution concerns.

Various pigment, binder and solvent combinations produce different types of paint. Their differences are reflected in coverage techniques, drying times, repairability and durability. In general, though, all paint materials are basically solid substances that have been mixed with a solvent and changed into liquid forms in order to be sprayed. Once solvents have evaporated, pigments and binders harden into colorful sheets that strongly adhere to autobody surfaces to offer pleasant visual appearances and oxidation protection for underlying metal.

In years past, auto painters were limited to either straight enamel- or lacquer-based paints. Enamels were relatively easy to apply and covered in just one or two coats. They did not have to be rubbed out, and lasted a long time. Nitrocellulose lacquer paint required lots of thin coats and numerous clear coats over color bases which had to be rubbed out in order to gain deep, lustrous shines. It dried fast and allowed minor flaws or nibs to be gently wet sanded and then painted over just minutes after paint was applied.

Recent advances in paint chemistry have brought new kinds of enamel and lacquer paint, referred to as acrylics. Acrylic simply means plastic. Although acrylic enamel and acrylic lacquer retain their same basic application and benefit characteristics, their durability and ultraviolet sun ray resistance have been greatly improved.

As acrylic enamels and lacquers underwent improvement, a new type of paint was introduced. Urethane paint products combined advantages of both enamels and lacquers to offer quick-drying ingredients that could cover in one to three coats and could also allow blemish repair soon after a coat was sprayed on. One of the biggest advantages urethanes offer is durability. In a sense, they were developed to resist the hazards of today's harsh airborne pollutants, acid rains and other oxidizing atmospheres.

Once again, although basic ingredients remain the same—pigment, binder and solvent—their chemical compositions give each paint its own

These instructions for the use of PPG's Deltron Acrylic Urethane are typical of those presented on product brochures, information sheets and application guides for most every paint product available through autobody paint and supply stores. As long as you are familiar with the basic procedures for mixing and spraying paint, you should easily be able to understand this information. If not, consult a jobber for answers to your questions. Deltron is a two-step paint system that includes clear coat coverage after the application of color. PPG Industries, Inc.

This is the information provided on the back of a Concept 8200 clear paint brochure, manufactured by PPG. Along with undercoat and color coat information, it includes mixing, application, air pressure and drying time instructions. Additional recommendations, instructions and general information can be found on the product information sheet available at autobody paint and supply stores. PPG Industries, Inc.

individual characteristics. The addition of chemical hardeners plays a significant role by improving the way pigments and binders bond together and adhere to painted surfaces.

Liquid hardeners (catalysts) are added to paint and solvent mixtures in established proportions as recommended by label instructions and informational guidelines. Along with instructions, labels and information sheets highly emphasize that fresh-air respirators be employed whenever hardeners are used. This is because hardeners contain isocyanate chemicals which have been deemed health hazards when inhaled or absorbed through skin.

Acrylic Enamel

According to PPG's *Refinish Manual*, "Alkyd [natural based] and acrylic [plastic based] enamels dry first by evaporation of the reducers, then by oxidation of the resin [binder]." This means that although the paint finish may appear to dry quickly through evaporation of its solvent base, the material continues to harden as resins combine with oxygen in the air. Heat from infrared lamps helps to speed this process.

As the curing process continues, a dry synthetic film solidifies over the top of the finish to offer a tough, shiny color coat. Wet sanding this coat to remove nibs of dirt or debris will destroy that film and require touchup painting to repair blemishes.

When compared to the durability of urethane products, alkyd and acrylic enamels fall short. Although they can cover in just one or two coats and do not require the use of isocyanate-based hardeners, they cannot hold up to the same kind of harsh environments or resistance to impact hazards. In addition, the application of any lacquer-based product over an enamel will result in surface wrinkling or crazing. This is because the materials in enamel cannot hold up to the strong chemicals in lacquer.

In order for an enamel paint to accept a top-coat of lacquer material, as for custom flames or artwork, a special sealer has to be applied first to prevent lacquer solvents from penetrating and ruining enamel bases. For situations such as this, you must consult an autobody paint and supply jobber for advice and recommendations that apply to your specific job.

Acrylic Lacquer

Acrylic lacquer resists ultraviolet sun rays, cracking, dulling and yellowing much better than nitrocellulose lacquer. It has been a favorite paint among auto enthusiasts for years because it is easy to mix, can be applied at relatively low pressures, dries quickly and can generally be repaired and recoated within ten to twenty minutes after the last coat has been sprayed.

By its nature, a number of lacquer coats have to be applied to achieve color and coverage expectations. After that, coats of clear lacquer are sprayed over color bases for protection and also for required buffing. If painters were to buff lacquer color coats, tints would be adversely affected. Therefore, clear coats are applied so that buffing shines them to a deep gloss without disturbing any underlying color characteristics. The process requires more time than enamel applications, but the extra-deep shine and lustrous finish are worth the effort.

Lacquer has also been used a lot by custom painters because of its quick-drying nature. Frequently, custom designs require multiple masking in order to achieve unique paint schemes. Because lacquer dries in ten to twenty minutes during warm weather, painters can apply masking tape over new paint and continue with their custom project without much interruption. To do the same thing in enamel, painters might have to wait for days until paint is dry enough to accept strips of masking tape without subsequent damage to its top film layer.

Most professional autobody painters recommend novices start out using lacquer-based paint. This is so they can repair nibs almost immediately and then continue with their work. Lacquer is very forgiving that way. Repaint efforts to repair scratches and cover areas exposed by bodywork are also easy to match on lacquer paint jobs. After mixing and spraying the matching original-finish paint color, painters can revive gloss and texture by polishing and buffing the finish.

Because of the amount of volatile organic compounds (VOCs) emitted by lacquer solvents, environmental restrictions imposed by regulatory agencies may soon curtail the use of lacquer paint, or, require it only be sprayed in down-draft paint booths equipped with special filters and air purifying systems. This is a factor to consider when contemplating a complete paint job for your car. Be sure to talk it over with your autobody paint and supply jobber, as he or she should be one of the first auto paint professionals to learn of any new restrictions.

Urethane Products

Perhaps one of the more familiar brands of urethane paint is DuPont's Imron. When it first became available, some auto enthusiasts thought Imron was an actual paint type instead of a name brand. Imron brand is a urethane type paint, just like PPG's Durethane and Deltron products.

Urethane enamels differ from alkyd and acrylic enamels in that their resins react chemically with isocyanates in the hardener. PPG's *Refinish Manual* states, "Urethane enamels dry by evaporation of the reducers and by a chemical reaction between the two principle [sic] base components (hydroxyls and polyisocyanates) which harden the paint film." In addition to maximum coverage and immediate high gloss without buffing, urethane enamels offer a much harder and more durable finish.

Acrylic urethanes are very versatile. They cover in just a few coats, dry quickly, can be wet sanded to repair minor nibs or blemishes and offer a very durable finish with maximum scratch, impact and ultraviolet sun ray resistance.

Urethane paint products dry much better when subjected to heat. Professional auto painters frequently use paint booths equipped with heaters or infrared lamps to help urethanes cure to their maximum strength in a short time.

At the factory, urethane paint jobs are baked at temperatures around 450 degrees Fahrenheit. This can be done because car bodies are bare and do not include any plastic pieces that would melt under those conditions. This baking process further hardens paint pigments and additives and helps them adhere to body surfaces better than ever before. Repaint efforts over baked-on factory

The attractive, yet delicate, graphic design on the side of this Volkswagen Bug would be ruined if wet sanding or polishing was done directly on top of the color coat finish. Therefore, coats of clear paint were applied after the color had dried. This enabled the painter to polish the clear finish to a deep, beautiful shine without any worry of disturbing underlying color. Custom painters like to use lacquer paint to complete custom effects, like this, because it dries fast and enables them to mask off successive patterns just a short time after paint was sprayed for the previous leg of the job. Dan Mycon

finishes are provided with solid bases as long as finishes are properly prepared and scuffed.

For repaint jobs, auto painters generally never exceed 140 degrees Fahrenheit when using heaters or lamps. This is because sensitive engine computers could be damaged or plastic assemblies caused to melt. They normally subject new paint to no more than 140 degrees Fahrenheit for about thirty minutes. Product information sheets list specific heat application times for particular temperature ranges.

Along with DuPont and PPG, other paint manufacturers, including BASF, Glasurit, R-M, House of Kolor and Metalflake, offer their own brands of urethane products. All of these companies believe they have the best products. Likewise, auto painters have their own personal preferences. But, just like with wax and polish brands, you can seldom get two auto professionals or enthusiasts to agree that one kind is better than all the rest. These decisions are based on all kinds of experiences.

Such would be where one painter applied a certain product over an incompatible base to cause a less than satisfactory result; another may have used the same product differently to arrive at a perfect finish with plenty of gloss and adhesion. As much as users may disagree as to which brand is best, manufacturers are adamant about two

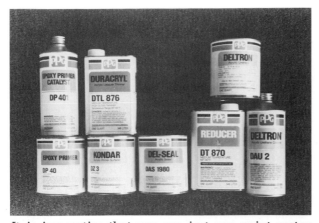

It is imperative that you use just one paint system throughout your paint project. This is just one paint system from PPG. It includes, from left to right: epoxy primer and catalyst; primer-surfacer and lacquer thinner; acrylic sealer; and acrylic urethane paint, reducer and catalyst. All of these products are compatible with each other but may not be with similar substances manufactured by other paint companies.

Autobody paint and supply stores carry a good assortment of respirators and their applicable replacement cartridges. You must be certain that the type of unit you wear is designed to filter out the hazardous materials you will be working with. Labels on respirator packages and information sheets inside their boxes generally list what the units will or will not filter. If in doubt, consult a store clerk or jobber.

things: First, painters must always use only those products included together as one paint system. In other words, if you decide to apply PPG paint on your car, be sure to use PPG reducer, hardener, primer, sealer, primer-surfacer, cleaner and paint throughout.

Never mix those products with any different brand. All products listed as part of a manufacturer's paint system are designed to be used together. Chemical bases and other important chemical combinations have been thoroughly tested and researched to give users the best for their money. Inadvertently mixing brands is asking for trouble. Should you mix brands, you are taking a risk that the new paint finish on your car or truck will wrinkle, craze, mottle, orange peel or otherwise suffer damage that cannot be repaired.

Painters' second area of emphatic agreement pertains to the use of all recommended personal safety equipment. In addition to spraying paint in well-ventilated areas away from all sources of heat or flame, they insist you wear respirators and augment that protection with a hood, rubber gloves and painters' coveralls. These recommendations are clearly printed on paint product labels which even go so far as to mention the kind of NIOSH (National Institute for Occupational Safety and Health) approved respirator to use when applying that particular material.

Because paint manufacturers must meet strict regulations and exacting product standards, it is quite safe to say that all of their products should perform as expected when properly mixed and applied. To further ensure that the paint finish on your vehicle exhibits the deep shine and excellent adhesion expected, be absolutely certain you follow all recommended surface preparation instructions. If you don't, the new paint you carefully spray onto your car's surface could dry to a separate film that would be easily peeled off in long sheets.

Remember, baked-on urethanes offer durable, hard paint finishes. Because of this, new paint solvents might not penetrate their surface to guarantee quality adhesion. You may have to spray on an adhesion promoter first before applying new paint. Information of this nature must be confirmed with your autobody paint and supply jobber for the specific job you are contemplating.

Metallic Paints

Many newer cars sport brilliant metallic paint finishes. Unlike custom paint jobs of the sixties, these newer paint products suspend tiny metallic flakes so small that you have to look at the surface from just a few inches away to distinguish their presence. Along with a pleasant color base, metallic particles offer extra shine and gloss to many paint schemes, in a sense, adding a flair of custom character to vehicles.

Painters can add recommended doses of metallic flakes to almost any paint base. They do this by scooping out small amounts of flake material with a spoon. They never touch the flakes with their hands because skin oils would tarnish their finish. Then, according to mixture instructions, they add ounces or fractions of ounces to the paint blend. A test panel is sprayed to visually check the outcome. If flakes are spaced too far apart, a little more might be added. Painters always start out with minimal metallic doses. This is because more flakes can always be added, but none can be taken out.

If you order a specific metallic paint from an autobody paint and supply store, flakes will be added in during the mixing process. Paint codes used by autobody paint suppliers account for all additives required to make new paint mixes match original standards, including metallic flakes.

When applying metallic paints, vigorously shake paint containers before filling spray gun cups to be sure that all metallic particles are equally suspended in the solution. If need be, visit the autobody paint and supply store just before painting and ask them to shake your paint container on their heavy-duty paint-shaking machine. While doing spray paint work, most professional painters shake their paint gun after each pass to ensure all particles remain thoroughly suspended and dispersed. This way, all parts of the vehicle being painted are assured of uniform metallic coverage.

For do-it-yourself painters who want to mix their own metallics, flakes are sold separately at most autobody paint and supply stores. They are displayed in small jars as a dry material; they do not come mixed with a paste or liquid. You can purchase metallic flakes in different sizes and colors. You can also order metallic materials through custom auto paint outlets like the Metal-flake Corporation and Jon Kosmoski's House of Kolor.

Pearl Paints

Have you ever glanced at a custom car and perceived it as white, and then during a subsequent glance realized it was light blue or pink? Chances are, your eyes are not failing you. Instead, the automobile in question has probably been painted with a pearl additive mixed in with paint.

This material consists of tiny chips of synthetic inorganic crystalline substances which are painted on one side and are clear on the other. Concentrates of pearl are sold at autobody paint and supply stores in four-ounce jars. Chips come mixed in a paste. They are added to gallons of paint in amounts of from two to four ounces. Small measuring spoons are used to remove material from jars and then transfer it to the paint mixture.

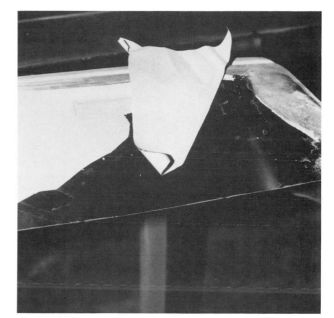

A plastic bumper is resting on a stand and displays a sheet of paint peeled from its surface. The painter who sprayed this bumper, a do-it-yourself repaint effort, did not understand that a bonding agent or adhesion promoter needed to be applied before paint. Using any paint product without following application instructions can result in problems like this. This bumper had to be completely stripped, cleaned, scuffed and then shot with a bonding agent before paint was finally sprayed.

When viewed from different angles, light reflection off pearl finishes causes painted surfaces to reflect different colors. The color presented is determined by the color of the pearl additive. You have to check paint chips at the paint and supply store to select which combination of color paint base and pearl additive to use for whatever color you desire. Now, if your car was originally painted with a pearl-type paint color at the factory, a paint and supply store should automatically include the prescribed pearl dose to your paint mixture. To be sure, ask the jobber at the time your paint order is placed.

If you are trying to jazz up a stock paint color by adding pearl yourself, you must make sure that pearl is compatible with the paint product you intend to use. In most cases, pearl works well with just about any paint base. But, why take a chance on ruining an otherwise clean paint job when all you have to do is ask an autobody paint jobber? Other than that, it is recommended you add just a bit less pearl than the prescribed amount listed on the information sheet or container label. Then, shoot a test panel and visually inspect the results. If more pearl is needed, add a little. This way, you should not have to worry about putting in too much pearl, which could ruin your paint job by making it look washed out or milky.

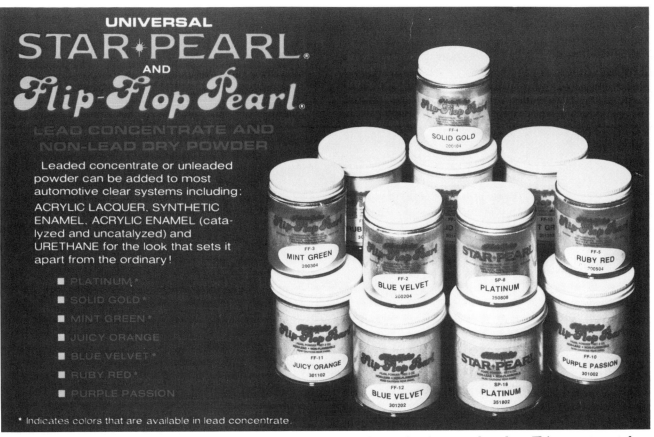
Especially used for custom paint work, pearl additives make certain paint jobs appear a different color when viewed from various angles. Tiny chips of synthetic inorganic crystalline substances are added to paint to cause the effect. They are generally painted on one side and remain clear on the other. This assortment from Metalflake Corporation shows some of the various colors available. User instructions recommend these products be used with a complete Metalflake paint system for best overall finish results. Metalflake Corporation

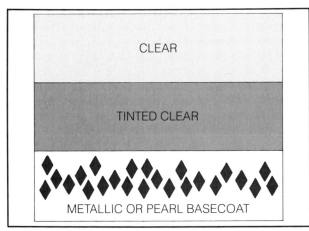

PPG's Radiance II three-step paint system produces results similar to candy paint jobs. After a base coat has been applied and cured, per directions, tinted clear coats are sprayed. Each successive tinted clear coat darkens the finish until the painter decides a perfect finish shade has been achieved. After the appropriate flash times have elapsed, pure clear coats are sprayed over the layers of base and tint coats for their protection. PPG Industries, Inc.

Clear Paint

Clear paint is just that, clear. It is sprayed over the tops of certain color coats to serve as a protective film which can be polished to perfection without the disruption of an underlying base of color, pearl or metallic. Until the last few years, clear was just about exclusively used over lacquer paint jobs because polishing lacquer color coats could disrupt their color uniformity. It also added resistance to sun rays and other potential paint finish hazards.

Today, clear coats are commonly found on stock factory paint jobs. According to PPG's *Refinish Manual*, there were two reasons for introducing base coat and clear coat finishes. First, the application of clear paint over light-colored metallic paint finishes greatly helped to increase their durability. Second, this process reduced the solvent needs for paint color applications to help manufacturers meet the government's emission standards. In essence, base coat and clear coat paint systems allowed painters to apply only a one mil thickness of color when it was covered with two

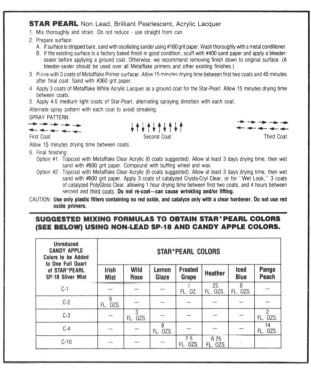

This is an application guide for Metalflake's Star Pearl product. Notice that the recommended spray pattern includes not only a back-and-forth movement, but an up-and-down application, as well. This paint spraying technique is employed for certain custom paint finishes to guarantee as close to perfect uniform application as possible. By applying Star Pearl in this pattern, concerns over streaking are minimized. Metalflake Corporation

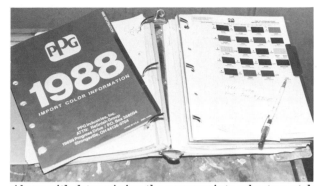

Along with determining the appropriate color to match the paint already in place on cars, catalogs explain whether or not the factory paint system employed included a clear coat finish. In this case, no clear coat was needed for the application of PPG #L90E, the appropriate color white needed for a spot repaint on Janna Jacobs' 1988 Volkswagen Jetta. Different paint color chip catalogs are kept on hand by painters, each designating specific auto make years of manufacture.

step involves color application while the second refers to clear paint coverage. Some new colors may require three steps, a fact that can be determined by color code deciphering or paint chip selection at an autobody paint and supply store.

Candy paint jobs require a base coat of gold or silver be applied before toners of another color are sprayed on. Basically, that base coat will always show through, somewhat, as toners are a light mixture of color blended in with clear paint. The first

mils of clear. Conventional paint color applications normally call for two to three mils of coverage.

Custom paint jobs almost always call for protective coats of clear paint. This is so polishing and waxing will not directly touch or adversely affect series of exotic color blends, metallic flakes, pearl additives or custom graphics. Along with that, certain clear coat products contain chemical ingredients that are designed to ward off the harmful effects of ultraviolet sun rays and help color coats resist premature fading.

To determine if your car has been painted with a base coat and clear coat system, bring the color code numbers from your factory-painted car to the autobody paint and supply store. Information in their paint books or computer will quickly tell what system was applied. If yours is a repaint, sand an inconspicuous spot with 600 grit or finer sandpaper. White residue is an indication of clear paint in most cases, providing, of course, that the vehicle is not painted white.

Two- and Three-Step Paint Systems

A base coat and clear coat paint system could also be referred to as a two-step paint system. One

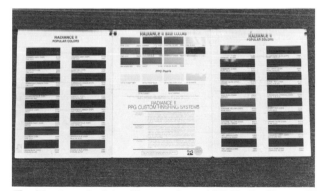

The black-and-white illustration of PPG's Radiance II color chip brochure cannot do justice to the vivid colors displayed. If you have decided that your car or truck is in need of a complete new paint job, you might consider the application of a customlike color from one of these kinds of three-step paint systems. About the only drawbacks to custom paints like this are that they take a little more work to effect, and spot paint repairs are not necessarily viable options. Because numerous tinted clear coats were applied to finally achieve a perfect tint, matching just a spot or panel may be difficult. Repairs could entail complete body side repaint from headlight to taillight.

toner coat may not seem to cover a gold base at all, but additional light coats of candy toners will eventually cover to an exciting degree but still allow shades of the base to be observed. The final semi-transparent effect is described as translucent. You can get an idea of this by holding a lollipop up to a well-lighted surface. Although the lollipop color will be greatly noticed, the surface color behind it will add some degree of color.

The same basic premise holds true for three-step paint systems. A base coat of white will make a color coat of purple, for example, a different shade than a base coat of gold or silver. The desired final finish color, along with the paint system brand selected, will determine what base color must be applied to achieve intended results. Application guides available at the autobody paint and supply store list recommended flash times between coats and any other pertinent information regarding use of that particular paint system.

The third step of a three-step paint system is the application of clear paint. With this type of system, wet sanding, rubbing out or polishing a color coat that has been applied over a base coat could remove enough color pigment to cause parts of the base coat to show through, creating a break in an otherwise uniform paint application. Therefore, coats of clear paint not only protect underlying color coats but also allow painters to buff and polish surfaces to deep, lustrous shines without ever touching color.

Volatile Organic Compounds (VOCs)

Many parts of our planet have become so polluted that government agencies and research institutes have taken bold steps to curtail the creation of any new pollution sources, as well as drastically cut back on sources that have been in existence for years. The automotive paint industry is not immune to these emission standards and has, in fact, done a great deal to curb pollution caused by paint overspray and solvent evaporation.

Volatile organic compounds (VOCs) are chemical substances that rise into the atmosphere from paint overspray and solvent evaporation to unite with nitrous oxides and produce ozone. Ozone is a major component of smog. Basically, VOCs are those elements in cans of paint that evaporate. Since pigments and binders (resins) are solids which form films on autobody surfaces, it is the chemical solvents that are responsible for VOCs. Solvent is a generic term used to describe the material in paint that keeps the mixture in a liquid state; lacquer paints have lacquer thinner, while enamels and urethanes have reducers. Any gallon of paint could include up to 90 percent solvent. Thinners and reducers are 100 percent solvent.

New laws have been passed in states like California, New York, Texas and New Jersey relating to the emission of VOCs by local companies, including automotive paint shops. In addition to mandating that shops install high-tech paint booths with down-draft ventilation systems, they insist that these booths be equipped with special filtering systems designed to burn off or otherwise filter out VOCs.

As an aid in stemming the amount of VOCs escaping into the air by way of paint overspray, some companies, such as Accuspray, have developed High Volume Low Pressure (HVLP) spray paint systems. These units are capable of producing 64 cfm (cubic feet per minute) of air at 5 psi (pounds per square inch). They also warm air to approximately ninety degrees Fahrenheit. Laursen used an HVLP to paint a mid-sized car. He was amazed at the reduction of overspray compared to conventional spray paint guns, and said that he used only three quarts of paint to cover a vehicle that normally took a full gallon.

Paint manufacturing companies like BASF have authorized their research laboratories to strive toward development of new paint products that will dramatically reduce the amount of VOCs escaping into the atmosphere daily. Waterborne paint products have been produced with mixed results, and research will continue until all avenues have been thoroughly examined. Bob Inglis, director of new product coordination at BASF Refinish says, "By 1992, we'll have to go to a high solids system or the water. As I envision it, it will probably be water-borne for the base coats, and high solids for single-stage, solid-shade base coats, and all clears. As far as lacquers are concerned, it's just not conceivable to get their VOC content down to the levels imposed by the new laws. Manufacturers have accepted that lacquers are going to be phased out. Shops have got to accept that also."

As confusing as this issue can be, the best way to stay on top of it is to maintain contact with your local autobody paint and supply store. Jobbers will be among the first to know of drastic changes in the auto paint industry. They will also be among the first to receive new and updated technical material on new paint products and compatible systems for use on previously painted automobiles in need of touchup. In the long run, rest assured that any new paint technology will be well researched with compatible systems developed so that repaint needs can be achieved for those vehicles painted with today's products.

Overview

If your car or truck is scheduled to be stripped to bare metal and you are contemplating a complete paint job, you can use almost any paint system. It could be alkyd or acrylic enamel for relatively easy two- to three-coat coverage with no rubbing out or buffing requirements or a complete three-step customlike system which will mean more spraying and rubbing-out work but a much more durable and bullet-proof finish. Preparations will basically be the same. You'll have to treat bare metal to coats of epoxy primer and primer-surfacer and then sand to perfection before applying either one.

Concerns over personal safety while using hardeners with isocyanate ingredients may cause you to opt instead for a lacquer- or enamel-based product. Should you decide to use a urethane product, consider renting a fresh-air respirator system from a local rental yard. For enamels, since nibs of dirt or debris cannot be wet sanded smooth, you will have to apply paint in an extra-clean and dust-free environment. Maybe lacquer would be the best choice, since there will be no need to use an isocyanate hardener which allows you to wear a filter respirator, as opposed to a fresh-air unit, and nibs of debris on its finish can be wet sanded and touched up with little problem.

By far, your best source for product information is your local autobody paint and supply store jobber. Along with concerns about your car's existing paint surface and any special mixing or application techniques unique to the new paint system you have chosen, local climates and weather conditions will play a significant factor in any auto paint endeavor. Jobbers should be aware of uncommon regional factors, which enables them to guide you through purchases of temperature-related thinners and reducers and other specific painting techniques required for that area.

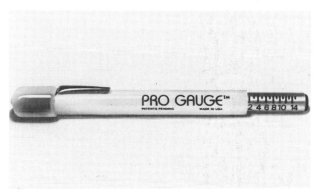

When a complete new paint job is called for and you are trying to decide whether or not to strip existing paint or spray over it, you might enlist the aid of Pro Motorcar Products' Pro Gauge. For a cost of only $35, this tool will measure the thickness of the paint already on your car, a very important concern. This lightweight magnetic device will measure as little as 0.001 in. Too much paint on a body surface will lead to cracks, checking, crazing and other related problems. Pro Gauge comes with complete instructions. Pro Motorcar Products

If a body panel exhibits signs that point to repaint needs, you may find that the use of this Spot Rot Autobody Damage Gauge from Pro Motorcar Products will help you determine if rust or previous body filler applications are present under paint. In some cases, you may find that certain panels need replacing. This tool sells for about $15. The magnet end is pulled out of the housing as the unit is moved away from body surfaces. The number ten indicates just one paint job over solid metal; a six to nine shows repainting has occurred, and from one to five warns of hidden rust or collision damage. Pro Motorcar Products

3

Paint Support Chemicals

The process of painting cars would be a lot easier and a heck of a lot less technical if there was only one paint product needed for all automotive uses. Wouldn't it be nice if all you had to do was buy one gallon of product and it would take care of all primer, sealer and color concerns? Unfortunately, that is not the case. Along with all the various paint bases that actually put color on vehicle bodies, there are numerous other products that must be used in specific situations to guarantee maximum color longevity, adhesion and sheet-metal protection.

Spraying paint directly onto bare metal will not result in the smooth finish you expect. The color may wash out, the paint may peel or crack and a host of other problems will quickly surface. Likewise, painting over the surface of cars that

have been subjected to lots of dressing applications on vinyl and rubber parts may include so much silicone material that fisheye problems persist almost everywhere paint is sprayed. And what about flexible urethane plastic parts, like bumpers and ground effects? Without a flex-additive, paint would just randomly peel and crack.

As with paint products, manufacturers supply autobody paint and supply stores with information

The end of a hectic day at Newlook Autobody might find the workbench in the paint mixing room in somewhat of a disarray. As you can tell, a lot of paint has been mixed here over the years. The empty cans under the bench are used for mixing paint, reducer and catalyst according to mixing sticks, seen just to the right of center in a 1 gal. can. Their straight sides are needed for accurate calibrations. It would be nice if only one kind of undercoat could be used with all color coats, but that is not the case. You must understand and follow paint product mixing and application instructions if you expect your paint job to turn out as intended.

K 200/K 201 ACRYLIC URETHANE PRIMER SURFACER   Form P-151 (11/89)

IDENTITY	CODE
Primer Surfacer	K 200
Primer Surfacer Hardener	K 201
Flexible Primer Hardener	K 248
Cool Weather Reducer	DT 860 (60 - 70°F)
Normal Weather Reducer	DT 870 (65 - 80°F)
Warm Weather Reducer	DT 885 (75 - 90°F)

BACKGROUND

K 200/201 Urethane Primer Surfacer, from PPG, is designed to provide fast film build properties with minimal coats, excellent adhesion, ease of sanding, and color hold out properties. It is to be used over properly prepared existing painted surfaces and/or properly treated bare steel, aluminum, or fiberglass. K 200/201 can be used under most PPG Finishes (see note for use under DURACRYL (DDL) Acrylic Lacquer) as a primer surfacer in any of the following ways:

- Normal build as a sanding primer surfacer (2 - 3 mils). Also, over flexible substrates.

- High build as a high fill primer surfacer (6 - 8 mils). Use gravity feed or primer gun.

DIRECTIONS FOR USE

Preparation:
- Clean all affected surfaces with soap and water then reclean with DX 330 ACRYLI-CLEAN™ Wax and Grease Remover.

- Sand well and reclean with DX 330.

NOTE: For maximum performance, treat bare metal areas with the PPG Metal Treatment System, and apply DP Epoxy Primer. Allow DP Epoxy Primer to dry one hour before applying K 200/201. If K 200/201 is used as a spot primer surfacer over DP Epoxy Primer, allow this system to dry overnight before topcoating.

MIXING:

Normal Build
- Mix K 200 Primer Surfacer in a ratio of 4 parts K 200; 1 part DT Reducer (see temperature ranges); 1 part K 201 (4:1:1). Stir thoroughly.

K 200		DT Reducer		K 201
4 parts/quarts	to	1 part/quart	to	1 part/quart

Application
- Apply with siphon feed gun using 40 - 50 pounds air pressure at the gun.

- Apply (2) full wet coats to produce a dry film thickness of 2-3 mils with a 5 - 10 minute flash off between coats. Note: Films of 2 - 3 mils can be sanded (wet or dry) and topcoated after 3 hours at 75°F or after force drying for 30 minutes at 140°F. For best sanding results and topcoat appearance, allow K 200/201 to dry overnight.

Note: Pot life of reduced & catalyzed K 200 is 3 hours at 75° F. Clean equipment with (DTL) Duracryl Lacquer Thinners or DT Reducers immediately after use.

© 1989 PPG INDUSTRIES, INC.

The front page of this information sheet for PPG's K200/K201 Acrylic Urethane Primer-Surfacer is quite complete. Additional information on successive pages lists the compatible and incompatible surfaces it can be used upon, as well as compatible topcoats, incompatible topcoats, cautions and test properties. Although some of this information may seem mundane to you now, a lot of it must be carefully read if you want your project to result in an even, uniform and professional appearing finish. PPG Industries, Inc.

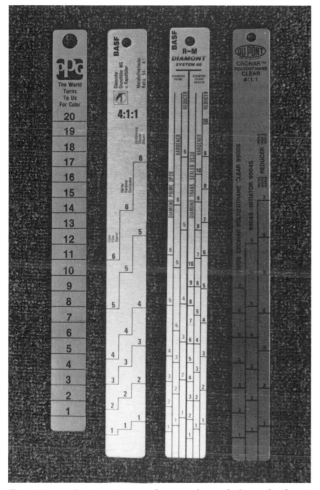

Two-step paint systems only require mixing of solvent with paint; three-step systems require that solvent and catalyst be mixed with paint. To be sure mixing ratios are accurate, paint manufacturers make mixing sticks available. These are samples of mixing sticks from PPG, BASF, R-M and DuPont. Be certain the mixing stick you use is calibrated for the paint system you employ.

Although these cans contain Glasurit brand reducer, each one has a slightly different chemical mixture. The one on the left is a fast mix; it will evaporate quickly. The one on the right is slow; it will take longer to evaporate. Reducer is added to paint in order to make it a more sprayable substance. Reducers are rated according to evaporation scales and are used during certain weather conditions. The fast kind might be used on cooler days when natural evaporation may take much too long. Conversely, on hot days, painters may need to use a slow reducer so paint does not dry too fast.

sheets and application guides for their sealers, primers, primer-surfacers, adhesion promoters, paint removers and cleaners. Mixing instructions and flash times are spelled out, just like for paint.

A complete paint system includes all the products needed to accomplish any paint job. Starting with wax and grease remover, paint manufacturers design all of their sealers, primers, thinners, retarders, reducers and paints to be compatible with each other. Mixing sticks from each manufacturer are calibrated so that as parts of one item are mixed with others, the outcome will be a perfectly blended paint product that will serve the purposes of metal protection, paint adhesion and color hold-out as intended.

Paint support chemicals refer to all of the products you will need to prepare autobody surfaces for paint (undercoats), as well as those additives designed to be mixed with paint to overcome specific problems. Since it is impossible to depict every kind of paint-related problem for every vehicle and every circumstance, you may have to confer with a paint and supply jobber, or professional auto painter, for unique problems. By being up-front with jobbers about the kind of paint job you expect to apply and your lack of painting experience, you allow them an excellent opportunity to share their technical paint knowledge with you and possibly solve more problems than you knew you had.

Thinners, Reducers and Retarders

In order for paint pigments and binders to cure and harden into a unified solid substance, the liquid parts of each paint mixture must evaporate. Those agents used to turn solid pigments and binders into liquids for sprayability are generically grouped and referred to as solvents. Thinners, reducers and retarders all fall into the category of solvents.

The chemical makeup of various solvents, although similar in design and purpose, varies according to the type of pigments and binders used in particular paint products. Lacquer thinners are designed to work with lacquer-based products. Enamels require solvents containing different chemical blends which are called enamel reducers. Lacquer thinner is not compatible with enamel products, and reducers are not generally compatible with lacquers. For all intents and purposes, the word thinner is associated with lacquer and the term reducer to enamels and urethanes.

The term retarder simply refers to either a lacquer or reducer with an extra-slow evaporation time. Retarders are used for paint jobs that are sprayed during exceptionally hot weather, typically above 95 degrees Fahrenheit. Their function is to evaporate much slower than other thinners or reducers so paint does not dry too fast to cause checking, crazing, cracking or other problems.

All of these paint solvent materials are designed for use during certain climatic conditions. They are rated according to slow, medium and fast evaporation abilities. In addition to temperature factors, you may need to use a specific solvent to compensate for very heavy or extra-light humidity. In essence, fast-evaporating solvents are used during paint work in cool temperatures, and slow ones employed during hot weather.

But using a fast solvent on a cool and very humid day could cause blushing, a condition where moisture is trapped in paint after the fast solvent has evaporated. In that case, a medium thinner or reducer is needed to allow moisture time to evaporate along with solvent so that the resulting paint film dries completely and evenly.

Paint products are designed to be sprayed under climatic conditions of 70 degrees Fahrenheit and 30 percent humidity. These are perfect conditions under which laboratory tests are conducted. Unless you live in an environment that commonly

PPG's reducers are labeled a bit differently than Glasurit's. These include the actual climatic temperature ratings each is designed for. In addition, PPG offers a retarder that can be used when temperatures exceed 90 degrees Fahrenheit, and an accelerant when paint spraying temperatures are below 60 degrees. The importance of this facet of auto painting cannot be stressed too much. Using a cool-temperature reducer in hot weather will cause paint to dry much too fast, and vice versa for warm-temperature reducer. If paint dries too slow, it may sag or wrinkle. If it dries too fast, it might crack, check or craze.

boasts this type of weather, you have to paint cars in a controlled spray booth equipped with a dehumidifier and heater to achieve these perfect conditions. To compensate for the lack of such a facility, which can easily cost $100,000 or more, paint chemists have designed various solvents which react differently under various atmospheric conditions.

To help inexperienced auto painters choose the correct solvent, labels on thinners, reducers and retarders include the temperature range in which they are designed to be used. For example, DuPont's Cronar brand of base color solvents are rated as follows:

Solvent Type	Required Temperatures (degrees Fahrenheit)
Non-Penetrating Basemaker	50 to 65
Fast Basemaker	60 to 75
Mid-temp Basemaker	70 to 85
Slow Basemaker	80 to 95

Other brands of thinner, reducer and retarder are labeled the same way, but with possible slight variations in temperature ratings.

Now, to assist you in deciding which rated solvent is best to use during specific humidity conditions for the region in which you live, consulting with an autobody paint and supply jobber is necessary. Jobbers are familiar with the atmospheric and climatic conditions in their areas in relation to spray painting. They want your paint job to result in a beautiful finish so you will be satisfied with their products and continue to buy merchandise from them in the future. Therefore, you should be able to confidently rely on their advice about the use of various products and their application techniques.

Definitive information sheets and application guides, available at autobody paint and supply stores, will list specific paint to thinner and reducer mixing ratios. Although paint has already been mixed with certain amounts of solvent, since it is a liquid while in the can, even more solvent is needed to make the solution sprayable. Mixing sticks are used for this function according to product label instructions. The specific calibrations on mixing sticks are designed for use of certain paint bases and solvent. You must be sure to use a mixing stick designed specifically for the use of the name brand paint product you use. Sticks are readily available at autobody paint and supply stores.

Fisheye Eliminators

Tiny surface finish blemishes that resemble small circles of popped paint bubbles which seem to occur almost as soon as paint hits an autobody surface could be fisheyes. These flaws are generally caused by silicone residue. Small traces of silicone do not allow paint to settle evenly, rather, they cause material to encircle the speck of silicone and form, more or less, a volcano-like shape.

Fisheye problems result from extended use of silicone-based vinyl dressings on body side moldings and other trim. Excessive dressing applications and their random overspray away from trim infiltrates surrounding paint surfaces to become embedded in finishes. Although these painted surfaces may be thoroughly cleaned before paint application, silicone particles commonly remain to cause fisheye problems.

Autobody paint protectants, like poly-glycoats and other silicone-based materials, can also cause fisheye problems. In severe cases, silicone materials are absorbed by paint finishes to the point where underlying metal becomes saturated with silicone to make quality repaint efforts an almost impossible task.

To solve this kind of problem, paint manufacturers have developed paint additives which overcome the dilemma of fisheyes and allow paint to flow uniformly and cover evenly. Various paint manufacturing companies label their fisheye eliminators under certain names, like PPG's DX 77 Fisheye Preventer, Glasurit's Antisilicone Additive and DuPont's Cronar Fish Eye Eliminator 9259S. When needed, be sure to use only that product designed to be mixed with the paint employed; for example, use PPG's Fisheye Preventer with PPG paint products.

Mixing instructions are provided on container labels. In addition, it is recommended you use the fisheye eliminator product throughout your entire paint job. Do not simply mix in a prescribed dose to paint one panel that seems to exhibit fisheye problems, rather, use that same mixture for the entire repaint. This way, all of the identical ingredients and mixtures will be used uniformly to guarantee that color tints and coverage smoothness is the same.

To reduce fisheye problems during future paint touchups or repaints, use multipurpose vinyl dressings sparingly. Instead of spraying trim pieces directly, spray dressing on a soft cloth first and then wipe it on parts in a controlled fashion. Afterward, be sure to wash the entire car thoroughly with a quality car wash soap to remove traces of lingering silicone residue.

Flexible Additives

Newer cars frequently feature flexible urethane bumpers, spoilers, splash guards and ground effects that are painted the same color as their vehicle's body. For the most part, paint products used to cover these pieces are the same as those used to paint bodies. However, since these types of parts are flexible, a special additive is mixed in with paint to allow its thin film to bend and conform along with the body part without cracking, peeling or chipping. This kind of additive is critical

In addition to appropriate mixtures of reducer and catalyst, painting plastic parts, like ground effects or bumper parts, will require the inclusion of a flexible additive. This material will allow paint to move along with flexible parts to prevent cracking or peeling. In this case, a flexible additive was not used, nor was the plastic bumper properly prepared for paint. It should have been scuffed and then treated to a coat of adhesion promoter before painting.

if you want the painted finish on flexible parts to last.

According to PPG's *Full Line Catalog*, their Flexative Elastomeric Additive can be mixed directly with acrylic lacquers, acrylic enamels, urethane-modified acrylic enamels and acrylic urethanes to repair flexible body parts. Specific instructions call for part surfaces to be clean and then sanded to promote paint adhesion. Once again, each paint manufacturer recommends its own brand of flexible additive be used with its brand of paint products.

In addition to flexible painted bumpers and bumper guards, be alert to using a flexible additive when painting any other similar material. This includes flexible spoilers, fender flairs, entire front nose pieces, mud flaps and the like.

Primers

A number of novice auto painters are confused with the term primers. Many believe this term simply refers to one product that adequately prepares car bodies for paint. Others think that a thick primer will hide dents and scratches, even out body surfaces and allow paint to cover evenly.

Simply put, primers are materials that are applied directly over properly prepared bare metal. Their category in the overall package of any paint system includes different products that are separately designed to provide a variety of surface preparation functions. Together, they could be clumped under the term undercoats: those materials applied to autobody surfaces in preparation for paint applications. Generally, these include epoxy primers, primer-surfacers, sealers and adhesion promoters.

Waterproof epoxy primers, like PPG's DP 40, are used to protect bare metal from oxidation problems. Mixed with a hardener according to label instructions, catalyst-type epoxy primers are applied with a spray gun. One to two coats are normally recommended. Painters usually apply these kinds of primers to bare metal before the application of any other product. This is done for two reasons: First, since they are waterproof, they protect sheet metal. Second, epoxy primers offer excellent adhesion to metal and serve as perfect bases for additional undercoat products and topcoats (paint).

As with other paint products, each manufacturer offers its own epoxy primer and you are advised to use only those designed for the paint system you have chosen. Although the basic purpose for epoxy primers is to protect bare metal and offer quality adhesion bases, other catalyst-type primers in the same category are manufactured for different purposes. Some are designed to comply with strict military standards that require excellent corrosion resistance and exceptional adhesion capabilities. Others are made for aluminum surfaces or fiberglass materials.

In order to maximize oxidation, rust and corrosion protection for sheet-metal car bodies in

When PPG's DP 40 Epoxy Primer is mixed with its DP 401 catalyst, it makes for an excellent waterproof primer over bare metal. Anytime you expose bare metal, whether it be during a restoration project or body repair, you should consider covering bare sheet-metal with an epoxy primer. Rust quickly attacks bare metal, even overnight, especially in certain coastal areas near salty atmospheres. To protect sheet-metal parts, particularly while they are in storage during a restoration, coat them first with an epoxy primer to ensure they will be in usable condition when you pull them out of storage.

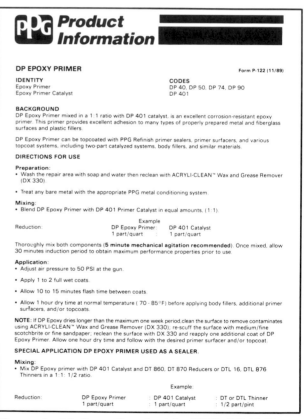

The product information sheet for PPG's DP 40 Epoxy Primer is detailed. Along with this first page, information is given relating to compatible topcoats and substrates, and just how users can employ it when sprayed over certain materials. Take advantage of this free information by picking up information sheets at the autobody paint and supply store on every product you have chosen to use. PPG Industries, Inc.

regions with exceptionally harsh corrosion environments, like ocean coasts and areas where winter roads are salted, autobody painters have applied catalyzed epoxy primers to bare metal and then again over subsequent primer-surfacer undercoats. If you live in such an area, you should confirm the need, usefulness and application procedure for additional epoxy primer coats with your autobody paint and supply jobber.

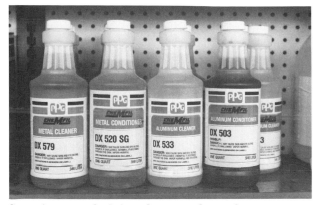

Sometimes, underlying sheet-metal panels are too contaminated with various forms of debris to allow good adhesion, even for the most potent epoxy primers. In those cases, you may have to wash and condition metal with a special product. Be absolutely certain you follow directions on the label of any such material you use. Especially heed warnings and always wear the recommended safety gear such as heavy-duty rubber gloves, eye protection and appropriate respirator.

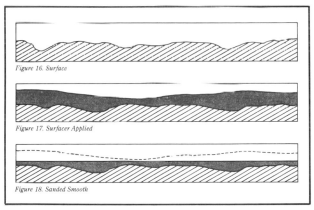

Figure 16. Surface

Figure 17. Surfacer Applied

Figure 18. Sanded Smooth

This illustration shows how a rather bumpy, on a minuscule scale, autobody surface can be covered with primer-surfacer material and then sanded smooth. Ideally, this only has to be done once. But, in reality, sometimes it takes three separate sessions of spraying primer-surfacer on and sanding it smooth and even. This material is not designed to cover or fill in dents! It is not nearly strong enough. Optimum usage dictates it should only be mils thick to cover such things as sanding scratches and very small and extremely shallow high and low spots left behind after body filler has been sanded. PPG Industries, Inc.

Primer-Surfacers

After an automobile body has sustained sheet-metal repair and received its required coats of epoxy primer, minor flaws might linger, such as sanding scratches. To cover them, painters use primer-surfacer products manufactured by the same company that produced the rest of the paint system products used. Because of their high-solids content, primer-surfacers cover tiny imperfections and allow painters to sand the coated surfaces to smooth perfection.

These products must not be confused with body fillers, however. The materials used in body fillers offer a great deal more strength and durability than primer-surfaces. Where properly applied, fillers are designed to cover sheet-metal imperfections up to ¼ in. in depth without cracking or chipping; primer-surfacers are only intended to be sprayed on surfaces to fill very slight sand scratches or other tiny blemishes. They are a final means by which to smooth body surfaces to perfection.

Primer-surfacers are the final undercoat products that are designed to be sanded and smoothed. Undercoats applied after them are simply used to seal base materials against the absorption of paint solvents, or to increase overall paint adhesion. Therefore, it is imperative that their coats be applied uniformly and all sanding be executed in a controlled and systematic manner.

Although some primer-surfacers may resist moisture to a point where wet sanding can be completed with no problems, other products can actually absorb water. Therefore, while your car sports only a primer surfacer finish, resist temptations to wash it or drive during periods of wet weather.

For some paint system applications, especially pertaining to particular colors, either a red or gray primer undercoat may be indicated. These two DuPont products have specific application properties. As recommended on information sheets or application guides, you will have to use one or the other when coats of primer-surfacer are needed.

Should moisture find its way into primer-surfacer finishes, it could become trapped inside this porous, talc-based material and remain there after paint has been sprayed and cured. At that point, moisture could find its way to bare metal and start a rusting process, or, if thwarted in that direction by epoxy primer, it may travel toward the surface to cause problems with the paint finish.

Different primer-surfacers are designed for specific applications. While one may be best suited for use over an epoxy primer and serve as a base for an acrylic enamel topcoat, another could be designed for use over aluminum or fiberglass surfaces in preparation for lacquer paint. Be sure to read information sheets and application guides for any primer-surfacer product you intend to use, and remember that selection assistance can always be provided by autobody paint and supply store employees.

Along with careful selection of the correct primer-surfacer brand and desired quantity, be sure to purchase enough sandpaper of the proper grit to smooth its surface after application. More than one sheet of sandpaper will be needed for just about every job, especially for those that entail entire panel repaints or full-body paint jobs. Terry Van Hee and Dan Mycon usually apply one coat of primer-surfacer and then block sand its cured surface with 150 grit. Another coat is sprayed on over the first and finish sanded with 320 grit and then perfected with 500 grit.

Sealers and Adhesion Promoters

A number of sealers and adhesion promoters are produced by paint manufacturers for an assortment of specific applications. Sealer functions include protection of undercoats from the materials and solvents in subsequently applied paint topcoats, and the addition of maximum adhesion capability for those topcoats. Adhesion promoters may also seal some undercoat bases, but are more likely intended to allow a different paint type to be satisfactorily applied over a non-compatible type of existing paint topcoat; for instance, lacquer over an original-finish base coat and clear coat enamel.

Especially when applying new paint over an existing paint surface, you must consider the use of a sealer or adhesion promoter, especially when you are not exactly sure what type or brand of paint is currently on the vehicle's finish. Most sealers and adhesion promoters do not require sanding after they have been applied and cured. They simply

Van Hee uses an attachment at the end of an air hose to blow off excessive sanding dust after meticulously sanding a final layer of glazing putty just before the application of primer-surfacer. Note the feathered edges and scuffed areas of existing paint surrounding the repair area. One sheet of sandpaper is not enough to accomplish all of this work. If you are not sure how much sandpaper of what grit you should buy for the job, let an autobody paint and supply jobber help out. Make sure you fully describe the job at hand so he or she can estimate accurately.

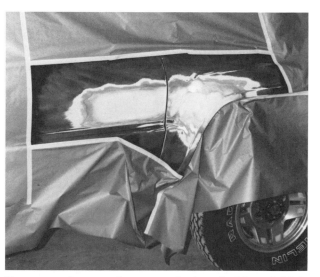

Because primer-surfacers are designed with such high-solids, masking requirements are rather minimal. This front door and fender section on a Toyota 4-Runner is masked sufficiently for that application. Van Hee will sand the initial layer of primer-surfacer with 150 grit to knock down the big stuff. He will then use 320 grit for fine sanding and finish it off with 500 grit for a really smooth surface. If initial sanding indicates minor low spots or other imperfections, another coat of primer-surfacer will be applied and sanded.

Sealers, like this one from PPG, are used to prevent undercoats from absorbing solvents from subsequent topcoats. They help to reduce sand scratch swelling by not allowing topcoat solvents to penetrate into the crevices and allow pigments and binders to follow. Be sure to confirm the appropriate sealer for the paint system you choose with your paint and supply jobber.

form a sort of barrier between the undercoat and topcoat.

Along with protecting undercoats from the absorption of paint solvents, sealers help to keep sand scratch swelling to a minimum. For example, let's say that some minor sand scratches are still present after you meticulously sanded the last coat of primer-surfacer. Absorption of a paint solvent will cause primer-surfacer sand scratches to swell and become more visible. As solvents evaporate, paint solids will fill the voids left behind by sand scratches to result in dull, scratchy appearing finishes.

Sealers and adhesion promoters also offer paint topcoats a uniform base to maximize color uniformity. A properly prepared surface sprayed with an appropriate sealer or adhesion promoter, as your paint system requirements designate, gives paint its best chance of forming an even film with uniform solvent evaporation to ensure all painted areas exhibit the identical color without blotches, clouds or bleed-through. This is especially important when painting a light color over an existing dark hue.

Adhesion promoters may be most advantageous for those jobs where new paint will be sprayed over factory finishes that were baked on at

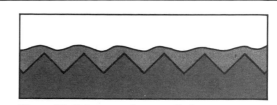

Figure 22. Primer-surfacer applied over sanded metal simulates the contours of the metal, with shrinkage more over deeper fills.

Figure 23. If sanded level before all solvents have evaporated, further evaporation of solvents will cause shrinkage leaving furrows over the sanding marks in the metal.

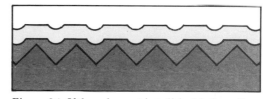

Figure 24. If the colorcoat is polished before all the thinner evaporates from the primer-surfacer and color, it will shrink back showing sand scratches. This condition may also be caused by using coarse rubbing compounds or too high of air pressure or too fast of solvent, when applying primer-surfacer.

This illustration clearly shows what happens when materials are sanded or polished before all of the solvents have had an opportunity to successfully evaporate. Pay strict attention to all flash times indicated on labels of paint material, information sheets and application guidelines. This problem can be accentuated from beginning to end with all materials applied to your car's surface if drying times are not followed. PPG Industries, Inc.

temperatures around 450 degrees Fahrenheit. Because those stock paint jobs are so hard and durable, new paint may have a difficult time penetrating the surface to achieve maximum adhesion. Mycon has had to repair more than one repaint job where inexperienced do-it-yourselfers just sprayed new paint directly over existing finishes without scuffing or sealing base surfaces. The results ranged from massive random paint flaking to the extreme where fresh paint layers were peeled off in sheets.

The application of sealers or adhesion promoters can make the difference between an adequate

The factory finish on this car was most likely baked on at a temperature around 450 degrees Fahrenheit. Because of that, it had a very hard and durable finish. In order for new paint to penetrate deep enough for solid adhesion, a bonding agent or adhesion promoter was sprayed on the surface before paint.

PPG's Acryli-Clean Wax and Grease Remover is a mild solvent used to rid autobody surfaces of wax, grease and other contaminants before the application of paint products. The use of such materials is imperative. Other paint manufacturers may call their pre-paint cleaners by a different name, but they are all designed to do the same thing: namely, remove debris or contaminants that would hinder the adhesion or uniform layout of paint materials. Be sure you acquire the appropriate cleaner along with the rest of your paint system materials.

paint job and an excellent one. Mycon and Van Hee almost always apply one or the other to the car bodies they paint, even those consisting of just small touchup areas. Confirm with the paint and supply salesperson the exact kind of sealer or adhesion promoter product to use with your paint system. Be sure to refer to application guides and information sheets for mixing instructions and other pertinent product user recommendations.

Wax and Grease Removers

Before any surface is ready for an undercoat or topcoat, it has to be as clean as possible. All traces of dirt, grease, oil, silicone and other contaminants must be removed. After a thorough and meticulous wash, car bodies must be wiped off with a wax and grease remover. Each paint system will have its own recommended product.

The best cleaning results can be obtained by using one cloth dampened with wax and grease remover to initially wipe surfaces with one hand, followed by a clean dry cloth in the other hand to remove lingering residue and moisture. Be abso-

lutely certain the cloths you use are clean and completely free from all traces of wax, polish, oil or anything else. To be sure, you might buy a yard or two of soft flannel material at a fabric store, wash it in your washing machine and then cut it into workable sizes about 2 ft. square. It can then be folded into a handy size where fresh sides can be unfolded for use when one becomes soiled.

Every part of any intended painted surface must be cleaned with a wax and grease remover product. If this chore is not completed, you run the risk of contaminants on the surface ruining an otherwise professionally applied paint job. Be sure to follow label instructions, including the use of rubber gloves and any recommended respiratory protective device.

To ensure that autobody surfaces are as clean as can be, supplement wax and grease remover

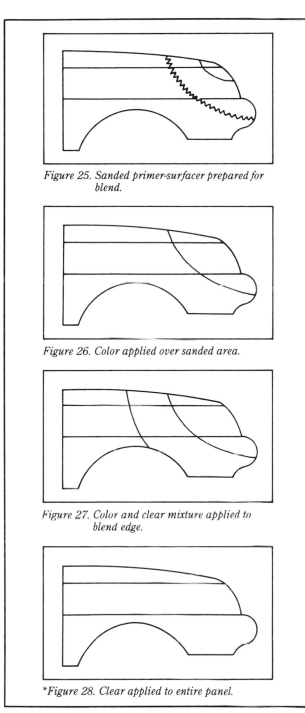

Figure 25. Sanded primer-surfacer prepared for blend.

Figure 26. Color applied over sanded area.

Figure 27. Color and clear mixture applied to blend edge.

*Figure 28. Clear applied to entire panel.

This illustration depicts how a two-step paint system is used for spot repair. The dark area in the top illustration denotes bodywork repair. The jagged line shows how far sanding efforts should extend for feathering with a primer-surfacer material. As indicated, color is applied to all areas where original paint was sanded off. The third illustration denotes how far a reduced color blend should be painted—a situation where clear paint and a tint of the color are mixed together for blending. Finally, the entire panel is shot with clear paint only. The total blend should be such that nobody would be able to tell that any repair or repaint work had been done.

cleaning with an additional wipedown using an aerosol glass cleaner. Ammonia in these kinds of glass-cleaning products helps to remove tiny traces of residual contaminant material and also assists in the removal of lingering moisture particles. Glass cleaner is simply sprayed onto surfaces and then wiped dry with a clean, soft, lint-free cloth.

Tack Cloths

The very last thing most painters do before actually spraying paint is wipe off body surfaces with a tack cloth. The special material used to make tack cloths allows them to pick up very fine particles of lint, dust and other debris. As mentioned earlier, imperfections on a primered surface are almost always magnified by coats of paint. The process of wiping off body surfaces with a tack cloth greatly helps to make certain bits of debris are removed so imperfections or nibs are not created.

You can buy tack cloths at any autobody paint and supply store. Their cost is minimal, especially

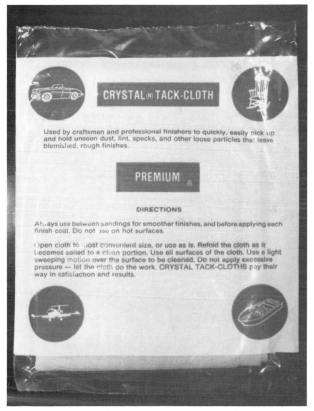

Tack cloths are saturated with a substance that makes them sticky. As they are gently rubbed across soon-to-be-painted surfaces, they pick up minute pieces of lint, dirt and other debris. Painters use tack clothes as a final step just before painting. In fact, they generally fill their paint guns and bring them to the booth just prior to tacking off surfaces for paint. The cost for these items is minimal when compared to the cost for paint materials, and you would be foolish to neglect their use.

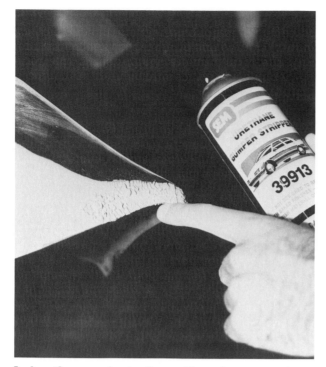

In less than a minute, the urethane bumper stripper Dan Mycon applied to this ground effect has wrinkled the layer of existing paint. Other products are made that will do the same thing to paint on metal. You must be certain that the product you apply to particular surfaces is intended for that specific use. Spraying a bumper stripper on an inappropriate surface may cause damage to the structural material.

This handy little Rust and Paint Stripper from 3M works well to remove accumulations of old paint and debris from autobody surfaces. It can be attached to the end of power drills or other designated rotary equipment. Tim Murdock, manager of Wesco Autobody, says that he has received nothing but compliments from customers who have used this item. They are happy with its paint removal capability and pleased that underlying sheet metal is not scratched to a point where it needs repair.

when compared to the kind of intricate dust and lint removal work they can provide. It works best to open and unfold tack cloths and then lightly fold them back again. This sort of fluffs them up to make them more manageable. Be sure to take note of any package instructions or user recommendations to ensure adequate and complete cleaning.

Paint Removers

Automotive paint is removed from car bodies in basically three ways: sanding, sandblasting and chemical stripping. Most endeavors to remove paint from selected areas for autobody repair work are done with coarse sanding discs on a high-speed sanding tool. More intense paint removal projects, like those for rusty and neglected hulks, are accomplished by controlled sandblasting. Both of these methods will not only remove paint, they will also take off undercoats and anything else covering bare metal.

Another method of removing paint down to bare metal employs chemical strippers which loosen paint material and make it easy to gently scrape off with a firm plastic squeegee or putty knife. The process is messy, as wet globs of paint are

scraped off and fall to the floor. You must also be concerned about personal safety while using potent chemical strippers. Wear heavy-duty rubber gloves, eye protection and a recommended respirator as suggested by the product label.

The use of chemical paint strippers is generally saved for complete new paint jobs, as opposed to autobody repair work to fix localized dents. For repair work, most autobody professionals quickly remove paint with a sander after the majority of dent repairs have been completed. This is because it is much easier to see surface imperfections, wrinkles and low spots on painted body panels than on those with bare shiny metal.

Using a 36 or 40 grit sanding disc, they can take paint off of car bodies in no time. The extra-coarse discs also do a good job of removing all paint or body filler remnants from tiny dings and other hard-to-reach crevices. The heavy pattern of rather deep sanding scratches on sheet metal also serves as an excellent base for filler material adhesion.

Chemical paint removers might be best employed on automobiles in need of a complete new

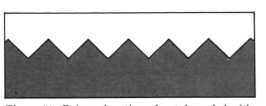

Figure 20. Enlarged section of metal sanded with 36 grit disc and followed with 80 grit paper still shows small combs and burrs.

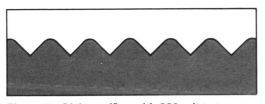

Figure 21. Light scuffing with 220 grit paper removes combs and will round tops of ridges eliminating much of the trouble with sand scratches.

After removing paint by way of a high-speed rotary sander and 36 or 40 grit sanding disc, sheet metal may present some very sharp, pointed sanding edges. To help eliminate future sand swelling problems, PPG recommends, and many painters comply, scuffing with a 220 grit sandpaper to round off sharp metal points. PPG Industries, Inc.

A special application gun is used to apply Rocker Schutz, a high-impact resistant undercoat material, to a front-end ground effect. The owner of this BMW preferred this durable material be applied on this part to help thwart rock chips on its surface. As with any surface material, you must be sure that scuffing and/or the application of bonding agents or adhesion promoters are in place before the application of the topcoat material. If you don't, you stand the chance that finish materials will not adhere as expected, possibly increasing the chance that they will peel or crack.

paint job when the body is in almost perfect condition. In other words, there is no compelling reason to roughen sheet metal with a sanding disc or take the chance that a mistake with sandblasting equipment could cause panels to warp or otherwise be damaged by high-pressure media blasting away at its surface.

Although chemical strippers can easily damage nonmetallic items such as rubber moldings or plastics, controlled applications and gentle material removal should result in a clean, shiny body surface with no ill effects. To further reduce the possibility of scratches or other scraping damage, consider using a heavy-duty plastic squeegee to remove wrinkled paint from body surfaces, instead of a metal putty knife.

A number of different brands are available, but you might want to seek an autobody paint and supply salesperson's advice as to which particular product might be best suited for your needs. Use a sheet of heavy-duty plastic or cardboard under the edges of your car while removing chemically impregnated paint residue. This way, once the body is stripped, plastic or cardboard can be removed and safely discarded, according to any local hazardous materials waste control regulations in effect for your area.

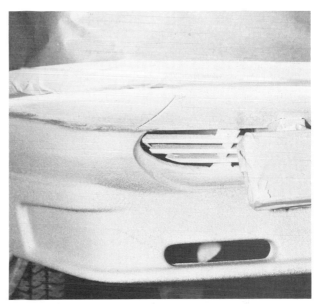

There is nothing wrong with this photo; Rocker Schutz goes on thick and offers a rather rough texture. Note the sturdy jack stand at the lower middle section of the picture. In order to satisfactorily reach the paint areas, Mycon had to raise the car. Never crawl under a vehicle unless it is supported by sturdy, heavy-duty jack stands. Also, foglights were masked off with strips of 2 in. masking tape, in lieu of paper and ¾ in. tape.

Overview

Compared to a few years ago, or so it seems, decisions regarding automobile painting have increased tremendously. Now, not only do you have tens of thousands of colors to choose from, you also have to determine which kind of solvent, primer, primer-surfacer, sealer and adhesion promoter to use. Or, for that matter, which products you do not need to use. The technology surrounding the auto paint industry has really become high-tech. Even professional painters sometimes have to suffer through difficult decisions relating to repaint procedures on cars that have been repainted one or two times with an unknown type of paint, or worse yet, more than one type sprayed onto different body panels.

The best advice professionals like Mycon, Van Hee and Laursen have to offer novice auto painters is to take plenty of time before starting a job to thoroughly research what has to be done to properly prepare the vehicle's surface, and just exactly which paint products will be needed to complete the job safely, effectively and with expected finish results. Haphazardly starting a project with little concern over a systematic and organized approach will do nothing but delay the overall process and probably cause frustration over missed completion dates and the extra work needed to go over areas that were not properly serviced the first time.

All automotive paint products are potentially dangerous to their own degree. Just about every product is flammable and you have to be keenly aware of all sources of heat ignition whenever working with them. Flash fires involving clouds of flammable gases will quickly engulf your shop, garage, carport and, most importantly, yourself. Have a fire extinguisher available at all times just in case of an accident.

Personal safety has become an intense issue with the use of automotive painting chemicals. Every label of every product will clearly recommend the use of certain personal safety equipment. Heed those recommendations to protect your health. Should you have any questions about the intended use or function of any auto paint product or piece of related equipment, do not hesitate to consult an autobody paint and supply salesperson, manufacturer information sheet or application guide, professional auto painter or paint manufacturer.

4

Tools, Materials and Safety

It is almost impossible to complete any job without the right tools, materials or equipment. Automotive painting is no different than any other chore and you must expect to buy, borrow or rent some rather specialized equipment if you expect to properly prepare any autobody surface and then paint it with results comparable to that of a professional.

Autobody paint and supply stores carry a wide selection of repair and painting tools and equipment. In most cases, this merchandise is designed for commercial use and will be of heavy-duty construction and quality. The cost may be high, but you could easily expect each item to last a long time. You might opt instead to purchase required equipment from tool outlets or other stores that sell the items. These other places might carry items built a little less heavy duty, which would cost less.

The Eastwood Company sells tools and equipment especially designed for both part-time and serious auto restorers, autobody repair technicians and painters. All of the tools and equipment they sell is tested in their field laboratory, a quality shop where auto restoration and repair projects are ongoing.

They advertise that each item listed in their catalog has been used in their shop with satisfactory results. Mycon has used some tools and equipment from Eastwood and was very pleased with their performance, construction and handling. Since Eastwood caters to the do-it-yourself hobbyist, you can be assured that the quality and prices of their equipment are very competitive.

In lieu of purchasing or borrowing tools or equipment, you could rent items at a local rental yard. Although most rental businesses make valiant attempts to keep all of their inventory in top condition, you may have some trouble finding paint guns that spray as expected. This is because tiny air and material ports are easily clogged with dry paint if they are not immediately cleaned after each use. Therefore, you might seriously consider spending a few dollars to buy your own spray paint gun so that you can be guaranteed it will be taken care of properly and operate as expected every time.

Work Area

If you wanted to apply a nonskid paint job to your car that was rough enough to prevent a sheet of ice from falling off of it, you could apply almost any paint in a desert sandstorm and call it good. A little smoother texture, you say? Then try painting

The paint booth at Newlook Autobody is frequently washed down with clear water. No sanding is conducted in that area, but paint overspray does accumulate into dusty residues. Before this Firebird is painted, all doors will be shut and the ventilation system allowed to operate for a length of time to remove dust particles from the booth atmosphere. You may not be able to duplicate the environment of a professional spray paint booth, but you can certainly do the next best thing by properly insulating your garage or shop with sheets of plastic, lath and duct tape.

47

your car in a carport with a dirt and gravel floor. But, if what you really want is a smooth, blemish-free, lustrous, deep-shine paint job, consider renting a regular auto spray paint booth or spending a little time to devise a makeshift paint booth in your garage or workshop.

Because of increasing restrictions regulating the auto paint industry, limitations are being placed on where and how auto paint can be sprayed. The advent of HVLP systems is a great help, but along with them, painters in certain regions are required to use high-tech spray booths equipped with down-draft ventilation systems and overspray capturing mechanisms.

To offset the staggering price of their booths, some paint shops make them available for rent—under supervised conditions, of course. You may be able to find rental booths through advertisements in your telephone book's yellow pages under the heading "Autobody repair and painting." You can also check with your autobody paint and supply jobber, auto parts store salesperson and even make a few calls to local bodyshops to determine if they rent their booths or know of any other bodyshops that offer theirs for rent.

A definite problem exists when renting paint booths, in that you have to transport your car to

that location. Whether it is driven or towed, masking will have to be completed at that booth's location, along with possible part dismantling, such as lights, and required cleaning. Be sure transporting is done on a dry day with dry roads.

Should you decide to paint your vehicle at home, you must provide a suitable work area. A garage or shop should be fine. Plenty of air ventilation must be provided and overspray concerns accounted for. You will need an air compressor, or suitable HVLP system, lots of light and an electrical source to operate a fresh-air respirator compressor if called for.

Rather than spray cars in an open garage and cover everything in the place with speckles of overspray, consider enclosing an area with sheets of clear plastic. Long, wide sheets of Visqueen are available at lumber yards and hardware stores. Roll an edge of plastic around strips of lath and nail them to the ceiling or rafters. Use heavy-duty duct tape to secure bottom edges to the floor. Consider placing plastic across open rafters as a makeshift ceiling to prevent dust from the attic space from falling onto your paint surface. Be sure plastic is not put too close to light fixtures, as hot bulbs could melt or ignite it.

To aid ventilation, put a large fan near the front of your work place. A hole can be cut in plastic for the insertion of a fan to bring in fresh air from outside the enclosure. Tape a thin, lint-free cloth over the fan's cage to trap dust or debris from entering the paint area. Leave the garage door open to assist in ventilation, but be certain that local breezes will not flow directly from the outside in through the open door. If that is a problem, determine when breezes are minimal, maybe early in the morning, and plan to paint at that time.

If a gravel or dirt driveway is located right outside your garage or workshop, you will have to thoroughly wet it down to keep dust at an absolute minimum. You might even have to leave a light sprinkler spray in place during paint work to keep dust particles from being kicked up and blown all over your painting surface. In addition, plan to wet down the floor in your paint enclosure to keep dust at bay while you walk around the vehicle.

Sandpaper, Sanding Blocks and Sanding Machines

Quality paint jobs cannot be accomplished when paint is applied to improperly prepared surfaces. Paint products are not designed to fill cracks, crevices or other blemishes. Rather, they will sink into these imperfections to magnify their depth and roughness. Therefore, you have to spend as much time as necessary to sand all coats of primer-surfacer or existing paint surfaces to absolute smooth perfection. Mycon and Van Hee consistently acknowledge that the vast majority of their time is spent preparing cars for paint, as opposed

Shown here are 360, 600 and 1500 grit sandpaper sheets. The 360 is coarsest among the three; the lowest numbers designate the coarsest grades of sandpaper. All three sheets display the name brand, Wetordry. This designation means they can be used with or without water. Be sure to obtain plenty of sandpaper of the appropriate grits in order to prepare and finish your project.

48

to actually spraying them. A variety of sandpaper grits and useful hand tools are available for smoothing chores.

Sandpaper is rated according to its relative coarseness. The coarser it is, the lower number it will have; for example, 36 grit sandpaper is extremely coarse and 1200 grit is super-fine, almost smooth. Autobody paint and supply stores carry the widest selection of sandpaper grits, both in the type used for dry sanding only and those that can be used dry or with water. Wet sanding is generally saved for those operations required to smooth blemishes on lacquer or urethane paints after they have been sprayed and cured.

To complement their assortment of sandpaper grits, paint and supply stores carry these products in various sizes and shapes. You can buy sheets of sandpaper measuring about a foot square that are cut or folded to suit user needs. You can also take advantage of sandpaper strips, with or without adhesive backsides, that are designed for use on long sanding boards, or, adhesive-backed discs that are put on the circular pads of dual-action (DA) sanders. Be sure to purchase enough sandpaper to complete your job, as one sheet is rarely enough for more than one small repair touchup operation.

For flat and even sanding you must use a sanding block or board. Using your hand alone will result in minute low spots or grooves, caused by the hand's irregular shape and nonrigid nature. Knuckle protrusions featured on the palm side of your hand cause the sandpaper under them to dig in while the rest of the sanding area receives only slight pressure and minimal smoothing. Sanding blocks and boards, on the other hand, provide flat,

This is a small assortment of hand sanding pads. They work great for smoothing surfaces in confined spaces where sanding blocks or boards will not fit. The hand blocks are designed for smoothing flat surfaces while the more pliable pads are better suited for jobs around contoured shapes and those in extra-tight spaces.

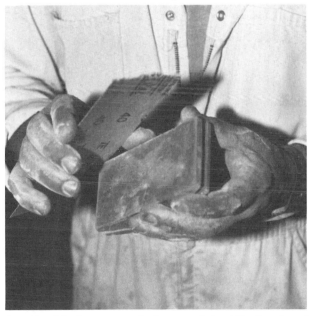

Sanding blocks commonly feature slots at the front and rear ends. Sandpaper is fitted into these slots where they are held in place by brads that extend up from the bottom base. In this case, an extra-long strip of sandpaper, designed for an air file, was measured and cut so it would fit this block perfectly. Some that feature adhesive backs work very well, as they stay in place on blocks much better than those without adhesive.

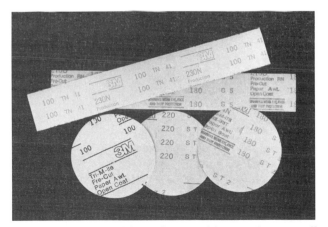

Sandpaper is available in discs and long strips, as well as in sheets. The materials above are for applications to sanding boards and air files, on the top, and dual-action sanders on the bottom. Some sandpaper comes ready-made with self-stick adhesive backs, and others require the use of a spray-on adhesive for their attachment to sanding boards or pads.

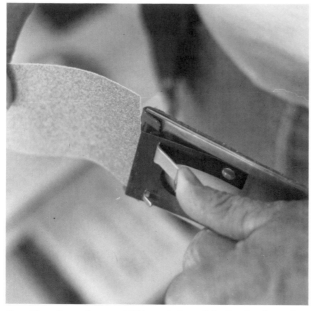

Sanding boards are different than blocks in that they are rigid boards to which sandpaper holding mechanisms are attached; they also feature comfortable handles. Here, a piece of sandpaper is fitted into an attachment mechanism. All you have to do is force up an operating lever to loosen the grab assembly and insert sandpaper. Once the lever is released, the mechanism securely closes over the edge.

In really tight spots, like this featured groove along a door panel, painters have to use their imagination in order to devise usable sanding blocks. In this instance, a wooden paint stir stick is used to sand a layer of glazing putty located inside a designed body panel groove. Normally, sandpaper is wrapped around stir sticks to ensure stability. It has been loosened for illustrative purposes.

rigid bases that easily receive and disperse identical pressure over entire sanding surfaces.

Sanding blocks and boards are available at autobody paint and supply stores, some auto parts houses and through catalog sales outlets like The Eastwood Company. Three sizes are commonly offered. The smallest, a little larger than the palm of your hand, is handy for reaching into tight areas confined by body designs or other obstructions. A medium size works great for sanding touchup areas that encompass small panel areas. Long blocks and boards work best for sanding chores on full panels, deck lids, hoods and the like.

Custom sanding blocks and boards have been designed for special applications. Rounded bases provide an excellent means for sanding curved body features, like grooves and arched fender flairs. Small hand pads work best for smoothing imperfections near ridges, acute corners and other unique spots too small for normal blocks or boards. Most of these items are also on display at your local autobody paint and supply store, and available through auto-related equipment and tool outlets like Eastwood.

Sanding machines basically consist of pneumatic or electrical-powered hand sanders. Their use is not always required, especially for small jobs. But, on complete repaints or vehicles that have undergone body repair, these tools can help to cut the amount of time spent sanding.

High-speed rotary sanders are most commonly used to remove paint, old body filler and rust deposits on sheet-metal panels. They can also be used to remove or smooth grossly jagged fingers of fiber-

This is a close-up view of a 3M brand, very fine grade, Scotch-Brite pad. They are used to scuff the shiny finish of existing paint surfaces to prepare them for the application of new paint. They can also be used to scuff trim pieces before they are sprayed. Assortments of Scotch-Brite pads are available at autobody paint and supply stores.

This high-speed rotary sander with a coarse-grit disc can remove paint, rust and other surface contaminants in just a matter of minutes. Note the sand scratches left behind after the sander passed over the surface. Although some relatively deep sand scratches will add a bit to the adhesive strength of epoxy primers, you may want to round off the sharp sand scratch tops with a 220 grit paper to make them a little less defined and help reduce sand scratch swelling for the subsequent application of primer and primer-surfacer.

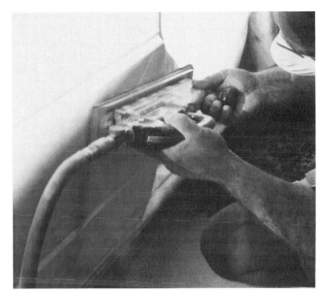

Air files are great tools for quickly removing the bulk of plastic body filler from repair areas on body panels. Various sandpaper grits can be attached to their bases, but, they may be too forceful for intricate work on primer-surfacer coatings. The rapid back-and-forth movement created by air file mechanisms require users to constantly keep the tools moving. Allowing them to sit on one spot for any length of time will cause grooves or low spots to appear. Before applying an air file to the surface of your car, be sure to practice with it on an old trunk lid or hood.

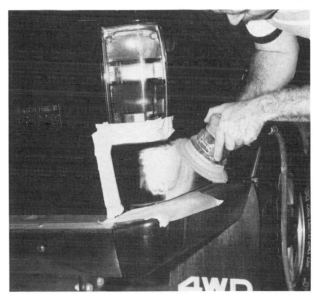

Van Hee is using a small dual-action sander to smooth an area covered with glazing putty before the application of primer-surfacer. The unusual vibration of these sanders can make users think they are not working very hard, but in reality, they can remove a lot of material in a hurry. Practice with these power tools is mandatory before applying them to the surface of your favorite vehicle. Sandpaper discs with adhesive backs work best on DA sanders.

glass that stick out from cracks and other collision damage to panels on fiberglass body vehicles. For the most part, these tools are employed by autobody repair technicians, although painters do use them to remove years of accumulated paint and rust deposits from vehicles scheduled for full paint jobs.

With bases shaped like long sanding boards, air files make quick work of smoothing layers of plastic filler on wide panels, like door skins. Their internal mechanisms operate bases in a rapid back-and-forth direction. Users must constantly keep these tools moving up and down because if allowed to rest on one spot, their forceful action will cause definite grooves, waves or other imperfections.

Dual-action or DA sanders are a mainstay in professional auto paint shops. Their unique design causes a circular pad to move in orbital directions instead of just spinning in a high-speed circle. An offset counterweight working in conjunction with an oval-shaped mounting mechanism allows DA pads to be forced back and forth and side to side in a very fast movement. Speed controls allow for intricate sanding, and assortments of sandpaper grit discs can be used for anything from initial sanding to fine finishing.

DA sanders are available in different sizes and power ranges. Large tools work best for body repair jobs, and small ones are handiest for paint preparation work. You will find DAs at autobody paint and supply stores, some tool houses and through companies like Eastwood.

Masking Tape

Almost everyone is familiar with masking tape. But, did you know there is a drastic difference between the rolls of masking tape found at ordinary hardware stores and those specifically designed for automotive painting jobs? There is, and the difference in their designs could make a definite difference in the outcome of your paint job.

Inferior masking tape was used to cover this body side molding mounting hole, evidenced by the debris on each side of it. Never use anything but masking tape specifically designed for automotive paint purposes. Besides lingering adhesive and paper residue, generic masking-type tape is somewhat porous and may let solvents or paint materials penetrate their surface to mar underlying finishes.

Ordinary household masking tape has not been treated to withstand potent auto paint solvents. Paint can penetrate weak tape to ruin the finishes underneath. In addition, adhesives used in ordinary masking tape are not designed to easily break loose from surfaces and can remain on painted bodies after the bulk of material has been pulled off. Lingering traces of tape and adhesive residue might require use of a mild solvent for complete removal, a chore that could threaten the finish of new paint applied next to it.

Whether your job consists of a very small paint touchup or complete paint job, you have to realize that automotive paint masking tape is the only product designed for such use. Using any other type of inexpensive alternative is just asking for headaches and hassles.

Autobody paint and supply stores sell masking tape in all sorts of widths. Sizes range from 1/8 in. to a full 2 in. Each masking job presents different needs, and having more than one size of masking tape on hand will help you accomplish those chores quicker and easier. For example, it is much simpler to place a few strips of 2 in. wide masking tape over a headlight than having to maneuver a sheet of masking paper over that same rounded area.

For masking designs, or to ensure perfect masking tape edges along trim and molding, many painters initially lay down a thin 1/8 in. wide strip of

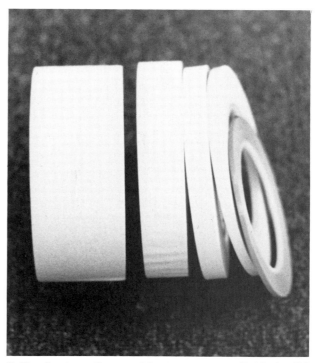

Rolls of automotive masking tape are available in different widths. To the far right is a thin roll of Fine Line plastic tape. Use various widths as necessary to accomplish masking jobs in a timely and proficient manner.

Fine Line plastic tape. Made by 3M, Fine Line is very maneuverable and will adhere securely around curves without bending or folding. It is easy to use as a primary masking edge along trim and molding edges. After it is placed, ¾ in. or larger tape can be attached anywhere along Fine Line without necessarily having to be right at the edge of the masked part.

Painters use more rolls of ¾ in. masking tape than any other. Its versatile size works great for securing paper and covering small items such as key locks. Tim Murdock, from Wesco Autobody Supply, recommends you have at least two rolls of 2 in. and three rolls of ¾ in. tape on hand for extensive masking jobs. If you contemplate masking along trim or molding pieces, have a couple of rolls of ⅛ in. Fine Line handy. Expect to pay anywhere from $1.75 to $2.50 per roll for quality automotive paint masking tape. Each roll is generally sixty yards long, the same as rolls of masking paper.

Masking Paper

Seldom will you find professional auto painters using anything but treated masking paper for any masking job. Newspapers have been used by some inexperienced painters with mixed results.

Although newspaper material may seem inexpensive and appropriate for paint masking chores, it is porous and can let paint seep through to mar surface finishes underneath. Murdock, Mycon and Van Hee all recommend you never rely on newspaper for any masking job.

Rolls of quality automotive paint masking paper are available at autobody paint and supply stores. Their widths range from 4 in. up to 3 ft., with 12 in. being the most frequently used size. This paper is chemically treated to prevent paint or solvent penetration, a most important asset. Two rolls of 12 in. paper should be enough for most jobs. You'll need a roll of wider paper to cover roofs, hoods and trunk lids, in situations where they will not be painted at all or will be sprayed a different color than body sides. A roll of 4 or 6 in. paper could be handy for intricate masking, as is necessary around doorjambs, trunk and hood edges.

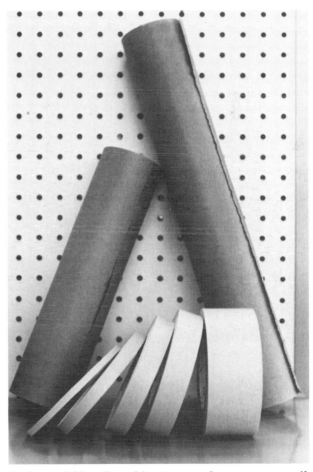

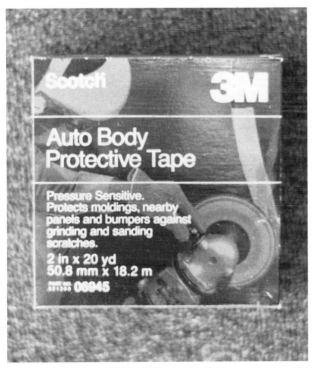

Many times, you will find that sanding requires working close to nearby surfaces that otherwise need not be removed. To ensure that sanding procedures do not accidentally mar those surfaces, apply pieces of Auto Body Protective Tape over them. This material is readily available at autobody paint and supply stores.

Various widths of masking tape and paper are available at autobody paint and supply stores. For the most part, you will need two rolls of 12 in. paper, two rolls of ¾ in. tape and one roll of 2 in. tape. This is the norm. For extensive masking jobs, plan your purchases accordingly. Costs are nominal, especially when compared to actual paint products.

Dispensers like this provide painters with sheets of masking paper with tape already affixed to their edge. Almost every professional bodyshop has at least one.

Moisture or oil in air supply lines will cause problems with paint finishes. At Newlook, the air pressure regulator on the right and air dryer on the left help painters to achieve just the right kind of air supply for the job they are spraying. Although the regulator may be a luxury item for most do-it-yourself auto painters, the air dryer should be a serious consideration. Small air compressors must work hard to supply the air demanded by many spray paint guns. The harder they work, the more condensation is allowed into the air lines.

To make their masking jobs easier, professional painters use masking paper and tape racks designed to allow paper to be pulled off with tape already attached to its edge. The Eastwood Company offers a small, hand-held model that can accommodate paper widths up to 9 in. To help you easily retrieve strips of masking paper, consider mounting a piece of heavy dowel on the side of your workbench with long brackets so rolls can rotate freely as you pull off needed lengths.

Air Compressor

You could buy the most expensive auto paint products made, spend weeks and weeks preparing your car or truck's surface to perfection, use the most highly advanced spray paint gun available and then *ruin* your paint job by relying upon an inadequate air compressor or a holding tank loaded with moisture and oil residue.

Jon Kosmoski, owner and founder of the House of Kolor, cannot overemphasize the importance of a clean, dry and controlled source of air pressure for any spray paint job. He stresses that minuscule particles of water, oil or rust will find their way from holding tanks to spray gun nozzles unless they are captured and retained somewhere between the compressor and gun. If allowed to accumulate and eventually exit a spray gun's nozzle, the paint finish being sprayed will be blemished with fisheyes, dirt nibs and possibly blushing problems all over the surface.

Most professional paint shops use a minimum 10 hp rated air compressor. These are big units that supply plenty of air for the operation of pneumatic tools and some painting equipment simultaneously. Mycon and Laursen recommend

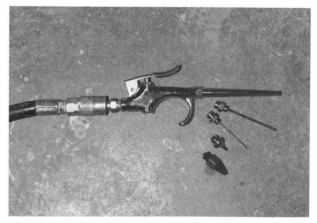

An assortment of air hose nozzle tips can be quite useful during paint preparation procedures. Thin tips allow air pressure to be blown inside tight spaces to dislodge sanding dust and other debris so it is not moved around during the paint process. Autobody paint and supply stores carry items like these, as do other tool outlets. Tools courtesy of The Eastwood Company.

units with at least a 5 hp capacity for most painting jobs. This is not to say that smaller compressors cannot be expected to work fine for small jobs, but that 5 hp machines offer plenty of compressed air without having to work overtime to supply it.

The more a compressor works, the physically hotter its air supply becomes. As heat continues to be generated, moisture is introduced into the air system through condensation inside piping. This is not good. You should want your air compressor to build up a reserve of compressed air in its holding tank and then shut off for a while to cool down.

About the best way to determine what size air compressor will work best for your needs is to compare the required cubic feet per minute of air needed with your spray gun and the application of particular paint products, to the cfm rating on the compressor you plan to use. If the compressor can easily supply the required cfm at the prescribed application pressure, you should have no problems. But, for example, if you need 12 cfm for your spray gun and your 2 hp compressor can only supply a maximum of 9 cfm, you will have to rent or borrow a higher rated unit to meet the minimum 12 cfm requirement.

Air filters are designed to trap elements like moisture, oil and debris before they enter the last leg of an air supply system, namely, your spray gun supply hose. This unit from The Eastwood Company does a good job. In addition to a filter, you might also consider the installation of an air dryer to better assist filters in removing all traces of oil accumulations or moisture condensation. The Eastwood Company

After you have figured out which air compressor to use, consider the installation of a piping system with a water trap or air dryer located at the end. Even for home use, a small air supply system with ¾ to 1 in. pipe could be advantageous. A copper or galvanized pipe running downhill away from a compressor toward a water trap or dryer will allow moisture accumulations in heated air to flow away from the compressor and toward the trap or dryer. Since the hot air will have time to cool inside pipes, moisture suspended in the air will condense into droplets that can be captured and retained as a liquid in the trap.

Kosmoski recommends do-it-yourself painters run ¾ to 1 in. copper or galvanized pipe up from their compressor location to the ceiling. Then, attach a horizontal section to the riser and run it downhill to the other end of a garage or workshop. Another section is attached to it and will go down to a convenient point where a water trap or air dryer is mounted. Working air lines will connect at the trap or dryer to be used for pneumatic tools and spray guns.

To keep portable air compressors mobile and to prevent their operational vibration from causing damage to solid piping mounted to walls, it is recommended you connect compressors to your piping system by way of a short, flexible air hose. This way, you can easily disconnect the compressor from the piping system to move it to wherever needed for other kinds of jobs.

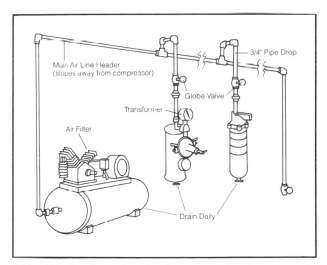

This illustration clearly demonstrates how an air supply system should be set up. Notice how the drop pipes come off the horizontal main line header from a U-shaped design. This element helps to prevent accumulated moisture at the bottom of header lines from entering paint gun supply hoses. To keep air compressors mobile and to prevent compressor vibration from disrupting air line supports on walls, connect flexible air line connections between compressors and the initial air supply riser mounted on walls. PPG Industries, Inc.

SIZE OF AIR HOSE	AIR PRESSURE DROP AT SPRAY GUN				
INSIDE DIAMETER	10 Foot Length	15 Foot Length	20 Foot Length	25 Foot Length	50 Foot Length
1/4 inch	Lbs.	Lbs.	Lbs.	Lbs.	Lbs.
At 40 lbs. pressure	8	9 1/2	11	12 3/4	24
At 50 lbs. pressure	10	12	14	16	28
At 60 lbs. pressure	12 1/2	14 1/2	16 3/4	19	31
At 70 lbs. pressure	14 1/2	17	19 1/2	22 1/2	34
At 80 lbs. pressure	16 1/2	19 1/2	22 1/2	25 1/2	37
At 90 lbs. pressure	18 3/4	22	25 1/2	29	39 1/2
5/16 inch					
At 40 lbs. pressure	2 3/4	3 1/4	3 1/2	4	8 1/2
At 50 lbs. pressure	3 1/2	4	4 1/2	5	10
At 60 lbs. pressure	4 1/2	5	5 1/2	6	11 1/2
At 70 lbs. pressure	5 1/4	6	6 3/4	7 1/4	13
At 80 lbs. pressure	6 1/4	7	8	8 3/8	14 1/2
At 90 lbs. pressure	7 1/2	8 1/2	9 1/2	10 1/2	16

The inside diameter of air hoses can affect the amount of air pressure delivered to a spray paint gun. This chart shows some basic pressure drops for 1/4 and 5/16 in. inside-diameter air hoses when used at specific lengths. Keep these calculations in mind when determining the correct pressure for spraying undercoats and paint so that spray application will be made at recommended gun pressures. PPG Industries, Inc.

Most professional auto painters use their own personal spray guns at work. This is so they can rely on the unit's operation time and again because they personally maintain it. All it takes is a small spot of dry paint residue in an air passage or material port to completely throw off the gun's ability to spray an even fan. You have to be conscientious about spray gun maintenance in order to guarantee the unit's dependability. Never force sharp objects into paint gun cavities or ports. Instead, use brushes, like these, to clean accessible areas so that your gun can spray as expected every time. Cleaning brushes courtesy of The Eastwood Company.

To ensure you have the recommended air pressure at the tip of your spray gun, hold the trigger on your gun wide open while adjusting air pressure regulator controls. Although a control gauge setting might show 40 psi while in a static condition, operating your paint gun may cause it to drop down to 30 or 35 psi. It is important to apply auto paint at the psi rating indicated on the container label or in the product's application guide literature.

Another factor that could cause false pressure gauge readings is the size of the air hose used to supply your paint gun. Small-diameter hoses will experience friction loss and cause pressures to dwindle once they arrive at the paint gun 25 ft. away. PPG's *Refinish Manual* suggests 1/4 in. hose is too small for standard production paint guns. It suggests a preferred hose size of 5/16 in. inside diameter in maximum lengths of 25 ft.

Paint Guns

Binks, Sharpe and DeVilbiss are three popular brands of automotive spray paint guns. You should be able to use equipment from any one of these name brand manufacturers with good results. Two types of spray guns are available. The standard production model is biggest and generally features a 1 qt. capacity cup. A smaller gun, referred to as a Detail Gun or Jamb Gun, features a 6 or 8 oz. capacity cup and has its trigger assembly mounted on top, as opposed to standard guns with handle grip triggers.

The difference between the full-size production spray paint gun and the detail model focuses around their maneuverability. As the larger unit is perfect for complete paint jobs and panel repaints,

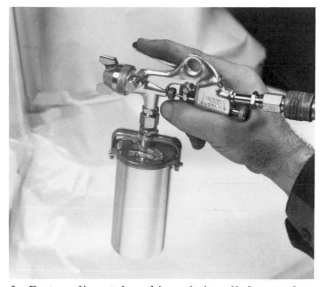

In Eastwood's catalog, this unit is called a touchup spray paint gun; other painters commonly refer to such units as detail guns or jamb guns. This is because these small paint guns are very maneuverable and work great for painting small surfaces like doorjambs. Custom painters use touchup guns for custom graphics where little paint is required, like for color blending flame designs. The Eastwood Company

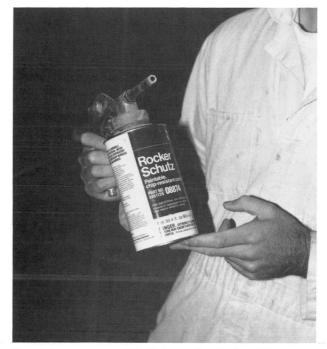

Special spray guns, like this one for Rocker Schutz, are available at autobody paint and supply stores. You can also find spray guns for undercoating materials for fenderwells and undercarriages, as well as airbrush units and HVLPs. Smart do-it-yourself auto painters plan their jobs long ahead of schedule so they can have all of the necessary tools and equipment at their disposal.

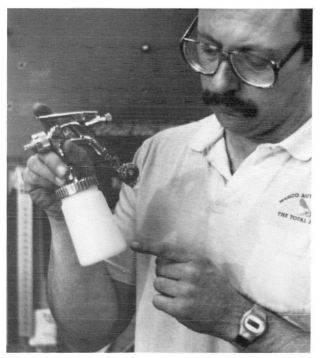

Tim Murdock is pointing toward the wide base on this detail spray paint gun's paint cup. It is made of plastic, which costs less, but the wide base makes it more stable when the unit is stood up. These paint guns are great for small jobs and their index finger control makes maneuvering easy. Consider using a unit like this for intricate jobs such as doorjambs and engine compartments.

the detail gun is perfect for intricate painting jobs, like small touchups requiring fine spray patterns and doorjamb painting. The top-mounted trigger on detail guns is operated by the full length of a user's index finger. This comfortable position allows painters to operate these lightweight units in confined spaces with maximum control.

A full range of various spray paint guns and their accessories are available at autobody paint and supply stores and through The Eastwood Company. Prices range from about $60 to $190 and up, depending upon the brand and precision quality. Paint cups are generally extra, costing around $25 for detail guns and $35 for production models. Along with paint guns, you can purchase air valves that attach to guns in line with their air supply. These valves help to fine-tune air pressure at the gun to perfect spray patterns.

Professional automobile painters heavily rely on their paint guns to provide uniform spray patterns with each use. To achieve this, they clean guns thoroughly after each use. Kosmoski tells his painters that he never wants to know what color was sprayed last through their gun, meaning the units had better be squeaky clean after each painting job.

In lieu of sophisticated air dryer and filtering systems, you may be able to get by with disposable air filters, as long as your air compressor is in excellent condition and is large enough that it does not have to work overtime to supply the air needed for your paint job. Seriously consider the use of these kinds of devices, especially if you have no other means of filtering the air from your compressor.

Spray gun quality is a number one factor when considering such a purchase. Better to wait to save up extra money to buy a top-of-the-line model, than settle for second best on an unfamiliar import. The problems with cheap paint guns relate to inadequate spray patterns and difficulty in finding new parts. It is recommended you seriously consider your paint gun purchase choices and opt for long-lasting quality instead of make-do availability.

High Volume Low Pressure (HVLP) Systems

As mentioned earlier, concern over our planet's atmospheric pollution has caused government agencies, civic groups, auto paint manufacturers, auto painters and paint equipment companies to acknowledge paint VOCs, overspray and material waste as pollution problems and they are therefore striving for solutions. One viable means of reducing VOC and overspray pollution is by use of High Volume Low Pressure (HVLP) spray paint systems.

This is a Binks brand high-volume, low-pressure spray paint gun. It sells for around $500. The gauge and control at the bottom of the grip are used to control supplied air pressure. Units like this are highly sophisticated and finely machined to provide the best fan spray and material application for the least amount of air pressure possible.

Binks has an HVLP paint gun available that works well with normal air compressors. It costs around $500 at autobody paint and supply stores. By increasing the volume of paint that can uniformly pass through a unit's ports and nozzle, a relatively low pressure is all that is needed to propel the paint material. The end result is more paint adherence to auto surfaces and much less— up to 50 percent less—waste through overspray by paint particles bouncing off surfaces at high pressures.

The Eastwood Company carries Accuspray HVLP automotive paint systems. These handy units come complete with their own compressor, hose and gun. They operate off of standard household electrical current, are lightweight and easy to use.

In capsule form, The Eastwood Company's *Auto Restoration News* shows how their Accuspray HVLP system works: "A relatively simple but high speed turbine fan draws air through a replaceable filter. It's forced through several stages resulting in a high volume of low pressure (less than 7 psi) air. Since air heats up as it is compressed, the air that is delivered is warm and dry, ideal for spraying paint." The report continues to explain that while conventional high-pressure systems are good for atomizing paint, particles are blasted toward surfaces to result in poor transfer efficiency and wasted overspray. In addition, "No oil is drawn into the air stream and the turbine delivers constant temperature, humidity, air pressure and volume."

Laursen successfully used an HVLP to paint a mid-size car. He used only 3 qts. of paint, where comparable jobs using conventional spray paint systems used one full gallon. He was amazed at the reduction in overspray and believes HVLPs would be great for those who must paint in garages or workshops because of this alone. If you do not currently own an air compressor or spray paint gun, you might seriously consider the purchase of a small HVLP system. Eastwood offers Accuspray two- and three-stage turbine HVLP paint systems for about $650 and $775, respectively.

Overall Safety

When asked what he wished someone would have stressed more heavily upon him during his apprentice years in the auto paint field, Laursen replied, "Safety!" After twenty years in the business, he now fully comprehends the health hazards involved due to the amount of sanding dust, paint overspray and solvents he has inhaled over the years. Although he feels fine and appears to be in excellent physical condition, he wonders what that constant exposure to painting chemicals has really done to his respiratory system and other body organs.

Especially with the advent of paint hardeners which contain isocyanates, painters have to be keenly aware of all the respiratory protection devices available to them. Although many painters still spray cars while wearing only heavy-duty filter masks for protection, smart painters opt instead for full-face, fresh-air respiratory systems. These units may be a bit cumbersome, but whatever inconvenience they involve is easily overshadowed by the amount of personal safety they afford.

Because of increased awareness to hazardous materials, government agencies have demanded chemical manufacturers comply with more and more standards relating to user safety. Therefore, you will commonly find recommendations of NIOSH-approved respiratory protection on almost all paint product containers. Be sure to read respirator package labels, too. They will list the types of

This dust mask will work well to prevent sanding dust materials from entering your respiratory system. At the least, you should use a device like this while sanding primer-surfacers or other body filler materials. Be advised, however, that this mask will not filter out dangerous isocyanate materials or other hazardous substances frequently encountered with automotive paint spraying. For those instances, you need to use a cartridge mask or fresh-air respiratory system.

The Eastwood Company offers this type of fresh-air, positive-pressure respiratory system for automotive painters. The full-face mask protects painters' eyes from material contamination, and the full-face shield allows for excellent visibility. If you do not have, or cannot afford such a system, and you plan to use a paint system which includes a hardener with isocyanate ingredients, you should seriously consider renting a fresh-air system like this from a rental yard. The Eastwood Company

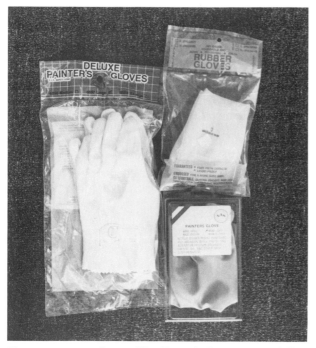

Veteran auto painters like Dennis Laursen and Dan Mycon remember washing their hands with lacquer thinner to remove smudges of paint. They also remember how dried out, chapped and tender their hands were after such escapades. Today, they both advise auto painters to use heavy-duty rubber gloves designed specifically for auto paint work. These gloves are just a sampling of protective gloves offered.

materials the filter will hold out and those which are *not* filtered at all. Autobody paint and supply stores carry assortments of filter masks and fresh-air systems. For assistance in selecting the proper protection for your job, consult a salesperson.

Since particles of paint overspray can readily enter your body through eyes, by way of moist tear ducts, manufacturers advise painters to wear goggles or full-face respirators. This is an important consideration during sanding, as well. Most autobody paint and supply stores carry a small selection of lightweight painters goggles.

Laursen and Mycon cannot remember how many times they have washed their paint-stained hands with lacquer thinner. However, they do remember how the skin on their hands used to dry out, crack and bleed from overexposure to potent chemicals, like lacquer thinner. Today, as an autobody paint and supply jobber, Laursen sees paint shops consistently buy monthly supplies of painters rubber gloves. Mycon wears them while spraying paint and does not notice any significant difference in his ability to handle a paint gun. You are encouraged to wear rubber gloves anytime you handle thinners, reducers, hardeners or any other paint product chemical.

In the spirit of recognizing how paint chemicals can enter painters' bodies through pores in their skin, paint manufacturers have developed

On the chance that your hands become soiled with automotive paint material residue, opt to wash them with a material designed for auto painters' hands, like this Cupran Special product. Not only do substances like this work, they also leave the skin on your hands feeling soft and flexible. Compared to washing hands with raw lacquer thinner, products like this are invaluable.

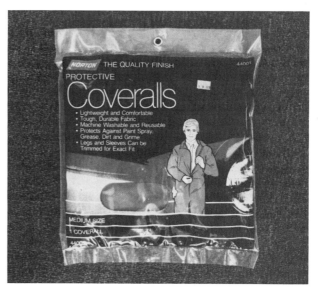

Some do-it-yourself auto painters may think wearing a special pair of coveralls is carrying things a bit too far. However, when you consider that painter attire like this is specially designed for car painting, you may think twice. Not only do painters coveralls protect users from paint contamination, they also provide a lint-free attire. This, in itself, eliminates one potential cause of paint finish blemish, that being lint debris from painters' clothing. These outfits are inexpensive and readily available at autobody paint and supply stores.

special impermeable coveralls. Designed to be used a few times and then discarded, disposable coveralls serve two functions. First, they prevent paint chemicals from coming in contact with your skin. Second, the material used to make the coveralls is lint-free, which means that concerns over lint falling off of your clothes and onto paint finishes is greatly reduced.

Professional painters who take full advantage of all personal safety equipment will suit up in the following way for maximum protection while painting: First to go on is a pair of painters coveralls and then rubber gloves. Both pant legs are taped closed around the ankles and both arm sleeves taped around the wrist. Then a painters hood is donned which covers the neck and entire head, except for the face. A full-face, fresh-air respiratory mask is next to be put in place and when connected to its air compressor supply hose will offer the user plenty of fresh, clean air.

This complete outfit gives painters full protection against harmful chemical liquids, paint overspray particles and vapors. Serious consideration should be given the use of all of these protective items. None of them is very expensive, except for the fresh-air respiratory system. But, rental yards may have these kinds of respiratory units available for rent at nominal and affordable fees.

5

Autobody Surface Preparation

Automobile painting consists of a series of tasks which ultimately combine to result in a quality paint job that looks great, feels smooth, adheres securely and lasts a long time. Each procedure must be completed satisfactorily. In other words, every time you set out to accomplish some kind of preparatory or actual paint chore, make sure it is done right the first time. Should problems arise, take whatever time necessary to adequately repair imperfections and make that phase of the operation perfect.

Autobody surface preparations include those jobs which actually get surfaces ready for paint application. Tasks may consist of, but are not limited to, part dismantling, old paint and rust accumulation removal, application of primer materials, finish sanding, and surface cleaning with wax

and grease remover and tack cloths. When any of these efforts are done haphazardly, the next operation cannot possibly be accomplished correctly.

In other words, cleaning with a wax and grease remover will not make surfaces smoother, even if undertaken two seconds after completing sanding. To reemphasize, all body surface preparation jobs are related to a single goal, a perfect paint job. But each has its own function which will not improve on another's lack of perfection. So, take your time during each preparatory phase and do not go on to the next step until satisfied that the work you just did has been accomplished accurately and completely.

Part Removal

With the exception of some expert masking work on vehicles repainted their original color,

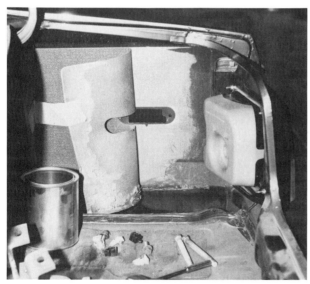

Some trunk spaces include cardboard inserts along the inner side of quarterpanels. They may have to be moved to allow for part dismantling, like side lights, or for masking. Here, a cardboard section has been folded over and taped in an out-of-the-way position for the removal of a side light and consequent masking over the hole left behind. Trunk spaces that include a number of different parts may warrant photographs be taken before and during dismantling to show how they are supposed to be put back.

Pete Noyes took all exterior parts off of his 1941 Plymouth to make paint removal work easier and less obstructed. The custom door handle has been left in place because it was welded in position. A lot of work with a high-speed rotary sander and 36 grit disc has already been completed, as witnessed by shiny metal and sanding scratch patterns. More sanding and sheet-metal work is needed to get the body in perfect condition before the application of any undercoat or paint products.

Autobody preparation steps are completed in a systematic order to ensure that the end result will be solid, smooth and blemish-free. Failure to correctly accomplish one phase will adversely affect subsequent work. Here, a couple of small dents were repaired and coats of body filler applied. If that material is not smoothed to perfection, too much primer-surfacer may have to be used to cover those problems, which in turn could result in excessive primer-surfacer shrinkage which would surely be visible after the last coat of paint was sprayed.

In order to reach the mounting mechanisms for the exterior door handle on this car, Doug Burrous had to remove the interior door panel. With most door handles, you have to feel your way around inner door spaces to locate and loosen door handle supports. Use a flashlight for inspection through one of the featured access holes on door panels. This way, you can at least look at those parts you will be working on before having to blindly dismantle them.

experienced auto painters and auto enthusiasts can always seem to determine which cars have been repainted and which have not. It is the goal of every auto painter to accomplish their work in such a way that their efforts cannot be distinguished. They want the cars they paint to look like they were painted only one time—at the factory.

Tiny strips of paint overspray on window moldings, door handles or light assemblies are telltale signs that an automobile has been repainted. Closer inspection of the surface finish next to these overspray blemishes might reveal slight sanding scratches which indicate bodywork has also been done. To a perspective buyer or car show judge, these things will raise red flags. A buyer may suspect that vehicles like this have sustained major collision damage and will be leery of their overall condition. A car show judge may deem subtle over-

spray patches and sanding scratches as inferior work, resulting in point deductions.

To guarantee that no overspray accumulates on mirrors, door handles, key locks, trim, reflectors and other removable body accessories, serious auto painters take as much time as necessary to carefully take off and store them. Along with alleviating overspray concerns, the removal of such items allows for controlled and thorough body preparation, as well as the prevention of paint build-up next to their edges.

Most autobody accessory parts such as door handles and mirrors are secured with screws, nuts or bolts. Some emblems, badges and trim on newer cars are attached with adhesive or double-backed tape. Before jumping into a part removal procedure with both feet, carefully inspect each item to determine just how it is mounted. Unnecessary prying force breaks parts, an inconvenience that also costs money for replacements.

Should certain screws present something other than slotted or Phillips heads, don't try to loosen them until you find a tool that fits correctly. GM, Ford, Chrysler and AMC vehicles feature some screws with multipointed Torx heads. Shaped

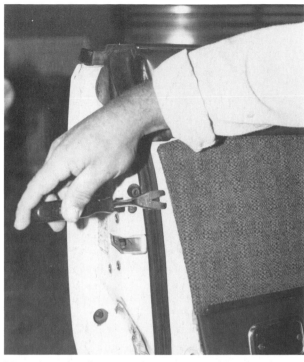

Many interior door panels are removed by simply popping them loose from metal or plastic pin clips. The plug puller tool shown here works well in most cases. You might consider laying a piece of cloth or cardboard on top of painted door surfaces before prying with tools like this to prevent unnecessary scratching. Note the light located at the bottom right corner. A set of electrical wires will be attached to this light fixture and must be unplugged before the panel is completely removed.

This door panel features white plastic pins along both sides and the bottom edge. They are pushed into corresponding mounts to keep the panel securely in place. In addition, large Phillips head screws are used to mount the armrest. These screws run all the way into the door's inner metal skin to also help support the panel. Should any pin break or mount crack, you will need to purchase replacements before panels can be put back.

somewhat like an asterisk or star, you will need Torx drivers or ratchet bits for their removal. These tools can be found at tool houses, auto parts stores and through The Eastwood Company.

Some door handles are removed by loosening a heavy-duty screw located on the door edge horizontally in line with the handle. Once the screw is removed, a handle is pulled out from the door skin so linkage arms can be dislodged. Most other door handles are secured by two screws or nuts accessed from inside the inner door space. Their removal requires interior door panels be taken off first for access to the handle support.

Interior door panels are secured by either screws or clips. You will have to examine the door panels on your car to determine how they are attached. If no screws are visible anywhere around the perimeter of the panel, chances are good that it features plastic clips that were pushed into retainer

Some window cranks and interior door handles are secured on their operating shafts by C-shaped metal clips. This tool works great to carefully push clips out of their slots for crank and handle removal. For the most part, C-shaped clips feature their open ends toward the length of cranks and handles. The position of this trim removal tool is correct; as it will be guided down to the base of the window crank, contact the open part of the clip and force the clip's sides out to dislodge from their retainer slot. Tool courtesy of the Eastwood Company

mounts. They are simply pried loose. But, before you start prying, be sure to remove armrests, window cranks and door handles.

Armrests are commonly secured by two large Phillips head screws. Window cranks on older cars are kept in place with a small C-shaped metal clip that snaps off the crank's operating shaft for removal. Newer cars may present dismantlers with cranks that have pop-off plastic caps designed onto their main arm that runs from the swivel knob to the shaft. Use a small-bladed screwdriver to gently pry off caps to access screws or nuts that hold cranks in place.

Door handles on older cars are removed just like their matching window cranks: by removing their C-shaped metal clips. Newer car handles will have a screw or two holding them in place. After screws have been removed, you might have to pry on the handle housing to pop it loose from the door panel opening in which it rests. Linkage arms from the handle to the door latch mechanism will have to be taken off, as well.

With interior door panels removed, you will notice a piece of plastic or other material located between the panel and door skin. This is a vapor barrier. Its function is to prevent water from entering the passenger compartment after it has seeped past window trim moldings. Be sure to keep those vapor barriers intact. You can simply roll them up to the top of the door and tape them in place out of the way.

If door edges are scheduled for new paint, you will have to remove weatherstripping. As with other body parts, you have to closely examine them to see just how they are secured in place. Some are attached with adhesive which requires the use of an adhesive remover, unless they are stout enough to withstand being pulled off. You could carefully use a heat gun or blow dryer to loosen adhesive as weatherstripping is pulled off.

Other kinds of weatherstripping feature plastic pins with large heads inserted into prefabricated holes along weatherstripping lengths. The protruding parts of these pins are pressed into holes around doors' perimeter edges.

Body side moldings and other trim pieces are secured to car bodies in several ways. Some feature protruding pins that snap into retainers, others have pins that are secured from the inside with flat metal retainers, and many are simply glued in place with adhesive or double-backed tape. To adequately determine how those parts are secured on your car, you will have to gently pry up an edge to inspect the backsides. Be very careful while doing this, because many plastic pieces are brittle and will crack or break if pried too far.

Light assemblies are normally secured with screws located on the backside of the housing assembly. Taillight units are removed from inside

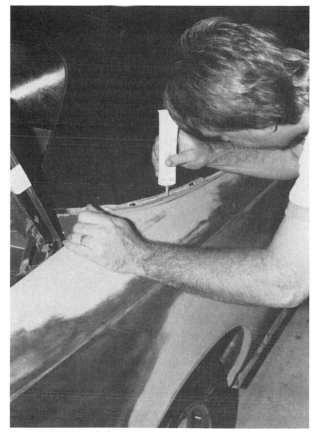

Van Hee noticed that the edge around this custom convertible top lacked the necessary amount of sealer. According to label instructions, new sealer is applied before paint work begins. This will allow time for the material to dry while sanding and masking are under way. Should you notice any areas on your car's body that require repairs or other work while preparing it for paint, take whatever steps necessary to accomplish repairs before paint is sprayed. This way, paint can be applied to the mended areas at the same time it is sprayed to adjacent body sections.

trunk or hatchback areas or pulled straight out from the outside. Some lights may require you to remove lenses first by taking out two or four Phillips head screws. Reflectors should be easily removed by loosening screws located at either end of the lens or from inside the corresponding interior compartment.

Grilles may be a bit tricky to remove. Automotive engineers have gotten quite ingenious with hiding mounting screws and clips in such ways that it is sometimes almost impossible to figure out how they are held in place. Look for Torx, Phillips or Allen head screws around the perimeter edge of grille sections. Although many grilles consist of a combination of parts, entire assemblies can sometimes be removed as single units if all the right screws are loosened. Separate pieces are held together with special clips.

Leave headlights in place if possible, especially if their current light beams are correctly adjusted. Should you decide that they have to be removed, do not touch the two screws that feature springs under them. These are directional adjustment screws used to move the headlight up or down, or from right to left.

Bumpers on older cars are a snap to remove. Their support bolts are in plain view and there is generally no question as to how they are dismantled. Newer car bumpers are not always that easy to figure out. Since many of these units consist of a number of different parts, it may appear that they couldn't possibly be removed. Splash guards and other urethane accessories may cover them to the point where the only visible part of the assembly's support is located under the front or rear section of the car. Take your time removing bumpers and get a helper if need be. These units are heavy and you should take precautions so they do

Newer style automobile bumpers frequently consist of more than one or two parts. The large piece on the left is the main bumper piece. It had been damaged in a collision. The smaller piece on the right was popped loose from the larger one and will be used on a new main bumper unit. The smaller piece includes studs which snap into the slots located along the center section of the larger bumper part. A section of molding is inserted over the metal strip support that runs along its center to make it look nicer.

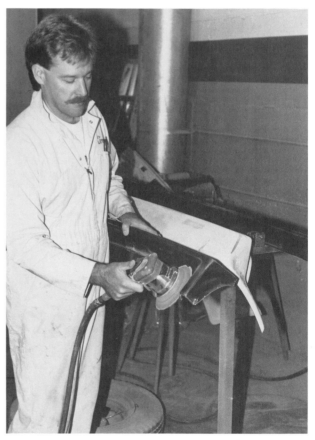

This is a bumper guard that has been removed for paint access near the corner of a quarterpanel. Between the two bolts sitting inside the guard is a round disc. The disc is used to cover up a bolt access hole located on the top corner of the bumper guard, just to the right of center in this picture. Manufacturers design their bumpers and other body parts differently than competitors. Therefore, you have to investigate mounting and support assemblies carefully before haphazardly prying or pulling on parts to prevent breaking them.

Mycon is using a small dual-action sander to remove lingering traces of old paint from this flexible ground effect part. Because a repaint was incorrectly applied, paint peeled off. Along with removing contaminants from the part's surface, sanding also produces a scuffed finish. This will help the ground effect better accept undercoat and topcoat materials, and also play a significant role in promoting the best adhesion possible for paint products.

66

Meticulous sanding has smoothed imperfections that resulted in exposing some of this ground effects' surface. Note how sanding has been feathered in order to allow new paint material to blend with the existing finish. Whenever painting plastic or urethane body parts, be certain you include required paint additives, like a flexible agent or fisheye eliminator.

To determine how well the sanding procedure is progressing, Mycon uses a wax and grease remover to clean the ground effect surface. This mild solvent does an excellent job of cleaning surfaces without causing damage to paint finishes. In this situation, it also helped to emphasize surface imperfections, like cracks, crazing or checks.

Mycon uses 320 grit sandpaper to smooth a layer of primer-surfacer applied earlier to this ground effect unit. Primer-surfacer filled in minute imperfections, like shallow stone chips, and will be sanded until Mycon is satisfied that the surface finish is as smooth and blemish-free as possible.

not fall on you while under the car loosening support bolts.

If you come across items for which you cannot determine a proper removal procedure, consult a service manager at a dealership, professional autobody repair shop or auto paint facility. It makes no sense to take chances on breaking parts when help is just around the corner.

If your experience working on cars is limited, seriously consider purchasing a detailed repair manual for the year, make and model vehicle you plan to work on. Be sure to scan the book first to make sure it offers you the tips and advice needed. Auto parts stores generally carry an assortment of these books. Sometimes, the stock operator manuals normally provided with new cars list names and addresses of companies that publish in-depth vehicle repair manuals. This may be an ideal source for specific information on your car.

Any attempt at body part removal must be complemented with an organized system of part

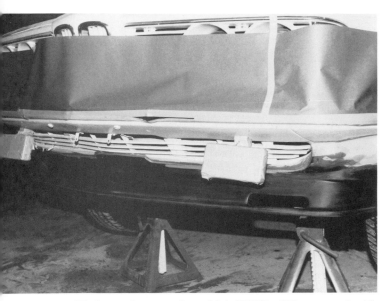

The lower front section of this BMW will be covered with Rocker Schutz before it is painted. Since that kind of chip-resistant material hardens to a bumpy texture, there was no need to prepare the ground effect with primer-surfacer. To allow for best working access to this area, raise the front end of the car and support it on sturdy jack stands. Never crawl under any raised vehicle unless it is securely supported by heavy-duty jack stands.

A vinyl graphic design was removed from the body of this vehicle by using hot, dry air from a heat gun; hair blow dryers work just as well. The remaining adhesive residue will be sprayed with 3M Woodgrain and Stripe Adhesive Remover so that it can be easily removed. Be sure to read and follow the directions on any label of adhesive remover you use to be certain the product's ingredients will not harm paint finishes in any way, like from being left on surfaces too long.

storage. What good will it do you to take off all those parts, if when you go to put them back on they can't be found? Have plenty of large coffee cans and boxes on hand when the project starts. Use a heavy felt marker to label boxes. Use one box for each general car section; for example, driver's side front fender and door, passenger side taillight, side light and reflector and so on. Be certain that small screws and nuts are put back in place after a part has been removed. This way, they will not be lost and will also be easily accessible when parts are put back in place.

Old Paint Removal

The degree to which old paint is removed from car bodies depends upon its condition at the time, whether or not bodywork is needed and how extensive the paint job will be. New paint can be applied over old paint if the existing finish is sanded to a point where all oxidized paint material is removed and the surface is left flat, even and smooth. If bodywork needs to be accomplished, paint on that area has to be removed to bare metal so that filler material has its best opportunity to bond completely.

These decisions are easy when obvious bodywork or deep paint blemishes are apparent. Questions arise when old paint looks dull and oxidized and you simply want to repaint it to look nice. Some

After an appropriate application of adhesive remover, glue residue appears to be melting. Outer adhesive residue layers have been heavily loosened while those layers closer to the painted finish are fast becoming soft. Masking paper and tape were used to cordon off the adhesive area so that remover overspray was not inadvertently applied to uninvolved body areas.

questions you should ponder are: Is existing paint too thick to support a new finish? Are rust accumulation traces present anywhere on the body? Does the entire car need a new paint job, or will repaint efforts to a couple of panels do the trick? Serious consideration must be given to the need for new paint, especially when contemplating complete paint jobs. A lot of work goes into the process, and materials can be quite expensive.

The means you choose for removing paint will be determined by the condition of the vehicle's existing paint surface. Cars with excellent bodies that require no sheet-metal repair should have paint removed using the mildest method. This would probably be a chemical stripper or mild paint-stripping scouring-type pad.

The Eastwood Company offers Strip Disc kits which include three 7 in. stripping discs and a

Van Hee directs hot air from a heat gun just ahead of where vinyl stripe material is being pulled off. Too much heat on vinyl stripes will cause them to snap off. Therefore, you have to apply just enough heat to loosen vinyl stripe glue and then immediately pull it away from the surface or direct it farther up the stripe. Not all vinyl stripes will come off in one piece. In many cases, you will have to be satisfied with pulling off short sections at a time.

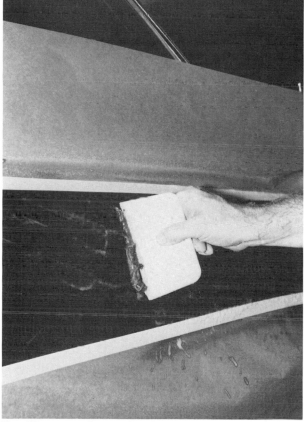

Van Hee uses a large plastic squeegee to gently remove lingering adhesive residue. After the bulk of residue has been removed, another application of adhesive remover will be applied. That application is wiped off with a clean cloth. When all noticeable adhesive has been successfully removed from body panels, plan to clean areas again with a quality wax and grease remover product. Any remover contaminations remaining on a body finish will quickly cause new applications of paint material to develop imperfections or fail to flow onto surfaces at all.

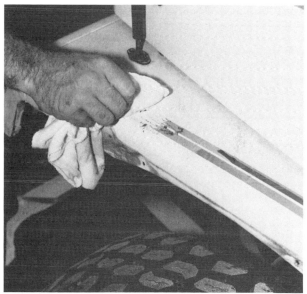

After vinyl stripes were pulled off of this Jeep fender, Van Hee dampened a cloth with adhesive remover to take off remaining glue residue. Some eager painters have used lacquer thinner for jobs like this, but were disappointed when that solvent caused paint to rub off also, even those paint products that included a catalyst hardener. Always be aware of what various paint chemicals can do to existing surfaces. It is better to spend extra time cleaning with a mild solvent than to use a much more potent one in hopes of making a job go faster.

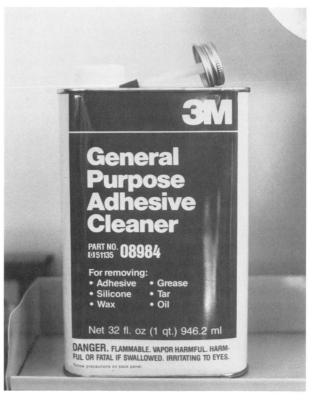

3M's General Purpose Adhesive Cleaner is a mild solvent used to remove remnants of adhesive, silicone, wax, grease, tar and oil. Used according to directions, it should be safe for applications to most paint finishes. If there are exceptions, they will be noted on the backside label. Although the label states that the material will remove wax and grease, you should consult an autobody paint and supply jobber before substituting this product for a wax and grease remover that was designed specifically for the paint system you intend to use.

3M brand Release Agent was developed for a specific purpose. Users must read the entire backside label to thoroughly understand how it is supposed to be applied and exactly what kinds of materials it will loosen. As indicated on the front label, Release Agent will work well to loosen those adhesives employed to attach weatherstripping. Most cans include thin nozzle tubes which help to direct material sprays into tight areas.

cushioned backing pad that attaches to angled sanders (buffers) with 6000 rpm maximum speeds. They are advertised to quickly and completely strip paint without creating excessive heat, and their design will not harm valuable body panels. It is recommended you use them after removing the bulk of old paint with a chemical stripper. Assortments of chemical strippers are available at autobody paint and supply stores. Be sure to read label instructions and plan to wear recommended protective equipment.

High-speed rotary sanders with coarse discs remove paint in a hurry. These work great for bodywork because the rough sanding scratches left behind make excellent bases for the application and secure bonding of filler material. High-speed sanders and coarse discs also work well to remove accumulations of rust from sheet-metal panels.

Besides personal safety, another caution you must be aware of is that sanding with high-speed power tools generates a lot of heat. Continued sanding on just one area can create enough heat from the friction of the disc rubbing against a panel surface that warping occurs, especially on the rather thin panels currently in place on newer cars.

Another alternative means for old paint removal is sandblasting. This equipment works especially well for older cars that have been neglected for years and suffer surface rust accumulations. Sandblasting media work fast to remove paint and traces of rust caught in tiny cracks, crevices and pits. You will have to contend with messy cleanup after work is done, but the extra work is well worth the effort as you'll discover that old paint and rust removal is done quickly and thoroughly.

Sandblasters require controlled use with a compatible pressure and media combination. Too much pressure mixed with a harsh media will cause sheet-metal warping problems and other damage. Safest results are found when all body accessories are removed, as sandblasting will take off chrome, paint and can quickly pit glass. Therefore, make sure all vulnerable body parts are removed or safely protected with heavy tarps or another suitable material. If you doubt the sandblasting resistance strength of your protective masking material, test it out beforehand by sandblasting against it while it is on the ground and before it is put in place on your car.

Charts are frequently provided with new sandblasters and are available at tool outlets which sell this kind of equipment that indicate which media should be used at what pressures for different kinds of jobs. Media are rated according to their size; the lower the designating number, the larger

Mycon will use this Eastwood sandblaster to remove scale and other surface imperfections from under the bumper area on this 1965 Chevy II. When used according to directions and with the correct media and pressure combinations, sandblasters can make short work of many surface preparation jobs. Note the heavy-duty sandblasting hood, gloves and respirator. Tools and equipment courtesy of The Eastwood Company

Mycon is carefully using a high-speed rotary sander with a 36 grit disc to remove paint from a small dent on the fender of Janna Jacobs' 1988 Volkswagen Jetta. The dent is highlighted by the white spot in the middle of the sanded area. Sander and face shield courtesy of The Eastwood Company

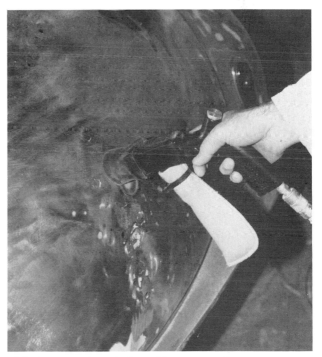

This is a very handy Spot Blaster sandblasting tool. It comes with five different heavy rubber tips which confine sandblasting to small areas at a time. The differently shaped rubber tips are designed to fit over edges, inside grooves and into tight spaces. Here, a spot of rust was quickly removed with just a couple of blasts. Most of the media used for the tool's operation returns to the pouch to be used again. The Blaster costs around $80. Tool courtesy of The Eastwood Company

particle sizes will be. For use on car parts and bodies, typical ranges would be from #40 (0.016 in.) to a smaller size of #12 (0.004 in.). Media also come in work mixes that combine different amounts of various-sized particles. Consult a salesperson at a sandblasting equipment store or jobber at an autobody paint and supply store for help in selecting the proper media.

Equally as important as media size is the pressure at which material is blasted. Since media can be propelled at speeds from 200 to 400 mph, you had better be sure that pressure settings are correct to prevent unwanted body damage. In addition, you need to protect yourself from sandblasting media. Always wear heavy-duty leather gloves, long sleeves and a quality sandblasting hood.

It is also recommended you wear a NIOSH-approved respirator. Certain media materials, like silica, produce dust particles that could be harmful to your respiratory system. Along with respirators and gloves, sandblasters and media can be purchased at autobody paint and supply stores. The Eastwood Company sells an assortment of sandblasters ranging from $40 sandblasting guns that siphon media from a bucket, to first-class units costing around $350.

Various sandblaster nozzle sizes require certain horsepower air compressors. For example, a $3/32$ in. nozzle requires the power of a 2–3 hp air compressor to supply 7 cfm at 80 psi. A $1/8$ in. nozzle needs a 3–5 hp air compressor to supply it with 15 cfm at 80 psi. Charts continue up to a $5/16$ in. nozzle which calls for a 40 hp air compressor to supply 125 cfm at 80 psi. Again, check the charts at places that sell sandblast media to be sure the nozzle size, media and air pressure you plan to use will work as a viable combination to complete the work you have at hand.

Sanding Body Filler Repairs

Regardless of the type of surface you plan to paint over, whether it be body filler or an existing paint finish, some sanding is required. This phase of any automobile paint operation is just as critical as any other. Remember that every blemish or surface flaw will be magnified by paint coats. This should help you be as meticulous as possible while working to accomplish all sanding and smoothing needs.

Top layers of body filler are initially sanded with 80 to 150 grit paper to smooth and flatten rough spots and to get the surface close to an even texture. Then, 240 grit is used to make that finish even smoother and flatter. Sanding must be done with a sanding board or block. After every two minutes, or so, feel the surface with your open hand to judge the progress being made. Note high spots or other problem areas and be sure to concentrate efforts at making them smoother so they blend in with surrounding surfaces.

Operate sanding boards and blocks in all directions. Do not simply maneuver them in a back-and-forth direction from the front to the back. Move them up and down and crossways diagonally, rotating the board or block as necessary for ease of operation. This multidirectional sanding technique will guarantee that all areas are sanded smooth without grooves or perceivable patterns.

Once sanding efforts with 240 grit have made surface areas flat with no remaining high spots, wrinkles, grooves or ridges, use 320 grit sandpaper to remove lingering sanding scratches and other shallow imperfections. Your work up to this point has been mainly concerned with the actual shaping of body filler to a point where it is flat and blends with panel areas adjacent to it. Sanding with finer sandpaper grits will focus on texture smoothness and the removal of sanding scratches, very shallow imperfections and the like.

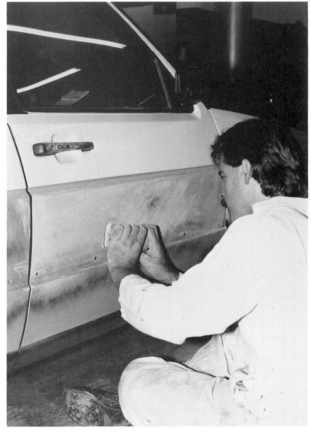

Mycon takes his time to carefully sand the primer-surfacer material on this door. He is using a sanding block to make sure that passes are uniformly applied. The streak of black paint on the lower door panel is a guide coat. As it is sanded off, low spots are highlighted to show where more sanding is needed. No matter what kind of a paint job you plan to undertake, expect to spend plenty of time sanding in order to get body surfaces smooth, flat and even.

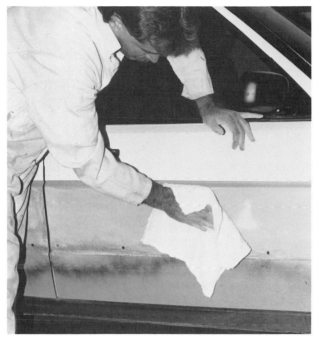

While sanding, painters continually feel surfaces with an open hand to better determine their progress. To accentuate their hand's ability to detect imperfections, many place a clean cloth between the work surface and their hand. Be sure that the cloth you use is clean and free from any kind of oil, grease, wax or silicone contamination. As you notice imperfections, use your sanding block to smooth and feather them into adjacent areas. Low spots will have to be refilled with primer-surfacer and the entire area sanded again.

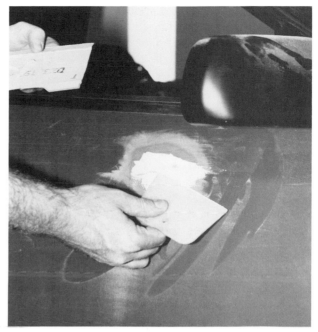

A thin coat of body filler is applied to a door ding with a plastic squeegee. Although it looks like a lot of filler, you must realize that most of it will be sanded off. Only a very small portion will remain to fill the void caused by the dented metal. Body filler materials and their appropriate hardeners are available at autobody paint and supply stores. Body filler adheres to bare metal surfaces better than anything else, although many professional autobody technicians have sprayed epoxy primer to bare metal first and then successfully put on filler.

To expose bare metal under a ding on the ridge of this door, Van Hee uses a small dual-action sander with 220 grit paper. Notice the different colored rings exposed by sanding. From the center of the area is primer, sealer and paint. By feathering out the edges of each material, subsequent applications of similar material will fill in voids until the last paint coat brings the repair area up to the same level as the existing paint finish.

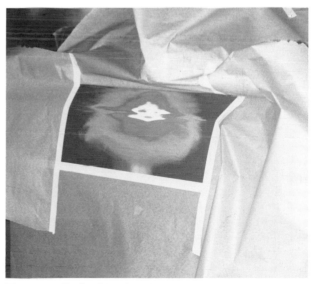

The coat of body filler has been sanded to a very smooth surface. Note the feathering of all materials, including scuffed paint extending around the repair for about 6 in. in all directions. The entire spot will be coated with primer-surfacer next. Masking is rather limited as the high-solids content in that material keeps overspray at minimum levels.

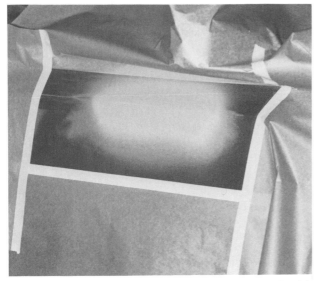

Entire masked areas do not need to be coated with primer-surfacer material, only those which have received sanding work. Smooth application of about four or five passes were made to gradually build up the surface. Primer-surfacer must be mixed according to label directions. With certain paint systems and colors, you may be required to use a red product instead of typical gray. This requirement should be confirmed with your autobody paint and supply jobber at the time your paint system is purchased.

Although it appeared that no primer-surfacer material was applied to anything but the repaired spot on this door, overspray is clearly noted with masking removed. Therefore, although primer-surfaces have such high-solids content and masking for that application is limited, it is needed nonetheless. This area will be sanded with 320 grit sandpaper for initial smoothing and then perfected with 500 grit.

Van Hee uses a small DA sander for a lot of this finish sanding work. He advises novice painters to practice with DA sanders before using them on their favorite car's body. Although DAs may not appear to be moving at all, they can remove a lot of filler material in a hurry.

When satisfied that your filler repair has been sanded to perfection, use 320 grit paper to gradually develop a well-defined visual perimeter around the entire repair area. This "ring" around the repair should expose an inch, or so, wide band of bare metal and then successive bands of equally wide exposed rings of primer, sealer, primer-surfacer and paint. Because undercoat and paint products consist of different colored materials, you will be able to clearly see your progress. The object, in essence, is to develop sort of a layered valley of smooth walls between the top surface of the body filler repair area and the top surface of existing good paint. This allows fresh applications of

Required sanding has been accomplished on this area where a ding was repaired. Just a hint of existing paint shows through on the ridge to each side of the actual repair. The streaks denote high spots where metal was ever so lightly raised when the ding was incurred. These high spots are noticed by color, but cannot be felt because they blend in with the surrounding filler and primer-surfacer material that has been feathered out to the perimeter of existing paint.

Air pressure pumped out through a nozzle quickly removes build ups of sanding dust and other debris from work surfaces, body panel gaps and other tight spots. In the paint booth, Van Hee uses clean air pressure to help dry off a quarterpanel that was just cleaned with wax and grease remover. Note the amount of feathering accomplished with meticulous sanding throughout the repaired areas. The rest of the existing paint on the panel has been scuffed with a Scotch-Brite pad.

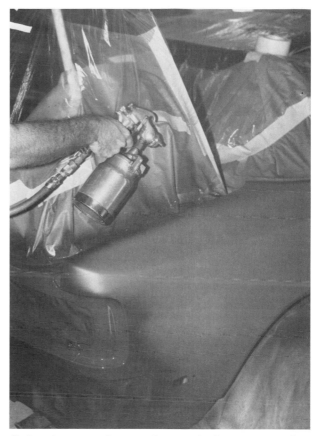

Sealer is sprayed onto the repaired quarterpanel to prepare it for paint. To achieve an even and uniform spray application, paint guns have to be maneuvered so that their nozzle tip remains perpendicular to the work surface. Especially with paint material, holding the gun like this could allow material that exits from the top of the fan spray to dry just a micro-second before the material from the bottom of the fan spray, because the top part has a longer distance to travel before reaching the surface. To perfect your paint gun handling techniques, practice on an old hood or trunk lid before actually painting your favorite car.

undercoat material to fill in to the same thickness as those same materials existing on the rest of the car's surface.

Accomplishment of this task will allow final color coats to be sprayed on in thicknesses equal to the rest of the paint finish to blend as best as possible and maintain the identical color tint and texture as surrounding paint finishes. This process is referred to as "feathering in" and is an important step toward successfully completing any touchup repaint work. Subsequent coats of primer-surfacer material will also be sanded to a point where the only depth difference between an existing painted surface and a repair area will be the actual thickness of the existing paint.

Sanding Existing Paint Surfaces

Applying new paint over old paint without properly scuffing up the old surface is a mistake, especially when dealing with factory paint jobs that were baked on at 450 degrees Fahrenheit.

Situations like this quite commonly result in new paint flaking off because it does not have an absorbent base to adhere to. The super-hard nature of baked-on paint jobs does not always allow new paint to penetrate their surfaces, thus causing those new layers to sometimes peel off in sheets.

Although painting over a perfectly good paint job might appear to be unnecessary or foolish, some enthusiasts may want to change a solid color scheme into a two-tone blend, or business owners may need to add certain bands of particular colors so new vehicles match the rest of the fleet. For whatever reason, paint surfaces that will be painted over must be scuffed first.

Fine-grade Scotch-Brite pads work great for scuffing baked-on paint finishes. The comparatively rough finish left behind makes a great base

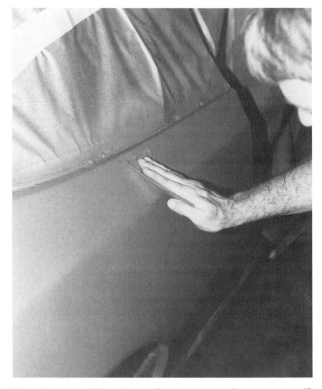

Van Hee uses 1200 grit sandpaper to gently remove a nib found on a coat of sealer material. He had to wait until the flash time elapsed before attempting the repair. Flash times indicate how long it normally takes for solvents in paint material to evaporate. If sanding was started before the material was dry, the imperfection would have only been made worse. Another coat of sealer will be applied.

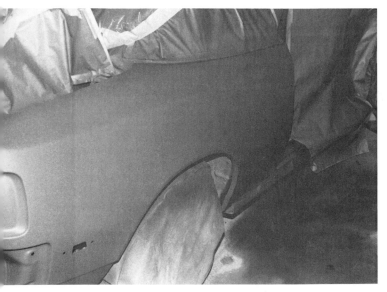

This is what the quarterpanel looked like after the appropriate amount of sealer was sprayed. Because sealers are not high-solids materials, no sanding is generally required after their application; although, nibs or imperfections should be sanded smooth and recoated.

for coats of sealer or adhesion promoter materials. You could also use 500 to 600 grit sandpaper to scuff shiny paint finishes. The overall purpose is to dull all shiny surfaces so new layers of material have something to grab onto. There is no need to scuff or sand in one direction only. You can, and should, sand in all directions in order to be sure all surface areas have been roughened up satisfactorily.

Cleaning Sanded Surfaces before Undercoat Applications

After sanding or scuffing has been successfully accomplished, a thorough cleaning is required to remove all surface contaminants. Painters normally use air pressure to blow off layers of sanding dust from body surfaces, as well as between trunk edge gaps, door edges, jambs and the like.

With the bulk of dry dust and dirt removed by air pressure, painters use wax and grease remover products to thoroughly wipe down and clean body

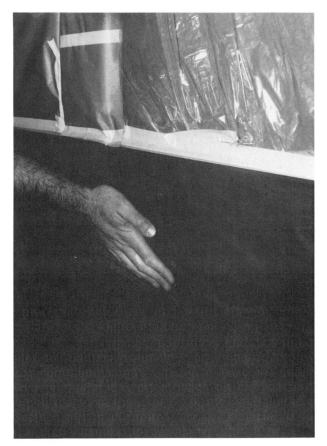

A Scotch-Brite pad is used to scuff an otherwise good paint surface. The pad does not have to be forcefully applied and expected to sand paint. Rather, it is used to essentially scratch painted surfaces to remove shines and allow for the best paint product adhesion possible. There is no need to scuff in any one direction only, in fact, it is best you maneuver the pad in all directions to get the most out of the process.

surfaces. Each paint manufacturer has its own brand of wax and grease remover that constitutes part of an overall paint system. You should use only those wax and grease remover products deemed part of the paint system you will be using to be guaranteed that it is compatible with the rest of your paint system materials.

Dampen a clean cloth with wax and grease remover and use it to thoroughly wipe off all body surfaces in the area of expected paint undercoat applications. Every surface should be cleaned except those that will be completely masked off. The mild solvents in wax and grease removers loosen and dislodge particles of silicone dressings, oil, wax, polish and other materials embedded in or otherwise lightly adhered to surfaces. To assist the cleaning ability of wax and grease removers, follow the damp cleaning cloth with a clean, dry cloth in your other hand. The dry one picks up lingering residue and moisture to leave behind a clean, dry surface.

To ensure super-clean and dry surfaces, go over finishes with an aerosol glass cleaner after using a wax and grease remover. The ammonia in such glass cleaners helps to disperse and evaporate moisture, as well as pick up missed spots of wax or dirt residue. Instead of wetting a cloth with glass cleaner, spray the material on surfaces and wipe it off with a clean, dry cloth.

In the paint booth, as a final cleaning chore just before spraying any paint product, wipe off body surfaces with a tack cloth. As mentioned earlier, these specially made cloths are designed to pick up and retain very small specks of lint, dust and other particles. Although wax and grease removers work well to get rid of contaminants, like wax and grease, tack cloths work best for removing tiny pieces of cloth fiber and other items which could easily cause imperfections in paint finishes.

Go over every square inch of body surface that will be exposed to paint product application to be certain that traces of lint are removed. This should guarantee that debris is not blown over onto painted surfaces during the paint process.

To be sure that the surfaces he paints are thoroughly clean, Van Hee prefers to wipe them off with an aerosol glass cleaner, which includes ammonia, after cleaning with an appropriate wax and grease remover. He generally sprays glass cleaner directly on surfaces and wipes it off with a clean, dry cloth. A lot of other professional painters also experience good results using glass cleaners this way. They believe the ammonia contained in aerosol glass cleaners not only helps to clean, but also assists in removing lingering hints of moisture. Van Hee and Mycon recommend using aerosol glass cleaners in lieu of concentrates which are mixed with water.

DuPont's Cronar Lacquer and Enamel Cleaner is basically a wax and grease remover designed for use with their Cronar paint systems. Differences between this product and other brands of wax and grease remover may be limited to simple chemical strengths, or could relate to actual ingredient properties. No matter the reason why, you are advised to use only those products designed as part of the overall paint system you employ.

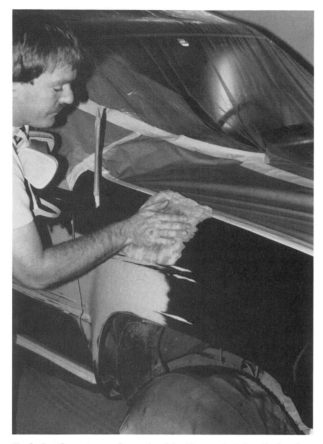

To help the atmosphere inside the paint booth be free from dust and other airborne debris, doors were closed and fans activated for about fifteen to twenty minutes before spraying. The final step before spraying sealer or paint involves wiping off surfaces with a tack cloth. Here, Van Hee uses a tack cloth to remove fine traces of lint and other debris. His paint gun has already been filled with sealer and the paint booth closed, with fans operating. Spraying will begin immediately after all work surfaces are tacked off.

Tack cloths have a limited life span. Therefore, you need to refer to instructions on package labels to determine how many times they can effectively be used. Do not try to get more out of them than expected. Once tack cloths are saturated with lint, debris and residue, they will no longer pick up new debris; in fact, they may spread accumulated materials absorbed from other cleaning jobs.

Applying Primer and Sealer

Epoxy primers and sealers do not have to be sanded, unless runs or imperfections occur on their surface. In those cases, a fine-grit sandpaper is used to smooth blemishes. Spots are then touched up with a new coat of material. As previously described, epoxy primers are sprayed onto bare metal finishes to waterproof and protect them. Most auto restorers apply epoxy primer

products, like PPG's DP 40, to bare metal items after they have had old paint and rust removed. Others prefer to apply body filler directly to bare metal and then seal repairs after primer-surfacer products have been sanded and are ready for paint.

For those body panels or vehicles that will receive complete new paint jobs only, primer and sealer materials are sprayed in a paint booth after masking. Because those items will receive no body repair or body filler applications, their surfaces are essentially ready for paint. Therefore, treat this paint phase as you would a normal topcoat application. After masking, clean surfaces with wax and grease remover, aerosol window cleaner and a tack cloth. Then, mix the primer or sealer product according to label instructions, don appropriate painting attire and begin.

For those jobs where only a part of a vehicle will be shot with primer or sealer, you should lay large strips of masking paper over unaffected areas such as hoods, roofs and trunk lids to prevent overspray accumulations. Use the minimum recommended pressure and fan spray to gently cover bare metal spots. Feather them into adjacent areas by slowly releasing the paint gun trigger toward the end of passes. This technique should be practiced before actual attempts are made on your car.

Complete repaint jobs where no bodywork has been performed and existing paint has been scuffed are also considered ready for paint. They need to be masked and then shot with a sealer or adhesion promoter, as recommended by your autobody paint and supply jobber or by the information in the paint manufacturers' application guides. These kinds of sealers and adhesion promoters will not have to be sanded, unless you botch a spot and have to sand down runs or other imperfections. Once the sealer or adhesion promoter has cured according to label directions, paint can then be applied.

Use of Primer-Surfacer

Use of primer-surfacer products are generally saved for those body parts that have undergone repair work or suffer very minor or shallow sheet-metal scratches. Primer-surfacers are *not* designed to be used as body fillers. Layers that are applied too thick will shrink to accentuate sanding scratches and other imperfections.

For example, after you have successfully sanded and smoothed a topcoat of glazing putty filler material, two to three coats of primer-surfacer are sprayed onto the repair area. Then 320 grit sandpaper is used to smooth that surface initially. After that, final finish sanding is done with 500 grit sandpaper. You might find that the first three coats of primer-surfacer did not produce the results expected. Very fine sanding scratches may prevail or a shallow low spot may be detected. In those situations, apply a couple more light coats of primer-surfacer and sand with 320 grit and then 500.

To aid in detecting the progress of primer-surfacer sanding, spray a light layer of SEM's Guide Coat over the surface. Sanding will immediately remove this coating from high spots and highlight low spots. In place of the Guide Coat, flat-black paint can be applied in very light coats.

Since primer-surfacers are so heavy, overspray is generally not much of a problem and masking can be limited to just the area involved. In other words, you do not have to meticulously mask the roof, hood and other areas when simply spraying primer-surfacer on a lower door panel. Large sheets of wide paper can outline the repair area with little worry of overspray marring other areas. In addition, because primer-surfacer will be sanded, there is no need to spray the job in a spray booth. A clean, dust-free area should be sufficient.

Because the high-solids content in primer-surfacers can easily flake off masking paper onto work surfaces, it is best you remove masking sheets used during primer-surfacer applications. Sanding dust will accumulate on the vehicle's surface and in gaps between doors and trunk lids anyway, which will require a complete cleaning with air pressure, wax and grease remover, an aerosol glass cleaner and tack cloth. After the application and sanding of primer-surfacer materials, you can begin the job of definitive masking for sealer or adhesion promoter applications and actual paint spraying.

Preparing Fiberglass

Repair work to damaged fiberglass auto bodies is done with resin, catalyst and fiberglass mat products. Exceptions are newer Corvettes, mini-vans and other vehicles which are made with a product called Fiber Reinforced Plastic (FRP). Those units require specific repair materials unique to their physical makeup and chemical design. Some autobody technicians prefer to cover finished fiberglass repairs with a skim coat of glazing putty to ensure against pinholes, as air bubbles in resin are common and pinholes on the surface sometimes impossible to avoid.

Primer-surfacer is mixed and applied to fiberglass repairs the same as for sheet-metal surfaces, except for any special fiberglass application instructions that may be listed on labels or designated information sheets. 320 and 500 grit sandpaper is used to smooth that surface, as well. Again, masking needs are limited to about 2 ft. in all directions as long as controlled primer-surfacer sprays are maintained.

After the primer-surfacer material has been sanded to perfection, dust is blown off and the car masked. Wax and grease remover is used for thorough cleaning and can be followed by a wipedown with an aerosol glass cleaner. When that is done, the body is tacked off and then sprayed with the appropriate sealer. When flash (drying) times have been reached, the body is tacked off again and then painted.

6

Masking

Masking paper and tape are strategically placed on various automobile parts to protect them against applications of paint materials intended for adjacent body sections. Although an initial estimate of the masking needs for your vehicle may appear to be rather limited and easy to accomplish, you must understand that less than meticulous masking will almost always result in obvious spots of overspray—imperfections that clearly indicate sloppy work or are regarded as signs of inexperience and unprofessionalism.

Some paint overspray can be cleaned off or painted over, but trim pieces and other assorted body items marred with thin strips of paint on their edges may not fair as well. A conscientious buyer or detail-oriented judge will quickly notice small lines of paint on windshield moldings, key locks, door handles, emblems, lights, reflectors and so on. To them, overspray on any item proves that an automobile has been repainted, and raises a red flag to hint that some other repair work might have had to be completed on the vehicle.

This Toyota 4–Runner is just about completely masked off for spot and panel painting. The painter will cover the tires with prefabricated plastic covers and enclose the hood, roof, rear end and opposite side with a large sheet of lightweight plastic after the rig has been moved into the paint booth. Note that masking on the right rear section follows along a vinyl graphic, and the taillight is masked with strips of 2 in. tape. Because actual color will not be sprayed over the door handle and key lock, they have been left in place and simply masked with tape.

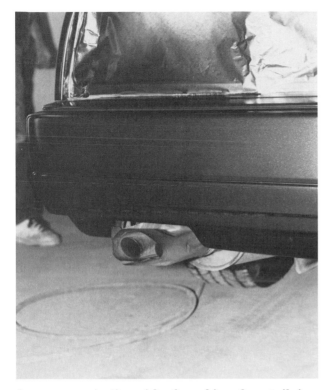

A more conscientious job of masking these tailpipes would have prevented overspray on their tips. Although they can be cleaned or painted with a high-temperature silver paint, just a few extra minutes with paper and tape would have alleviated that task. As you mask, be sure to look at areas below rocker, front and rear panels for parts or assemblies that might be subject to paint overspray. In cases where extensive sanding is anticipated, many painters plug tailpipes with rags to prevent sanding dust from entering the exhaust system.

A car or truck that has been involved in a collision may not be as inviting as one that has never been involved in any accidents. Questions could arise in potential buyers' heads as to the quality of repair work performed by autobody technicians and to just what extent the vehicle was damaged. They might ask themselves, "Is this person selling his or her car because it does not perform like it did before the wreck? Was it a total that has been put back together? Am I considering the purchase of a vehicle that might completely fall apart 100 miles down the road?"

Do you see how just a small bit of overspray can arouse a multitude of suspicions? At car shows, judges may deem overspray as a sign that other restoration efforts were also completed in a less-than-perfect manner. Because of this, you might find them deducting valuable points or looking closer into corners and other out-of-the-way places to find additional flaws.

When asked what was the most meticulous and exacting chore he faced as a professional

This brand-new red Chevrolet pickup truck will have a band of white added to its lower body as well as the roof so it will match the rest of the fleet from a construction company. This was Mycon's first step in masking the lower section: a long strip of tape placed from front to rear in one step. Tape was attached at the front first, then unrolled and pulled taut away from the surface so it ran the entire length of the truck. In one movement, he was then able to attach it to the body in a perfectly straight line as he looked down the side along the tape's top edge.

painter for Newlook Autobody, Todd Shrewsbury replied, "First, of course, is color matching. Then it's masking." Since your autobody paint and supply store will mix paint blends and tints, your most precise work revolves around masking. To make this job as simple as possible, be sure you use only those tape and paper products designed for automotive paint masking, devise and follow a systematic masking plan and then allot enough time to complete those tasks with strict attention to detail.

Outlining with Extra-Thin Tape

It is not always easy to lay down a perfect strip of ¾ in. masking tape along edges of trim or other body parts. Around curves, especially tight ones, this kind of tape material tends to bunch up and fold, causing flat spots instead of smoothly and evenly following contours. Masking rounded items is even more difficult when sheets of masking paper are attached to tape strips. As a matter of fact, placing paper and tape together along exact edges in one move is not easily accomplished on any body part.

Professional painters rely on quality workmanship and effective time management to make money. To them, it would be foolish to waste a half an hour masking trim when only five minutes would be needed to remove the part. Likewise,

In order to meticulously mask along the pinstripe edge, a strip of thin Fine Line tape was placed first, as indicated in the center of this picture. To the Fine Line, a sheet of masking paper with tape was attached. Notice how much easier it was to place the wide tape and paper to a strip of Fine Line than it would have been to carefully match the pinstripe edge.

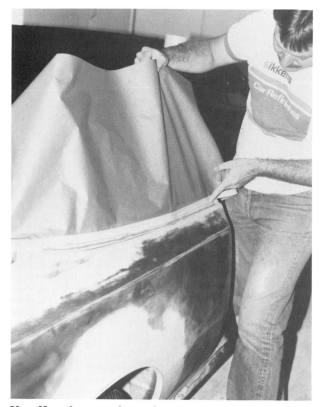

Van Hee places a sheet of paper and tape to the body panel edge where new sealer was applied earlier along a seam on this car with a custom convertible top conversion. Masking the window in this instance is easy because sections of trim have been removed and the paper is wide enough to cover glass with one strip. The extra paper bulk he is holding in his right hand will be folded over and taped so it lays flat and is not moved around by air pressure from a paint gun.

rather than hassle with a piece of tape and a sheet of paper to closely mask along a section of window trim, they lay down a thin strip of Fine Line brand masking tape first and then attach wider strips of tape and paper to it; a much less meticulous task.

Placing a thin ⅛ to ¼ in. strip of plastic Fine Line masking tape right along molding or trim edges is made easy because of its manageable size and texture. It gently follows curves without bunching or folding, and its smooth edges are easy to match along body part edges for perfect masking every time.

The only function of Fine Line tape is masking those part edges next to body panels that are slated for new paint. Additional strips of regular masking tape and paper are attached to Fine Line. That job is made easier because you will have ⅛ to ¼ in. of tape material to mask to instead of having to match a slim part edge. It gives you a wide base to work off of for the quick and simple application of wider tape and paper.

Although most professional auto painters prefer to use Fine Line for outlining intricate masking jobs, you could also use ¼ in. paper masking tape. It works very well along straight sections, but tends to bunch and fold around corners. In addition, the slightly rough texture of this material sometimes allows tiny gaps to form along masked edges which allow paint materials to build up and form spots of overspray.

Another beneficial feature of Fine Line masking tape is its thin nature. In cases where only a section of a body panel is planned to be repainted, masking will be done along a design ridge or at the edge of an existing stripe. Thick paper tape will allow paint to build up and create a definite lip. Thin Fine Line limits that paint edge, or lip, to a minimal thickness along with a very smooth and definite line edge.

Masking Windows
Painting body panels around windows always presents problems associated with overspray on

Sometimes, it is much easier to cut excess masking paper to make it fit tighter and neater. Here, Van Hee uses a sharp razor blade to trim excess paper that was attached in a vertical position. A new strip of tape will be used to secure the loose paper edge.

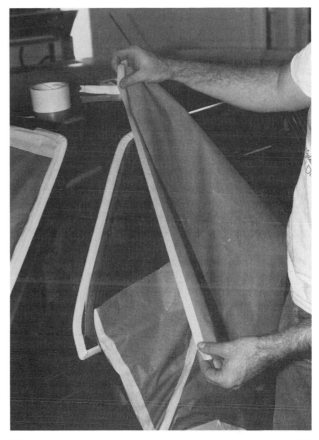

Since window trim edges were already masked with strips of tape, attaching sheets of paper will be easy. Neither the paper nor the tape attached to it will have to match trim edges perfectly, as they can simply be placed anywhere on top of the existing tape. This gives the painter a much broader base to work off of and also allows the masking job to proceed much quicker. In other situations, Fine Line tape might have had to be used to perfectly match more detailed trim edges.

belt moldings and those trim pieces encompassing glass. By far, the surest way to avoid overspray on their surfaces is to remove them. Barring that, use Fine Line tape to outline outer molding edges next to those panels to be painted. Strips of wider masking tape and paper will be attached anywhere along Fine Line's width; just make sure there are no gaps between the inside edge of Fine Line and the wider tape.

Only one strip of masking paper is needed to cover windows as long as it is wide enough to reach from top to bottom. Fold paper as necessary to make it fit neatly along the sides. Use strips of tape to hold paper in a secure position and to cover any resulting gaps. A single sheet of automotive masking paper will prevent paint from bleeding through to underlying surfaces. If you have chosen to use a masking material other than recommended automotive masking paper, you might have to apply two or three layers.

Masking paper does not always come in widths that fit window shapes exactly. Most of the time, especially with side windows, you end up with a tight fit along edges and bulges in the middle. To avoid bulges, fold excess masking paper so it lays flat. Not only does this make for a tidy masking job, it prevents bulky paper from being blown around by air pressure from a spray paint gun. All you have to do is lay one hand down on an edge of the paper and slide it toward the middle. With your other hand, grasp the bulging paper and fold it over. Use strips of tape to hold it in a neat fold.

Whenever masking, always remember that paint will cover everything it touches. Very small slits between tape and masking paper will result in paint coverage to the surface exposed through them. Lightly secured paper edges will blow open during spray paint operations and allow mists of overspray to infiltrate spaces beneath paper. Therefore, always run lines of tape along the length of paper edges to completely seal off underlying areas. This is especially important when the edge of one piece of masking paper is lapped over another.

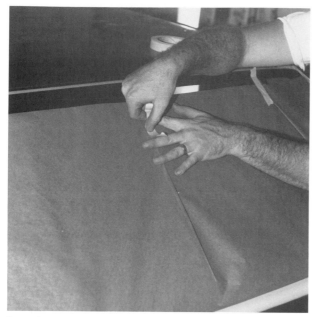

In order to prevent paper bulges from being blown open during spray paint work, fold excess paper and tape it in place. Here, just a small fold was needed to gather loose masking paper that was formed as a result of masking around a contoured rear window. Another fold was made and taped in place just to the right of the fold Van Hee is working on in this picture. Since paint work on this car will be limited to lower panels, the roof will be covered with a sheet of plastic that will be taped to this paper.

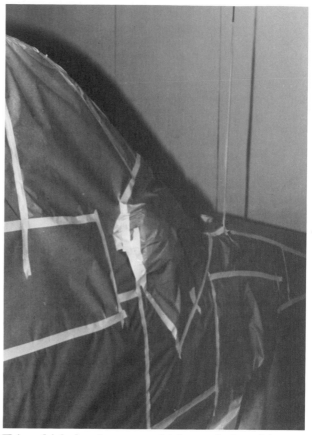

This vehicle has been completely masked and is now ready for paint. Notice the amount of tape that was used to seal off all paper edges. This was done to prevent air pressure from the spray gun from blowing open those seams and forcing in paint overspray. All masking must be tightly secured to prevent accidental openings or weak points where air pressure can force them open.

The taillight and side light have been removed for painting. Since paint will be sprayed over the body area encompassing those assemblies, masking was achieved from inside the trunk space. Strips of masking tape are visible along the trunk to quarterpanel gap and have also been trimmed around the decal next to the fuel filler door that says, "Unleaded Only." Additional masking will include the mud flap, wheel, roof and driver's side body. The bumper has been removed to facilitate unobstructed painting.

Windshields and rear windows are generally quite big. You might have to use two or three strips of paper horizontally placed in order to adequately cover all glass. If trim pieces are not removed, consider placing a strip, or strips, of Fine Line tape around their outer edges before working with wider tape and paper. Rear window deflectors must be removed when paint work will be undertaken on body areas next to them.

Rubber moldings that lap against body panels—rubber windshield moldings along roofs, A-pillars and cowlings—present difficult masking challenges. To make the job of placing tape directly over the molding's outer edge easier, consider putting a length of thick, nonscratching cord under it.

The Eastwood Company carries a Weatherstrip Masking Tool that is designed to insert long strips of plastic cord under the edges of molding and weatherstripping. It raises these edges up off body surfaces to allow complete masking under them. This way, paint is allowed to be sprayed

A Weatherstrip Masking Tool is used to pull up and secure a section of windshield molding so that masking tape can be attached under and over it. This handy tool works great to quickly place a plastic cord under flexible trim to facilitate masking. Made of plastic, the handle assembly will not scratch and once the cord is started it is easily guided along trim while leaving cord deep under the trim flap. Tool courtesy of The Eastwood Company

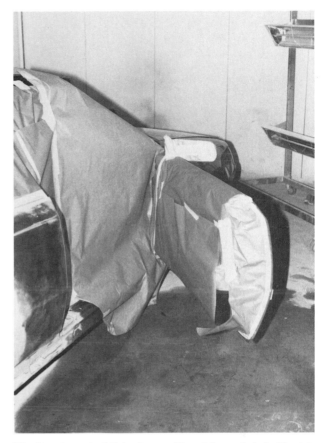

The front part of this door will not be painted. That is why it can remain open while the doorjamb and quarterpanel are sprayed. An extra-wide sheet of masking paper was used to cover the door opening and prevent paint overspray from entering the interior compartment. Careful masking with plenty of forethought must go into a project like this to completely eliminate any chance of paint marring interior panels or surfaces.

under molding edges instead of just up to them. Worries of inadequate molding edge masking and distinctive paint edge lines next to moldings are eliminated.

For those restoration projects where windows and moldings have been removed, you will have to be sure that masking tape and paper are properly positioned to prevent overspray from entering the interior compartment and to form the correct paint edge along window opening perimeters. Generally, exterior paint colors are applied to the middle of window openings. You could lay down strips of wide tape inside these openings and fold it over toward the inside for side windows. Along the spot-welded metal edge of windshield openings, simply apply perimeter tape and paper from the interior compartment side.

Emblems and Badges

As with trim pieces, it is best to remove emblems and badges before painting. They are secured in place by clips, pins, screws, adhesive or double-backed tape. Be extra cautious while attempting to take these items off of any vehicle. Too much prying pressure will cause them to break. Unless you can see that their protruding support pins are secured from inside a trunk space, inner fender area or other location, you will have to carefully pry open an edge to determine just how they are mounted.

If you are not sure how to remove those items on your car, consult a dealership service representative, autobody paint and supply jobber or professional autobody painter. Should an emblem or badge break during dismantling, don't despair. Even professional autobody technicians break these plastic items once in a while.

Although most painting jobs call for the removal of emblems and badges, there are two occasions where they can be left in place. They are when clear coat paint is the only material that is scheduled to be sprayed over them, and when spot painting work will require only a light melting coat be applied close to their edge. With that, careful masking must ensure that no overspray is allowed to build up on their edges.

Intricate masking with tape is needed to ensure emblem and badge edges are completely covered while no part of the tape extends over onto the painted surface. You have to take your time placing tape over item edges first before being concerned with masking their faces. Again, Fine Line tape may be the best choice of material for this meticulous task. After attaching the tape's end to a corner of an emblem, maneuver the roll with one

hand while carefully placing and securing the tape with your other hand. Practice is essential, so do not expect to accomplish this kind of unique masking on the first try.

Van Hee makes this job easier by covering emblems with wide strips of tape first. He then uses a sharp razor blade to cut tape along emblem edges at the exact point where they meet the painted body. He has to employ a very delicate touch in order to avoid cutting into paint or missing the mark and leaving an open gap along the piece he is masking. If you should decide to give this technique a try, opt for very light passes with the razor blade, even if it takes two or three attempts to cut completely through tape. This will prevent excessive pressure on the razor blade from cutting deeply into paint.

About the only way to mask vinyl decals, like those under gasoline filler housing that say "Unleaded Only," is to cover them with masking tape and cut off excess with a *sharp* razor blade. The word sharp is emphasized for a reason. Dull razor blades, even those that have been used to make only three or four cuts, will cause masking tape to tear instead of being cleanly cut. Again, avoid the use of too much pressure on razor blades to prevent unnecessary damage to underlying paint.

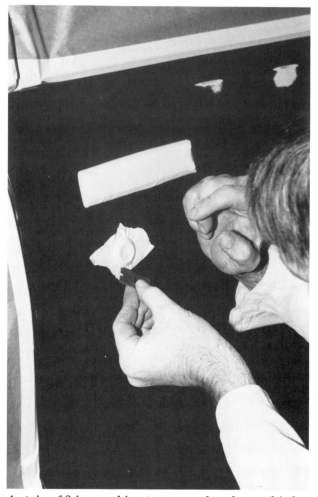

A strip of 2 in. masking tape was placed over this key lock and is now being trimmed with a sharp razor blade. This is a quick method for masking small items like door handles, key locks and certain vinyl decals. You have to have patience and use only enough force on razor blades to cut tape and not dig into underlying paint. Here, Van Hee forced his thumbnail around the key lock circumference to make sure tape was securely attached before he started cutting it along the part's edge. If you plan to paint color, as opposed to clear, around objects like this, you would be best off removing the part rather than rely upon perfect masking to prevent overspray blemishes.

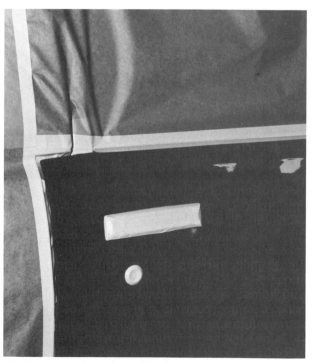

The door handle and key lock have been masked and are ready for paint. Any gap around the edge of either part will display paint overspray after painting. Notice that masking material has been secured inside the doorjamb and window areas to prevent overspray from entering those spaces.

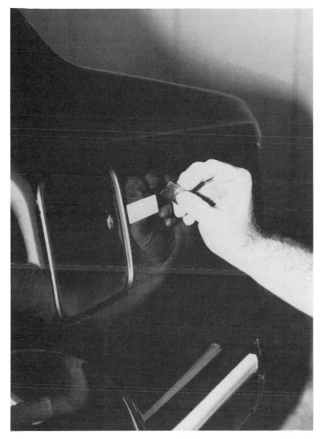

The Unleaded Only decal has been covered with a strip of masking tape that was trimmed off with a sharp razor blade. This area of the car will be painted with clear only, which is why the trim piece below has been masked and not removed. The fuel filler door lock was taken off because it was much easier and quicker to remove than to mask. Notice that the existing paint finish is clean and polished, a chore completed in anticipation of feathering coats of clear.

Door Locks and Handles

Because door locks and handles are secured right next to painted door panels, the same kind of meticulous masking is required for them as for emblems and badges. By the same token, it is recommended they be removed for paint applications next to them, except for clear coats and light paint feathering or melting in maneuvers up to their edge.

Some door handles are removed without having to take off interior panels. These feature a large Phillips head screw on the doorjamb just above the latch mechanism and directly in line with the handle. When the screw is loosened, the handle is tipped outward so you can disconnect linkages. Be certain you secure linkage arms with tape or string so they do not fall into the open space between the inner and outer door skin. If they do, you will have to remove the interior panel to gain access for their retrieval.

While the door is open, masking tape has been placed over the jamb area. Tape will also be placed along the door edges that meet these areas. This has been done to prevent paint overspray from landing on any part of the doorjamb area to mar the surface. In this case, the exterior door skin will be painted along with a spot repair section on the quarterpanel. Masking has been allowed to cover part of the body behind the doorjamb because it will be completely masked anyway.

Door handles are best masked using tape for the entire process. Paper, even 4 in. widths, is just too cumbersome to work with. Use ¾ in. to mask the perimeter edges and then 2 in. to completely cover the unit. If your car presents a rather unique handle, employ whatever means necessary to cover it. Use your imagination. Tape can be applied initially from the backside to offer sticky edges that extend out past upper and lower edges and can be folded over to cover the front. Remember, the most critical part of masking is along the edge where items meet painted panels. Wide strips of tape can easily cover faces and other easy-to-reach parts.

Key locks are easiest to mask using Van Hee's method. Simply cover them with a wide strip of 1 or 2 in. tape and then cut excess from around the lock's circumference with a sharp razor blade. Before cutting, though, use a fingernail to force tape down along the circumference to be sure coverage is complete and that the tape is securely in place.

Doorjambs

Many novice painters forget to mask doorjambs before spraying undercoats or topcoats. This oversight always results in overspray accumulation around doorjamb areas, including the inner side of door edges. As paint is sprayed through the gaps between doors and jambs, it bounces off surfaces to land anywhere it can. The same problem exists inside the gaps along the tops and bottoms of doors. The mess created by this kind of overspray can be difficult to remove.

Painters commonly prefer to coat doorjambs and edges first before any other parts when paint jobs call for them to be sprayed along with the exterior body. After those areas have cured, doors are closed so that painting their exterior portions will be uninhibited. In addition, attempts to paint doorjambs, door edges and outer door skins all at the same time will require doors to be moved so that their front section, which swings inward past the rear part of the fender, can be reached. This movement damages wet paint on hinges.

This is the same procedure followed when painting brand-new doors. It is much easier to paint the interior side and perimeter edges of doors while they are off of vehicles. When paint has dried and the door assembled with window and latch mechanisms, units are installed on vehicles so that their exteriors can be sprayed in one painting sequence. During the exterior painting process, jambs must be masked, even those freshly painted with the same color that will be applied on the outside.

Shrewsbury likes to apply 2 in. tape along the edges of rear doorjambs with the sticky side facing out. Only about half of the tape strip actually goes on the jamb, the rest is folded over so that it is perpendicular. Another strip is placed on the rear door edge in the same manner; half of it sticks out with the sticky side facing out. This way, when the door is closed, both strips of tape are attached to each other to effectively seal the gap between the door and jamb.

The same technique is used along the lower door edge. For front doors, tape is applied to the front edge of the rear door to match the rear edge of the front door when it is closed. A little practice and some patience are required to perfect

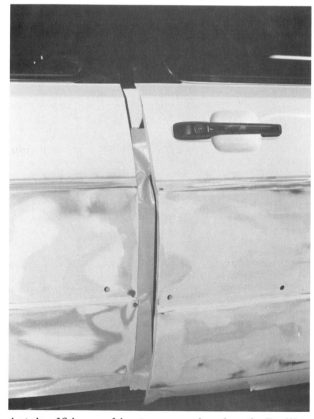

A strip of 2 in. masking tape was placed on the B-pillar post with its sticky side facing out. The theory is, when the door closes, tape on its edge will make contact with the 2 in. tape to effectively seal off the door gap area. This is a tricky operation which takes some practice to perfect. Should tape not secure as expected, paint will enter the space and mar doorjamb surfaces. Further masking will cover the upper door area starting at the top of the designed ridge just above the primer-surfacer area, which is why the door gap area has only been taped up to the handle.

Because the rocker panel area will not be painted, strips of 2 in. tape have been placed along the bottom door edge with their sticky sides facing out. Sheets of paper will be attached to them to effectively mask the lower body section while the door is painted. Here, the strips of tape in the door gap have made contact and will work well to seal off that space from paint overspray.

In case paint must be feathered into the area behind the door and above the fenderwell, a strip of tape has been placed along the rear doorjamb, with its edge protruding out from the body. This was done to make paint essentially bounce off of the tape so that a definite paint edge would not be formed by the application of a feather coat. Wide strips of tape were used to cover the fenderwell trim piece, a much easier method than relying on tape and paper.

Masking has been placed along the doorjamb and around windows. Since window trim edges are already covered, a sheet of masking paper with tape will be attached to the tape on this side window. Maneuvering a large sheet of paper and tape along a trim or molding edge is very difficult. Using tape alone initially makes placing the paper much easier and faster. At the bottom of the window, excess paper is folded and taped into position.

these maneuvers. Tape does not always stick the way you would like it to and sometimes, the air movement caused by a door closing is enough to throw off the tape's ability to match up with a corresponding strip.

Mycon and Laursen have used strips of 2 in. tape and 4 to 6 in. paper to mask doorjambs and edges. Consideration must be given to the location where tape edges are placed. If they are set too far out, they may allow a paint line to be visible through the gap between the door and jamb. This is an important factor when painting a color on the exterior that is in contrast with the shade on doorjambs. You have to decide where the dividing line will be and make sure that tape is positioned symmetrically.

Trim

Most body side moldings and other trim pieces do not look their best when painted over or marred

with thin strips of paint overspray along their edges. Therefore, when paint work is called for on body sections presenting them, plan their removal for painting and later installation, after paint has dried and all rubbing out or buffing operations have been completed. By waiting until polishing is done, you prevent the unnecessary build-up of compound along trim edges, as well as their designed grooves or wrinkled surfaces.

Drip-rail trim is generally secured by being snapped over the welded drip-rail edge and then screwed tight at each end. Careful dismantling, with the assistance of a helper on long pieces, will prevent these items from bending in the middle to form creases. When masked, attention must be given the top inner side as well as the facing portion. Place tape of an adequate width to the inner side first and then lay it down over the face. Should another strip be needed, apply it to the bottom edge first and fold excess over the front to overlap the previous strip.

On many cars, metal trim around windshields and rear windows sticks up just a bit above the vehicle body. Take advantage of this gap to insert masking tape into with the sticky side facing up. Gently slide the tape strip back and forth until you can no longer force it any deeper into the gap. Then, fold it over on top of the trim section. You may need to stand on a sturdy stool to reach top trim pieces, and you might need a helper to assist you from the opposite side. Employ the same technique for the side and bottom sections.

Applying tape to other types of trim does not require any special skill, other than patience and attention to detail. Edges next to body panels are covered first and faces last. Hold a roll of tape in one hand and position the extended strip with the other directly on top of trim sections. Be absolutely certain that trim edges are covered and that tape does not extend to the body. Small pieces of tape that do touch body parts will block paint from the surface to cause a blemish.

Always inspect your masking work after tape has been positioned. Use a fingernail to guarantee tape is securely attached along edges. On the bottom sides of body side trim, you may have to lie down in order to accurately place masking tape. Do whatever it takes to accomplish your goal of masking in such a way that nobody will be able to notice that any paint work was done, except that the car body looks great.

Other Exterior Body Features

Radio antennas can be taken off for paint work on fenders or quarterpanels. Many of these items will unscrew from their bases, leaving a large gap between the car body and remaining antenna unit. If you decide to leave the antenna in place, do not wrap tape around it from top to bottom. Although it might seem quite easy to put tape on in this "barber pole" kind of way, it is a pain in the neck to take off.

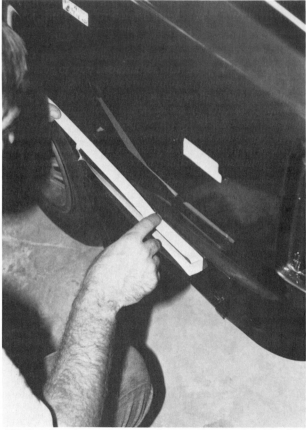

All it takes is patience and attention to detail when placing strips of tape along moldings or trim. With the roll of tape in one hand, let your other hand carefully guide tape on top of parts so that the edges next to the surface are perfectly covered, with no excess jutting out onto the body. Use your finger to make sure tape has securely adhered to the surface. If the first attempt at this is not successful, pull tape off and try again. You should be able to attach and remove a section of tape three or four times before its adhesive strength is weakened.

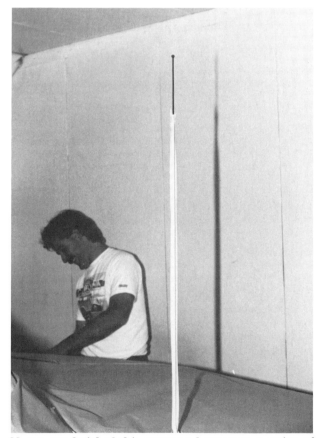

Mycon sandwiched this antenna between two strips of masking tape to protect it against paint overspray. More tape will be needed to conclude the chore.

Instead, sandwich antennas between two long strips of masking tape that run vertically from top to bottom. Secure the lowest edge with a short strip of tape. Van Hee prefers to make a skinny cover for antennas out of a strip of masking paper, much like those paper covers used to package drinking straws. He pulls off enough paper to match the height of the antenna and then rolls it into a cylinder. Tape is used to hold it together. It is then slipped over the unit, folded at the top and taped securely at both ends.

Taillight and side light units are usually quite easy to remove. Most newer cars feature taillights that are quickly dismantled by loosening four to eight nuts on their housing backsides. The assemblies are then simply pulled away from the body from the outside. Side lights are removed the same way.

However, should you decide to mask taillights instead of removing them, plan to use strips of 2 in. tape. Because their designs commonly feature curved corners or awkward shapes, masking is accomplished much easier, faster and more completely by placing overlapping strips of 2 in. tape

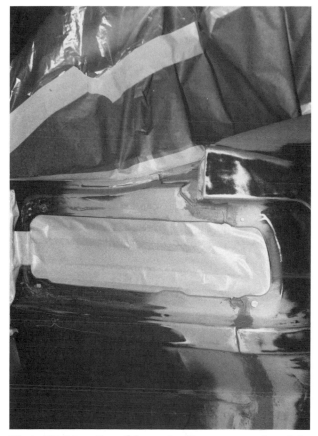

The taillight unit on this car has been removed and the opening left behind masked off from inside the trunk space. The tape you see covering the taillight opening is actually the sticky side. Masking paper above the taillight opening runs up to the trunk lid, which remains open to facilitate painting around the trunk opening. Plastic has been attached to the masking paper at the top of the picture and continues over the car to cover the roof and hood.

Van Hee likes to roll up strips of paper and then slip them over radio antennas for masking. It does not matter which method you use, as long as antennas are protected from paint spray.

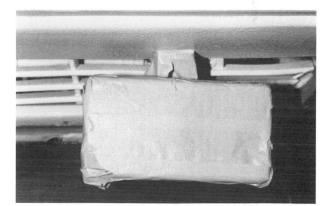

This is a foglight that has been masked with strips of 2 in. tape. Masking paper and tape are used to cover the upper grille, while coats of Rocker Schutz and paint are applied to lower grille areas and the stripped ground effect located directly behind the foglight. Rather than using masking paper for all chores, consider using masking tape alone for smaller items, like foglights.

over their entire surface. Be sure that each overlap extends to at least ¾ in. to prevent paint seepage into seams. Side lights are masked using the same procedure as for emblems and badges.

Bumper designs range from out-in-the-open pickup truck dock bumpers to wraparound, closely fitted urethane-faced models. Again, paint work around these units requires they be unbolted and removed. This will allow plenty of work room around them while painting, and eliminate any overspray possibility.

Masking requires the use of regular masking tape and paper. If possible, insert a strip of tape between body panels and those parts touching them. Fold it over and then attach paper and tape to it. Fold paper over the top and face of bumpers. If more paper coverage is needed, start from the bottom and fold over the top to overlap with the preceding piece.

If you intend to touch up only a quarterpanel and just the side-mounted bumper guard is in your way, consider dismantling the guard alone. These are attached to bumpers with nuts and bolts. They are flexible, for the most part, and bending them out of the way should allow you good enough dismantling access. If not, maybe that piece can be pulled away and secured with tape to allow adequate painting access.

License plates and their holders are very easy to remove. You are much better off dismantling them than attempting to mask and expecting to be able to spray paint behind them. If inset into actual housings, consider the entire unit's removal. For those that insist upon masking, follow the techniques described earlier to maintain adequate top, side and bottom edge masking coverage.

Vinyl graphics, stripes and decals cannot be easily removed. They cannot be stored either. The procedure involved with their removal destroys them. Therefore, carefully placed masking is defi-

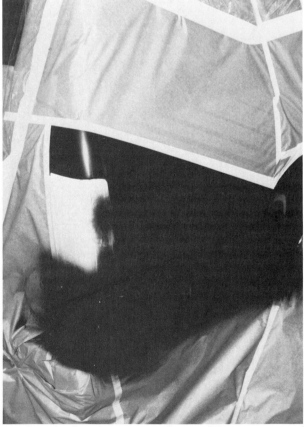

Black paint has been sprayed over this quarterpanel area. Because the spot repair was located away from the taillight and upper decal graphic, only feather coats of paint are needed next to them. In fact, this picture illustrates what the project looked like after the second coat of black was applied. The first coat encompassed only half of what the second coat covered, which did not include areas next to the taillight. The third pass of the spray gun will include all of the masked area.

Van Hee uses a razor blade to cut plastic away from a paint area. Definitive masking was accomplished around windows and other assemblies first, while plastic will quickly cover large areas, like the roof, for overspray protection. Notice how neat and tight fitting the masking paper is on top of the rear window. This is how all masking jobs should look.

Initial strips of masking tape have been carefully placed along the edge of this mud flap. Paper will be attached to this tape to complete the masking chore. Tape has to be perfectly fitted along edges that meet body panels scheduled for paint. Away from the body, like on the mud flap, tape ends can cross and do not have to be placed in any special fashion. If your masking job requires tape be placed inside fenderwells, be sure those areas are clean, as tape will not adhere to dirty surfaces.

The mud flap has been masked using paper that has completely surrounded it. One sheet was placed horizontally around the flap and taped in place. A second sheet was placed along the vertical edge to cover the top part of the flap. You can use more than one piece of paper to cover unusually shaped items, like mud flaps. When painting near wheels, make sure the tread is masked along with the fenderwell to prevent paint overspray blemishes.

nitely required when painting near or around them. Because vinyl graphic and stripe material presents such perfectly smooth and even edges, use thin Fine Line tape.

Meticulously mask the outer perimeter edges of vinyl graphics, stripes and decals first. Be sure Fine Line tape is placed directly on top of the item being masked and perfectly in line with its edge. When touchup or spot painting is scheduled for just a body section below such items, you only need to mask the bottom edge. The rest can be covered with paper and regular masking tape.

However, should you need to paint areas between vinyl graphics be sure to outline the entire scheme and then fill in with wide tape or paper, whichever is most appropriate. With a two- or three-step paint system, where clear paint will finish the job, you could remove masking after color coats have been applied and then cover everything, including the graphic, stripe or decal, with clear. This effort will fill in the gap between color paint layers and vinyl to make the entire panel smooth with no distinguishable paint edge or lip.

Be sure to confirm the effectiveness and compatibility of this procedure with your autobody paint and supply jobber, as various vinyl graphic, stripe and decal materials may not be compatible with the paint system you employ. In addition, be 100 percent certain you want that vinyl adornment to remain on your car or truck for a long time. Once you spray clear over its top, you will have to remove the clear coat first before you can remove the vinyl material.

Grille

Most grille sections are quite easy to dismantle once you determine how they are secured. With the hood open, you should be able to see sets of screws or clips that hold these pieces in position. Other means of support are visible from the front, such as screws, clips, bolts and so forth.

Masking for grille sections is best accomplished with wide strips of paper. Attached to the top of the unit first, paper will hang down to cover a majority of the assembly. Use ¾ in. tape to secure

The spot repair in the lower left part of this picture will be painted. Successive paint coats will extend up to the vinyl graphic. A section of tape has been carefully placed along the lower edge of the graphic for initial masking. Paper and tape will be attached to it next. Vinyl graphics cannot be taken off without destroying them. For spot painting on areas near them, take your time to mask their edges in lieu of removing them.

The area surrounding this spot repair on a Toyota 4-Runner has been completely masked. Although the taillight could have been removed, the painter decided it would be easier and faster to simply mask it off with 2 in. tape. Feather painting will extend out to almost the entire masked area. Painting will stop at the gap between the quarterpanel and tailgate. Notice how big an area is involved for just a small, spot paint repair. This is to guarantee plenty of room for paint feathering to ensure a perfect color and paint edge blend.

paper on the sides. There is no significant need to mask each individual facet. If you have 12 in. paper and need to cover a top to bottom grille of 20 in., simply tape paper edge to edge and attach the extra-wide sheet as a unit.

Intricate painting on the grille side of fenders requires the grille be removed. No amount of masking will allow adequate spray paint gun maneuverability. However, if all you need to do is paint the front part of your ground effects system, then start masking from the bottom of the grille and work upward. When masking, always keep in mind the painting requirements for the job and the sequence you plan to follow.

The most important part of masking involves those items secured adjacent or perpendicular to the area to be painted. It is the edges of those items that will expose overspray and the paint build-up edge so predominant with repaint efforts. Be sure the first piece of masking tape placed along the

edges of those items is secure, adequate and accurate.

Wheels

A lot of street rods, as well as other specialty automobiles, have painted fenderwells and special wheels. It would be a shame to mar them with overspray. So, for paint projects that include fenderwells, remove wheels. It's just that simple. (Be sure the vehicle is securely supported on sturdy jack stands.)

On those that command a new paint job or spot painting and already have painted fenderwells, take time to adequately cover them with masking paper and tape. Cars with normal everyday driver fenderwells covered with undercoat, do not need to be masked, unless you want to. On those, cover overspray imperfections with new layers of undercoat or black paint. The choice is up to you.

Most paint shops, like Newlook, have covers designed just for wheels and tires. In addition, there are packages of plastic tire and wheel covers available. They easily and quickly fit over tires and wheels to protect them against overspray. If you do not have access to such items, plan to mask tires and wheels as you would anything else. Should some paint be accidentally sprayed on tires, use thinner or reducer, whichever is appropriate with the paint system employed, to scrub them clean.

Wheels are a different story. Polished wheels will not look the same after you attacked overspray on them with harsh solvents, #0000 steel wool or other abrasive. Chances are, you will have to get them polished by a wheel restoration service. To save the expense, and hassle, take a few minutes to mask them appropriately. Use enough paper to cover them completely, and plenty of tape to make sure paper seams do not open under the pressure exerted by a spray paint gun. The best means of affording overspray protection is to remove them from the vehicle during paint work.

As with all masking efforts, tape will not stick to dirty surfaces. Grungy tires and filthy fenderwells will not allow masking tape to adhere. Even if tape does stick initially, air pressure from your paint gun will quickly blow them off. That quick second where masking comes off will be just enough to allow paint overspray access to the area marring the surface. So, before you bring your car or truck in for masking, make sure you spent plenty of time washing those areas where tape will be placed.

Unaffected Body Areas

Automobiles scheduled for complete paint jobs should have almost all exterior body parts removed, the more the better. For spot paint projects, part dismantling will be minimal and unaffected body panels will have to be protected against overspray. Just remember, even with the best HVLP system, there will always be paint overspray. Therefore, before you begin your project, plan to mask every part of your car that will not receive paint.

A large sheet of plastic covers the bed on this new Chevrolet pickup truck. Because paint overspray will land on everything in its path, you have to remember to cover uninvolved pickup truck beds.

This tire and wheel have been covered with a piece of material especially designed to cover wheels and tires during paint work. For your projects, you could use plastic, tarps or masking paper. Be sure that any cover is securely held in place with tape so it does not blow around while spray painting operations are conducted nearby. Plastic will be used to cover the roof, hood and sides of this car, while the C-pillar area and top of the fenderwell lip remain exposed for paint feathering.

Two-inch masking tape has been attached to the fender edge with its sticky side toward the fender. It will be rolled up and over the hood to present a curved edge for paint to reflect or bounce off of. This was done to prevent the formation of a paint line edge along the top of the fender as paint is feathered into the area. The first coat of paint will cover the repair, and the two subsequent coats will each feather out a little farther until the third covers the fender edge.

This does not mean you have to meticulously mask the trim pieces on the driver's side when all you will be painting is the passenger side quarter-panel. It simply means that the driver's side of the car must be covered so overspray from the other side does not land on anything on that side.

At Newlook, painters use large sheets of plastic to cover everything beyond the immediate painting area. Tape is used to hold plastic in place, as air pressure could certainly blow it around. Meticulous masking is accomplished at the paint site, followed by general coverage provided for everything else.

In lieu of large plastic sheets, you will have to use masking paper. Think of your car as a large present. You want to cover everything so the recipient will not be able to steal a clue from an uncov-

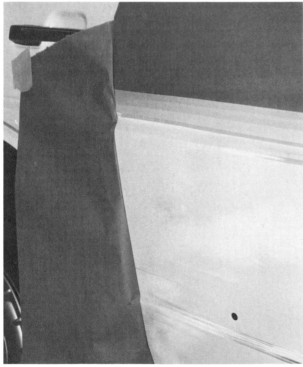

Masking paper has been folded back over itself to produce a rolled edge for paint to bounce off of, thus eliminating a definite line where paint stops. Likewise, a section of nonstick tape has been placed along the top edge. This special tape features nonstick edges which can be folded at a ninety-degree angle to reflect paint spray. The lowest and darkest line on the top strip of masking tape denotes an edge that has been folded up.

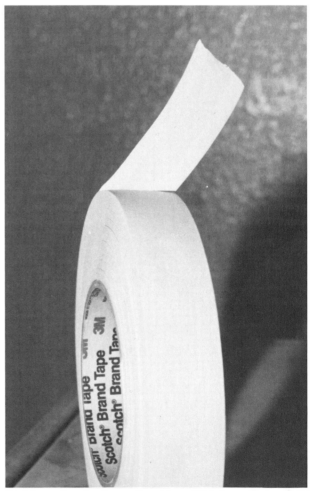

Lighter color shades on the sides of this tape show where material is located to prevent the edges from sticking to a surface. The center of this tape is sticky and will adhere like normal automotive masking tape. Once this particular tape is attached to a body surface, an edge can be folded up to a ninety-degree angle so paint will reflect off of it to effect a smooth, feathered edge. It is available at autobody paint and supply stores.

ered spot. Using large sheets of paper, cover the roof, hood and trunk lid and secure it with masking tape. Overlap successive sheets by an inch, or so, and seal the seams with tape the full length. You can never mask too much.

Individual panel painting requires masking at the edge of each panel. This is a simple process. You can place a strip of tape down first and attach paper and tape to it. Or, if you have the means, roll off a section of paper with tape attached and secure it as necessary.

Paint feathering or melting requires a little different technique. Mycon, Van Hee and Shrewsbury prefer to mask off panels by applying a taped sheet of paper over the area to be painted and then folding it over toward the area to be masked. This forces tape to roll over backward. So instead of a clean edge, the curved tape contour forces paint to bounce away to create a soft, gentle edge. After all coats have been applied, they empty all of the paint from their gun cup except for about ¼ in. To that, they add about ¾ in. of reducer. The mixture is about three to one.

That section of masking paper that was rolled over itself is then removed. The overreduced paint mixture is then sprayed over that newly exposed area. The extra reducer melts old paint, in essence, and allows just a hint of new paint to infiltrate the surface. The result is a perfect blend and feathering of new paint edges into old.

7

Paint Application

Regardless of the task at hand, almost anyone who is able to follow detailed instructions can successfully complete the job. That is, of course, if nothing unexpected crops up between the time that task is started and finally completed. It is when unfamiliar problems suddenly arise that novices run into trouble. The sign of a professional, in this sense, is his or her ability to quickly remedy problems and then get back on track afterward to accomplish satisfactory results.

Nobody ever expects a "first timer" to be able to anticipate problems with any job if they have never been exposed to that particular type of work before. This is why many trade professions and other careers demand apprentices serve an intern-

ship before being allowed to work on their own. However, do-it-yourself auto painters who have not attended trade schools or other training sessions are not able to enjoy the security of an experienced veteran painter looking over their shoulder to identify and help correct problems.

Therefore, novice do-it-yourselfers must rely upon personal practice and trial-and-error experience. Before you jump into an automotive paint project with both feet, get an old hood, trunk lid or door and practice your new hobby. Mix paint products according to label instructions and apply them with the air pressure recommended on the same label, or from information sheets and application guides.

Try painting with different fan patterns and pressure settings to see which combinations work best for intricate work in confined spaces and which perform better on large panels. Practice holding paint guns at perpendicular angles to work surfaces; see what happens when you don't. Use cans of inexpensive paint, and practice until you become familiar with the techniques required for good paint coverage. When paint has dried, practice wet sanding, rubbing out and buffing.

Use your new dual-action sander to remove those coats of paint to get a feel for its operation. Put a deep scratch into your practice panel and repair it, instead of practicing on your favorite car or truck. Become proficient with the tools and materials you expect to use while fixing your special car before attacking its precious surface with power tools and harsh chemicals. Practice, practice and practice some more.

This will be your personal training session, or sessions, where novice mistakes can be corrected and your ability to quickly recognize problems in the making will enable you to stop before they get bigger. In addition, your hands-on experience will help you to discover just what needs to be done to correct problems in ways that allow you to continue with the job, just like professionals.

Paint Mixing

Because there are literally tens of thousands of different automotive paint colors, mixing the precise shade for your car is a critical science. Accord-

Directly in the center of this picture, you will notice a small piece of plastic extending out into the paint area. Unless this problem is remedied early, corrective work will have to take place after the panel has been cured. In this case, the plastic was pulled out of the way and subsequent coats of paint were able to rectify the problem. It is this attention to detail and the corrective action taken to repair mistakes, that separate mediocre paint jobs from professional ones.

Information from the microfiche pertaining to a specific paint color mixture was retrieved and written down on a sheet of paper. Because the amount of paint needed was less than that presented on the screen, a calculator was used to divide paint mixing proportions. A straight-sided, empty paint can sits on top of the scale, which registers zero. According to calculations, specific weights of paint will be added until the desired color is finally derived.

Before a paint mixture is used, it must be thoroughly shaken. This is done to completely suspend all pigments and binders in the solution. Some colors include heavy ingredients which quickly settle to the bottom of paint cans during shipping and also while sitting idly on shelves. Just before using the paint you purchased, consider asking the jobber at your local autobody and paint supply store to put your can of paint on the store's shaker.

ing to stock vehicle color codes or those selected from paint chip catalogs, autobody paint and supply personnel use highly sensitive weight scales to measure drops of color tint in hundredths of a gram to finally arrive at prescribed colors. This work is done for you as part of your paint system purchase.

However, in most cases, you will have to thin down those concentrated colors with solvent (thinner or reducer) to dilute them into a sprayable mixture. Along with that, specific quantities of hardener must be added for those products that call for it. You might wonder why paint stores cannot simply put all of the required ingredients in a single container and sell it to you as a ready-to-use product. The answer is simple.

Paint materials are shipped from manufacturing plants in concentrated forms. This helps to keep the heavy pigments and other solid materials from settling. Solvents are added to make those products sprayable. Also, according to PPG's *Refinish Manual,* "The temperature at which the finishing material is sprayed and dried has a tremendous influence on the smoothness of the finish." Thinners and reducers come in different temperature ratings, remember? If you bought paint mixed according to manufacturer recommendations on a day that was hot and sunny, the thinner or reducer used would be suited just for those climatic conditions.

Now, if you could not apply paint on that particular day as planned, how could you be guaranteed that the next available painting day would offer an identical temperature? Furthermore, some products are designed to be more heavily reduced for spray painting than others, depending upon the task at hand. DP 40 Epoxy Primer, for example, is mixed with catalyst and reducer when used as a sealer, but without any reducer for primer applications. By purchasing paint products with a basic content, painters are able to mix proper amounts of solvent as recommended for the current temperature and application requirements.

As far as hardener is concerned, once it mixes with paint the hardening process begins. As you will note on application guides and information sheets, catalyzed paint has a pot life of only so long. Hardener, therefore, is only mixed with paint just before spraying begins.

To take the guesswork out of paint and solvent mixing, as mentioned earlier, paint manufacturers have designed calibrated stir sticks. According to mixing directions, an amount of paint is poured into a clean, empty can with straight sides (not a spray gun cup) up to a certain number located along one vertical column on that paint system's designated stir stick. Solvent is then poured in until

Paint sticks with calibrated numbers arranged on specific columns are used by painters when mixing solutions of paint, reducer and hardener. Each paint manufacturer has its own sets of calibrated paint sticks. Failure to use an appropriate mixing stick can easily cause improper paint solutions which will not flow, adhere or smooth out as expected. Sticks are available at autobody paint and supply stores.

Before dumping paint into your spray gun cup, always place a paint filter over the cup opening. Here, a Sikkens brand filter was used to pour paint from this can into a spray gun cup. After the cup was filled, the filter was simply placed on top of the can. Filters work well to catch small globs of undiluted paint material and other contaminants that would otherwise clog paint spray gun ports or tips.

the fluid level in the can raises to a corresponding number on the next column over on the same stick.

If a one-to-one ratio of paint to solvent mixture were indicated on label directions, for example, paint would be poured into an empty can up to the number one. Reducer is added until that total mixture reaches the number one on the next column over. If more paint was needed, because of a large job, simply mix the ingredients up to a higher number.

When using a paint system that requires the mixing of paint, solvent and hardener, a corresponding stir stick is required. Instead of just two columns of numbers, it will have three. Again, paint is poured to whatever number desired depending upon the amount of material needed for the job. Solvent is poured in until the fluid level reaches the identical number in its column, and then hardener is added until the content reaches the same number in the hardener column.

Not all paint systems are based on a one-to-one ratio. By looking at a paint-mixing stir stick,

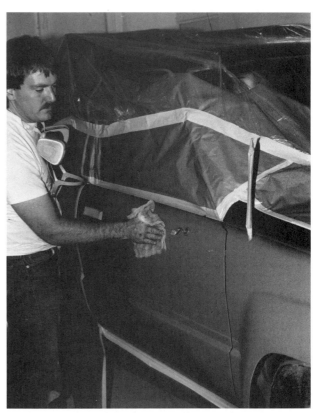

Just before spraying paint, Van Hee uses a tack cloth to carefully wipe off the vehicle's surface. Even though wax and grease remover and an aerosol glass cleaner were used previously, tack cloths are designed to pick up minute pieces of lint and other small debris. This should be the last thing you do just before donning your respirator and spraying paint. This door and fender have already been sprayed with sealer, as noted by the uniform color.

Nozzle Orifice:		Siphon: 1.5 (0.059″) — 1.8 (0.070″) Gravity: 1.2 (0.046″) — 1.5 (0.059″)		

SPRAY GUN	NEEDLE	NOZZLE	AIR CAP
DEVILBISS	EX	EX (0.070″)	30,80 or 43 (JGA,86)
MBC/JGA/JGV/GFG FF	FF	FF (0.055″)	30,80 or 43 (JGA,86)
	FW	FW (0.062″)	30,80 or 43
BINKS BBR	AB	A047(0.046″)	AS 17 or 20
	AB	A061(0.059″)	AS17
#7	35	35 (0.059″)	SC
#7	36	36 (0.070″)	SD or SG
#18	65	65 (0.059″)	SG or SH
#62	365	65 (0.059″)	SG or SH
#69	565	65 (0.059″)	SG or SH
SHARPE #775PI/71	03-45N	71-04-055 (0.055″)	71-02#10

Recommended Spray Gun Setups:

Air Pressure at the Gun:		Siphon: 35-45 PSI
		Gravity: 25-35 PSI
Application:		Apply two to three medium coats until desired hiding and match are achieved. Cross-coat if needed for mottle control.
Cross-Coat:		Often times the CRONAR® base color will appear to mottle. As it dries the flake usually orients itself, eliminating any mottle, and no cross-coating is necessary.
Fish Eyes:		If fish eyes occur: Allow CRONAR to dry. Wet sand the fish eyes smooth with 600 grit or finer. Re-apply the CRONAR color.
Flash Time:		2-5 minutes between coats. 5-10 minutes after final coat and before applying the clear option of your choice.

This is just one page of the application sheet for DuPont's URO Clear paint which is designed to be used over Cronar Base Colors. As you can tell, instructions are quite clear with reference to nozzle and air cap descriptions. Air pressure and other factors are included.

Application sheets are generally set up in this manner to make it easier for users to understand and implement suggested recommendations. Courtesy of DuPont Refinish

Viscosity:		17-19 seconds in a Zahn #2 (DuPont M-222) cup.
Nozzle Orifice:		Siphon or Gravity: 1.4 (0.055″) — 1.9 (0.073″)

Recommended Spray Gun Setups:	SPRAY GUN	NEEDLE	NOZZLE	AIR CAP
	DEVILBISS MBC/JGA/JGV	FW FF EX	FW (0.062″) FF (0.055″) EX (0.070″)	30,80 or 43 30,80 or 43 30,80 or 43
	BINKS BBR BINKS #7	AB 36	A072 (0.073″) 36 (0.070″)	AS17 SG or SK
	SHARPE 775	0.070	CC-70 (0.070″)	CC

Air Pressure at the Gun:		Siphon: Spot/Panel—35 PSI Overall—45-55 PSI
		Gravity: Spot/Panel—35 PSI Overall—35-40 PSI
Application:		Apply 2 to 3 medium-wet coats until desired appearance is achieved.
Retarder:	Retarder 8100S	Use Retarder 8100S up to 10% by volume.
Fish Eyes:	Additive 259S	Use Additive 259S up to one ounce per ready-to-spray gallon of URO™ Clear.

The application sheet for DuPont's Cronar Base Colors also includes a page with specific spray paint gun setup recommendations. Should this information be foreign to you, be sure to confirm nozzle settings and other recommendations with your autobody paint and supply jobber. In addition, should you be using a spray paint gun other than DeVilbiss, Binks or Sharpe, be certain to match the needle, nozzle and air cap specifications to those recommended.

you will see that sometimes the numbers on the reducer or hardener column are not twice as high up the stick as those in the paint column. This is a very accurate way of mixing paint, solvent and hardener. You must follow the manufacturer's recommendations and instructions to be ensured of a quality blend.

Once your paint product has been carefully blended, use the stir stick to swish the contents around in the mixing can. Pointed tools, like screwdrivers, are not recommended for stirring. The flat-bottomed, rather wide nature of stir sticks works best. Stir for at least two minutes. Then, place a paint filter over the opening of your spray gun cup and pour in the mixture. Your paint product is now ready for spraying. Be sure to put the caps back on containers of solvent and hardener, as well as paint. This will prevent unnecessary evaporation or accidental spillage.

In the paint booth, tack off your car or truck's surface immediately. Then start painting. Some paint products and colors are designed with a lot of heavy solids that could settle to the bottom of paint cups in just ten to fifteen minutes. If you were to take your time tacking and then wait a little longer while your paint gun sat idle, solids could settle, possibly causing the color to change. This would be a catastrophe, especially with spot paint projects.

Spray Gun Controls and Test Panels

The high-tech world of automotive painting extends past basic paint material mixtures and safety equipment to the fluid tip and air cap dimensions of spray paint guns. Companies, like PPG, recommend specific spray gun setups for application of their products. Such a specification is this recommendation for base coat spray guns: "DeVilbiss JGV–572; Fluid Tip—FW (0.062 in.); Air Cap #86."

The same kind of recommendations follow for their enamel spray guns and lacquer spray guns involving DeVilbiss, Binks and Sharpe gun models. You can obtain this information from information sheets and application guidelines. Or, check with your autobody paint and supply jobber.

Two control knobs are typical on most full-sized production spray paint guns. One controls the fan spray, while the other manages the volume of paint that exits the nozzle. They are located at the top rear section of most models. About the only way to determine proper spray patterns and volume combinations is to practice spraying paint on a test panel. Various paint products and their reduction ratios will spray differently, especially when recommended air pressures are varied.

To assist in perfecting fan and volume match, many painters keep test panels in their spray paint booth. Usually, these are nothing more than sheets of wide masking paper spread and taped to a wall. On the test panel, they can spray paint and then make adjustments to control knobs until just the right pattern and volume are established. At that point, they begin actual painting.

Periodically during paint jobs, painters may notice a flaw in their gun's fan pattern. To check it, they turn to the test panel and shoot a clean section with a mist of paint. If the pattern is not uniform, it is noticed immediately. Controls are checked, as well as air pressure. If the pattern is still flawed, the paint gun is disconnected from its supply hose and cleaned. Chances are, a small port or passage has become clogged and must be cleaned before the job can continue.

Accordingly, as maneuvers are focused onto body areas confined by their design, like some front-end areas, painters must reduce pressure or change fan sprays to accommodate smaller surface areas. By checking the spray pattern on a test panel, painters can accurately make adjustments as needed without having to guess while actually spraying body surfaces.

Spray Gun Maneuvering

Spray paint guns apply their most uniform and effective paint finishes when they are held

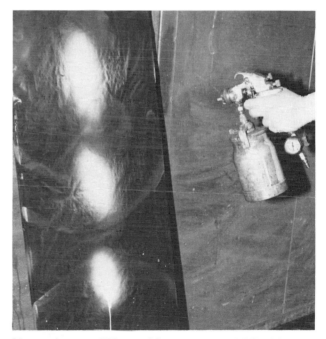

Most painters will have either a test panel, like this, or a sheet of masking paper available for checking the condition, size and shape of spray gun fan patterns. As you can see, the test pattern at the top is perfect, the one in the middle is too short and the bottom is so short paint runs quickly developed. Just above the painter's hand, you'll see two knobs. The top knob adjusts the fan pattern and the bottom knob controls the amount of material that sprays through the gun. Practice with your spray paint gun to get an accurate feel for how it operates and how fan spray patterns are adjusted.

Correcting distorted spraying patterns

When the gun is adjusted properly and held at the right distance from the painting surface, the pattern should resemble Figure 9. As you can see, it's an elongated ellipse with a uniform distribution of material over the entire area.

A split spray (Figure 10) or one that is heavy on each end of a fan pattern and weak in the middle is usually caused by atomizing air pressure too high for the viscosity of the paint material. Reduce the air pressure, then check that the fluid adjustment is open fully. Do not lower air pressure below the recommended pressure of the product being sprayed.

Where the air pressure is correct, a split pattern may be caused by attempting to get too wide a spray with thin material. To correct, open material control "B" (Figure 7) by turning counter clockwise, then turn spray width adjustment "A" clockwise (Figure 7). This reduces the width of the spray but will correct split spray.

Dry material in a wind port "M" (Figure 8) restricts air passage through it and produces a crescent shaped pattern like Figure 11. To correct this, dissolve

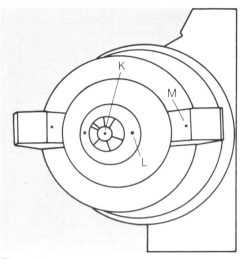

Figure 8.

material in the wing port with thinner, and clean out the port, but do not use metal instruments.

A spray pattern heavy and wider, at either top or bottom (see Figure 12), indicates that material has dried around the outside of the fluid tip.

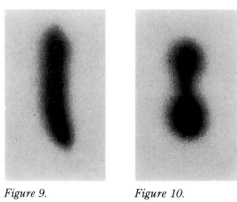

Figure 9.

Figure 10.

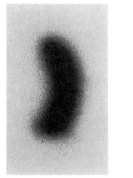

Figure 11.

Figure 12.

Here are a series of inadequate fan sprays and the reasons why they have been affected. Dirty wind ports and other paint gun surfaces must be cleaned using quality solvent and only those brushes designed for paint gun cleaning. The use of hard-metal instruments can quickly and permanently damage paint gun components. PPG Industries, Inc.

perpendicular to the surfaces being sprayed at a distance of from 8 to 10 in. PPG's *Refinish Manual* clearly states, "If the gun is tilted toward the surface, the fan pattern won't be uniform. If the gun is swung in an arc, varying the distance from the nozzle to the work, the paint will go on wetter where the nozzle is closer to the surface and drier where it is farther away." This all adds up to imperfect or blemished paint finishes because some of the product dries just micro-seconds before it reaches the surface while other parts of the same fan spray go on wetter than intended.

About the only time painters can fan paint gun passes is on small spot repaints. These situations call for a reduced amount of paint material around the feathered perimeter of spots as compared to center sections. This is done with wrist action to lightly blend edges only. Practice this technique before attempting it on your nice car or truck.

Because automobile roofs, hoods and trunk lids lay in a horizontal plane, paint guns must be held at a horizontal angle in order to effect smooth, even and uniform passes. To prevent drips of paint from landing on body surfaces, Kosmoski advises his painters to tie an old tack cloth or other absorbent and lint-free rag around the top of the cup where it makes contact with its support base. Even with paint guns that are reported to be dripless, this may not be a bad idea.

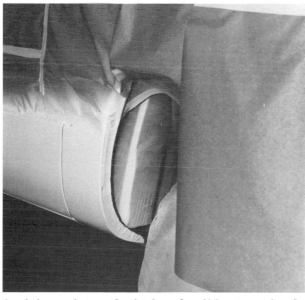

Applying paint on the fender edge did not require the same spray pattern or full trigger operation as the body panel next to it. Some painters prefer to adjust their fan sprays and throttle the trigger on their guns down while painting small sections or in confined spaces. Again, this effort requires practice to refine. In addition, paint overspray on the fenderwell area of this truck will have to be painted over in black to make the paint job look professional.

Holding paint guns so that the nozzle is perpendicular with the surface is very important. Lock your wrist and elbow and walk along panels to ensure a right-angle position. Do not rely solely upon your arm to swing back and forth. Move your body with your arm and shoulder steadfastly anchored. Again, this takes practice, especially when you have to move from one panel to another in a smooth, steady and even walk.

Each fan spray should overlap the previous spray by half. In other words, the center of the first pass should be directed along the masking line: half of the paint on the masking paper, the other half on the body surface. The second pass should be

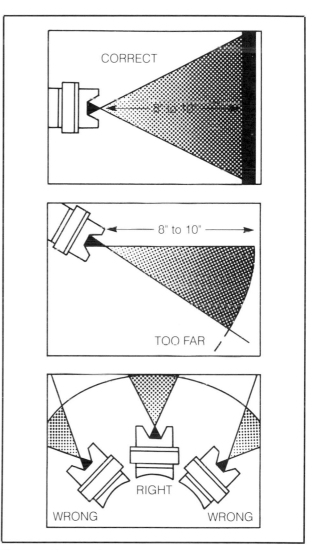

Spray paint nozzles must remain perpendicular to the surface upon which they are spraying. Deviations from this pattern will result in paint sags, build-up, orange peel and a host of other problems. Practice on a test panel will help you to lock your wrist and elbow, making your body move so that the spray gun remains in the same plane while spraying. PPG Industries, Inc.

Using the correct filter mask, coveralls and rubber gloves, Mycon holds his paint gun at a perpendicular angle to the roof he is painting. Notice that he holds the air hose with his free hand so that it is out of the way and does not interfere with the painting operation. For painting roofs, especially those on large vehicles, you must have a sturdy step stool or ladder available in order to reach the center of the roof and still maintain the proper holding angle for your paint gun.

As he maneuvers toward the outer roof edge, Mycon tilts his paint gun slightly to accommodate the rounded section of roof. His index finger activates the trigger while the gun unit pivots on his middle finger. The last two fingers are used to support the bottom part of the paint gun and also tilt it as needed toward the front. Maneuvering a paint gun like a professional takes practice.

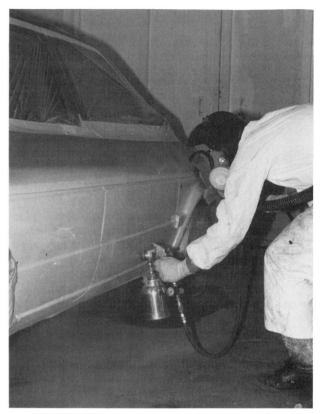

Todd Shrewsbury operates his spray gun along the lower door panel of Janna Jacobs' 1988 Volkswagen Jetta. Note that he is wearing a full-face, fresh-air respirator because the hardener in the paint mixture includes isocyanate material. In order to keep the paint gun perpendicular with the surface, he has to bend over and concentrate on the position of his hand, wrist, arm and shoulder so that they remain locked on one plane.

directed in such a way that the top of the fan rides right along the masking line. Then, each successive pass should overlap the previous one by half. Maneuver each pass with the same speed and at the same distance away from the surface: 8 to 10 in.

Look at your painting results. If you have practiced with your equipment on an old hood or trunk lid, chances are good that your efforts are proving worthwhile. If not, you might be experiencing runs or other gross abnormalities. Runs are generally caused by too much paint landing on the surface at one time. You may be holding the gun too close or walking too slow. Whichever, you have to adjust. This is where practice will get you in shape for perfecting paint spraying maneuvers.

Spot Painting

Whether your project involves a minor body repair or complete repaint, the rules of right-angle application and controlled spraying remain in effect. The difference is in the amount of paint needed and efforts required to blend new paint into old finishes.

Nonstick tape did a good job of preventing the formation of a definite paint edge along this door. It is good that the tire and wheel were masked, as paint overspray has been directed onto them. The tire was wet down with water before the application of plastic to help keep plastic tightly attached to the tire. The masking paper extending down to the tire has prevented overspray from infiltrating into the fenderwell area.

The quarterpanel and doorjamb needed to be painted after sheet-metal work was performed. Paint was feathered into the back half of the door to help blend the new paint job into existing color. You can tell that only the back half of the door was painted since only half of the masking tape on a piece of body side molding is covered. This black-and-white picture does not accurately reflect how well the feathering job matched the front part of the door.

The primary concern with any spot paint job is an accurate color match. This has to be accomplished with the deciphering of paint codes or color chip matching through paint manufacturer catalogs. After that, you have to be in tune with methods that guarantee new paint will flow and melt into old paint.

One of the basic concerns autobody painters are faced with are obvious lines that separate new paint from old. You could visualize this by imagining a piece of masking tape running along a panel with new paint applied only up to the bottom edge. Once the tape is removed, the build-up of new paint will have formed a lip, or edge, to at least its own thickness or the tape thickness. This is not acceptable.

One way to get around this problem is to mask along a definite ridge, groove, vinyl graphic or stripe. Depending upon the type of paint used and the degree to which that lip is presented, some delicate wet sanding could make the scar almost invisible. Professionals opt for a different method. First, an edge or stopping point is masked with tape rolled over upon itself.

Let's say that you want to spot paint a ding repair near the driver's side taillight on the quarterpanel. Masking was done along a piece of body side molding on the bottom and a design groove on the top. But, toward the front and back there were no definite breaking points. Lay a piece of masking paper at both the front and rear ends of this repair as if they were going to cover more of the paint surface than needed. At the front of the repair area, the paper's tape edge would be toward the front, with paper extending toward the rear of the car, over the repair area. At the opposite end of the repair area, the taped edge would be toward the rear with paper extending toward the front, over the repair area. In essence, it would look like they were trying to cover up the repair area.

However, once each piece of paper is placed, they are rolled over toward the tape edge in such a way that only the sticky side of the tape is exposed. The paper is moved 180 degrees forward for the forward section and rearward for the rear section. This leaves the repair area clear and both the front and rear areas masked with a strip of tape that has been rolled back over itself.

The purpose of all this is to create a means by which paint can bounce off a curved section

The loose piece of masking paper at the front of this Jetta has been placed in this position to allow for paint feathering. If need be, the painter can remove it for a final coat of heavily reduced paint to perfect the feathering job. Note the amount of overspray on the front tire as each paint pass was continued past the body edge to ensure uniform paint coverage with every pass.

To feather in, or melt, a paint edge, painters have had good luck adding about ¾ in. of reducer to ¼ in. of paint in their paint-gun cup. The overly reduced mixture causes baked-on paint finishes to loosen and allow a hint of color to penetrate their surface. The results are generally very good: paint edges are not noticeable and new paint is melted in with old to produce perfect color matches.

of tape and become overspray, with only a portion of it actually adhering to the surface. This completely removes the possibility of a well-defined line being introduced, and helps paint to feather into a great blend.

Now, to help that kind of situation even more, painters like to reduce paint to about a three-to-one ratio for melting. Once the spot has been successfully painted, they will remove those rolled-over strips of paper and tape and then empty their paint gun cups to about ¼ in. full. To that, they will add ¾ in. of reducer. This makes for a very hot mixture, a blend which will loosen old paint and allow just a tint of the new paint to melt in. The results are great, as it is difficult to find where the new paint starts and the old paint leaves off. If nibs are found, they are gently wet sanded smooth, except for uncatalyzed enamels.

The most important thing to remember about spot painting is that there is a valley that has to be filled where old paint and sealer have been removed. It might only be mils thick, but never-

The loose piece of masking on this fender is gently lifted up to allow a light coat of reduced paint to enter the area for feathering (melting). Shrewsbury is wearing a fresh-air respirator and also has an air pressure regulator attached to the base of his paint gun to more accurately set appropriate working air pressures. The trigger on his paint gun is not fully activated for this kind of intricate work. Instead, he uses light trigger action to apply just a small amount of material to the space.

theless it has to be filled if the overall surface is to be flat, even and smooth. New sealer and primer-surfacer will fill up most of the valley, but paint must fill in and then blend with the adjacent surface.

To achieve this, a paint mixture extra rich with reducer literally opens up the existing paint to let a touch of new pigments fall into place and join with the old to form a new surface that is flat, even and smooth. It is the very last step of a paint job, after the appropriate flash time has passed for the final spray paint pass for the center of the repaint.

Warning: Before attempting this kind of spot repair technique on your car, confirm its value with your autobody paint and supply specialist. It works great for some urethanes and lacquers, but may not fair so well with certain enamels. It all depends on the brand and type of product you use, the paint currently on your car, the color and what additives, like metallic or pearl, are involved. There is no clear-cut rule to follow and each case is unique.

Full-Panel Painting

Automobile and paint manufacturers advise professional auto painters to repaint complete sides of certain cars even though there may have been need for only one minor body repair and repaint on a single panel. As ridiculous as this sounds, there is a method to the madness. This type of overkill repaint involves those vehicles factory painted with products including pearl or other special additives.

The reasoning is simple. Especially with pearl, it is very difficult, at best, to reach a perfect match between a new repaint and an old existing finish. When paint has dried, there very possibly could be lines or grossly visible separations between panels, instead of a satiny smooth finish evenly uniform over the entire side of the vehicle.

This is a dilemma that must be faced on certain cars that feature new-style paint schemes. To find out if this affects you, check with your local autobody paint and supply store. Pay attention to recommendations, as they are not passed through corporate channels without reason.

Painting just a panel or two is generally no big deal with noncustom paint products. Masking can begin and end on definite body design breaks. You have a clear understanding of what has to be

Maneuvering paint guns around vehicles will entail a certain amount of attention be given the air hose. Unless hoses are manipulated correctly, they could be dragged across fresh paint surfaces or get caught up under tires to cause imperfect paint passes. Here, Van Hee holds the air hose behind his back to keep it out of the way and still offer plenty of working slack to operate the paint gun correctly. For maximum personal safety, he should be wearing a hood, eye protection, rubber gloves and painters coveralls.

In order to accurately spray paint the lower section of this rear body panel, Van Hee has to squat down. The paint gun is still maintained at a perpendicular angle to the working surface to maximize application uniformity. You will have to move your body as needed while painting cars in order to keep nozzles at right angles to work surfaces. Failure to do so can result in runs, sags and other problems.

painted and know that virtually everything else has to be masked. But what if your car or truck is a little on the old side and you are concerned about matching the new color with the old? Who wants a door and fender to look like new while the quarterpanel, hood and roof look old and oxidized?

These kinds of situations are not unique. Mycon has found that many times a complete buff job on old paint surfaces makes them look just like the new paint he sprayed on doors or fenders. In other cases, he has had to feather in a blend between the new paint and old.

Feathering in is similar to the melting in described earlier. After a panel is completely painted, masking is removed and a heavily reduced mix of paint and reducer is lightly sprayed onto existing paint. This works well for certain products but not at all for others. You have to check with your autobody paint supplier to compare your new paint with the compatibility of the product currently existing on your car to see if this is a viable option.

To blend in panels with paint finishes that are compatible, painters complete their main job and then take off strips of masking from adjoining panels. With a heavily reduced paint mix, they gently melt in a feathered edge. These edges may extend out to 6 in. With other paint products, no melting in or feathering takes place. The type of paint used will not support such an effort, so they must rely upon a perfect color match to make newly painted panels match old ones adjacent to them.

Flash Times

Earlier, mention was made of how solvents evaporate from paint and how pigments cure chemically to make freshly painted surfaces dry. It is important you understand that spraying second, third and successive coats cannot be done until enough time has elapsed for preceding paint coat solvents to evaporate. This is critical! If you spray a new coat of paint over one that has not had time to flash (dry), you will be trapping solvents underneath the new layer.

Solvents have to evaporate. Even if trapped, solvents will not remain in place for long. Their inherent nature is to escape from the paint mixture into the free atmosphere. So, when suffocated beneath a surface of new paint, they will try to escape through the overlying material. In the process, that action can cause blistering, checking, crazing, cracking, dulled finishes, lifting, sags or

To paint the angled part of this quarterpanel, the paint gun has to be held at a slight angle so the nozzle is perpendicular with the surface. This picture illustrates just how much paint overspray can be formed while painting cars. Material contained in this paint mist is not good for anyone's respiratory system, nor should it be absorbed through skin. This painter should be wearing rubber gloves and coveralls.

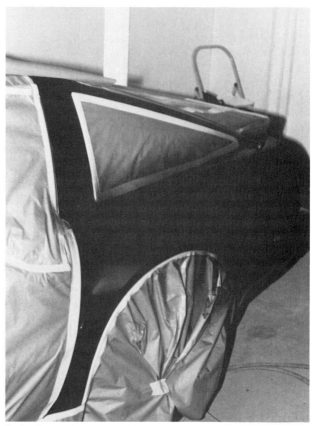

Only the rear corner of this quarterpanel was in need of paint, as it was the only part that underwent sheet-metal repair. However, to guarantee that paint was able to blend in with surrounding surfaces, feathering coats were applied up the hatchback section and pillar. Very light air pressure was used to melt in the feather coats. Clear paint will be shot over all exposed body areas.

DIAMONT SYSTEM 88

Procedure for painting a spot repair:

PRODUCT NEEDED:

12. Apply the second coat of Diamont Basecoat Color over the same area as the first coat and about 4 to 6 inches beyond where the first coat ended.

13. Apply the third coat, (if needed), over the same area as the second coat and about 4 to 6 inches beyond where the second coat ended. Normally 2 to 3 coats are required to obtain hiding. Do not melt in the dry edge of the basecoat color after finishing the blend — the clearcoat will take care of this.

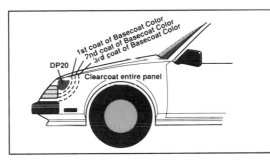

R-M Automotive Refinishing Products

This is a page from BASF's Technical Reference Manual for the spot painting application of R-M brand Diamont System 88 paint. As you can see, to make a spot paint repair to the front of this fender, each base coat is sprayed just a little farther away from the actual repair area. Finally, the entire fender is painted with clear. This is a typical procedure for spot painting operations.

---

other such imperfections on the final surface finish.

Flash times are clearly indicated on all information sheets and application guides for all paint products. Second and final coats may require longer flash times than initial coats. Read and follow the directions for the individual paint system employed. They are not all the same. This goes for undercoats, topcoats and clear coats.

Clear Coat Finishes

Along with offering better protection for metallics and other paints, the application of clear coats helps to reduce the amount of color material that has to be sprayed on car bodies, thus reducing some of the overall solvent needed to help manufacturers stay within governmental guidelines. Clear coat finishes are also good for smoothing out sharp paint lines left behind along custom graphic paint edges. Painters also use clear to help feather in repaints along adjacent panels and old paint perimeters.

The application of clear is no different than any other paint. You have to maintain a close eye on your work so that each pass is made uniformly. Exterior body parts, like door handles and key locks, can be masked for clear paint applications without as much concern about overspray blemishes as with color coats. This is because it dries to a clear, invisible finish.

Instructions for mixing solvents and hardeners in with clear paint material are provided on product labels, application guides and information sheets. Of utmost importance is recognition of the flash time between the last color coat and application of clear. Spraying clear coats on before the solvents in color coats have sufficiently evaporated will cause checking or crazing.

RECOMMENDED SPRAYING SEQUENCE

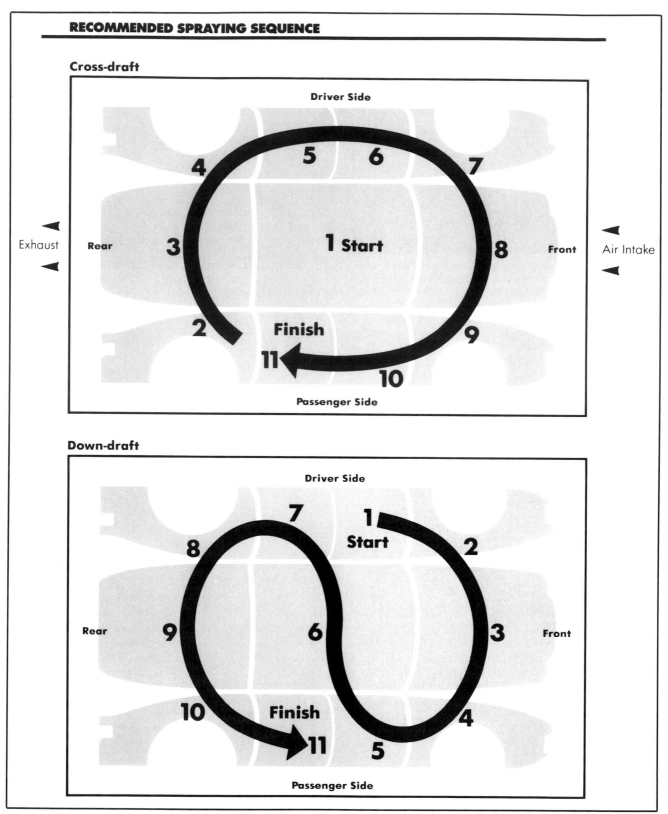

Cross-draft

Driver Side

Exhaust ◄

Rear

Air Intake ◄

Front

Passenger Side

Down-draft

Driver Side

Rear

Front

Passenger Side

To help users apply their paint products as uniformly as possible, DuPont includes *Recommended Spraying Sequences* like this on their application guides. Since it is best that paint be applied to each panel completely before painters move on to adjoining panels, you need to have a painting pattern developed before entering the paint booth. Here, sequences are displayed for both down-draft and cross-draft ventilation spray paint booths.

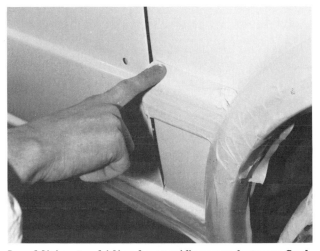

In addition to abiding by specific manufacturer flash times, many painters prefer to touch masking materials to see if paint is dry enough for second, third and subsequent paint coats. If strings of paint come off on your finger, the paint is still too wet to safely accept another coat. On the other hand, if it is still just a bit sticky to the touch and no strings come off, and the appropriate flash time has elapsed, the surface should be ready for another paint pass. Do not touch body surfaces, though, only masking material.

Applying clear paint requires no special maneuvers or techniques other than those used for color coats. You must maintain the same perpendicular angle between your paint gun nozzle and the work surface, and maintain the same distance away from the surface as you did before. Since clear might be more difficult to see once it has been sprayed, you may have to concentrate a little harder to be able to distinguish just where the last pass stopped and the new one begins.

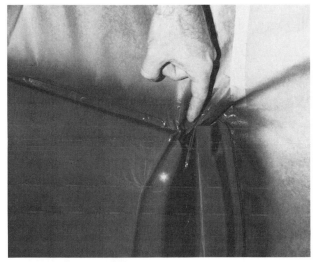

As he did while spraying the color coat, Van Hee touches a piece of masking material to see if the previous coat of clear is dry enough to accept a second pass. Again, if strings of paint appear between the masking paper and your finger, the surface is still too wet to accept new paint material. And, if both the flash time has elapsed and no strings are featured, you should be able to apply an additional coat of clear.

Three-Step Paint Systems

Reserved for more custom paint finishes, three-step systems include base coat, color coat and clear coat applications. The reason a base coat is applied first, is to give the color coat a compatible base to blend with. For example, a purple color coat sprayed over a silver base will have a different tint than the same color coat sprayed over a white base.

All of the pertinent information for the combining of specific base coats and color coats is readily available at autobody paint and supply stores. In essence, you will be putting three different paint products over the surface of your car when enlisting three-step paint systems.

As you would any other paint, you apply base coats to cover all intended new paint surfaces. After the recommended flash time has elapsed between the last applied base coat and beginning of color coat application, you simply spray on color coat material following established auto paint practices. Again, you have to heed listed flash times between coats as you would for any paint product.

When you have completed spraying the correct number of color coats and the proper flash time has passed, you put on the recommended number of clear coats. Once it has all had a chance to cure, as indicated on product labels and application guidelines, you will be able to wet sand blemishes and buff those areas you deem in need of extra polishing. The clear coat finish will prevent wet sanding or polishing from distorting the

The very fine line just below Mycon's finger shows where clear paint was stopped by masking tape. Normally, this is not acceptable. However, this custom paint job will include a section of black paint that will run from this clear paint line up to a black section that runs along the tops of windows. That black paint material will butt next to this clear line, through definitive masking with Fine Line tape, to eventually smooth out this section so that no paint edge will be distinguishable.

This is the paint gun cleaning cabinet at Newlook Autobody. Gun assembly siphon tubes are placed over cabinet pipes, and triggers are held in an open position by a wedge featured at the end of the chain and inserted horizontally into the trigger area. When activated, cleaning solvent is forced through spray tips at each corner of the cabinet and also through the pipe over which the siphon tube sits. With triggers maintained in an open position, solvent is allowed to spray through paint guns for optimal cleaning. In addition, painters at Newlook also clean their guns by hand, using prescribed brushes and clean cloths.

blended color achieved between the base coat and color coat.

Paint Gun Maintenance

Spray paint guns need consistent and conscientious cleaning and maintenance. Very small air and material passageways are easily clogged by bits of dry paint or debris. Once they become plugged, it is difficult to clear them.

Mycon, along with all other professional painters, cleans his paint gun after each use. Kosmoski reminds his painters that he does not want to know what color paint was sprayed through their gun last, meaning that their equipment must be completely cleaned after each spray session. Each paint system will have certain wash solvents designated as part of the overall paint system. Be sure your autobody paint and supply jobber describes which cleaning product is best suited for the system you employ.

Professional bodyshops have special enclosed cabinets they use for gun cleaning. Solvent is forced through gun assemblies under pressure while trigger units are maintained in an open position. Without a cleaning cabinet, you will have to fill your gun cup partly full with solvent, swish it around and empty it to remove the bulk of remaining paint product. Then, refill it again with clean solvent and spray it through the unit. This should clear out the inner passageways.

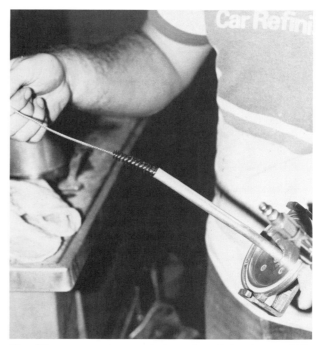

Van Hee uses a spray paint gun brush to clean out the siphon tube on his unit. Use only those tools designed for cleaning spray paint guns. Anything else could scratch wind ports or other passageways to render fan sprays useless.

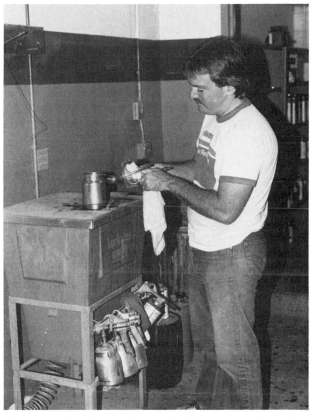

Flexible body parts, like ground effects, must be sprayed with paint mixtures that include a flexible additive. If not, the chances that cured paint will crack once the part is flexed are greatly increased. Although this ground effect was first covered with Rocker Schutz, subsequent color painting required the use of a flexible additive. To make the painting job more accessible, Mycon raised the car onto heavy-duty jack stands. The front tires have been covered to protect them from overspray.

After cleaning his gun by hand with designated brushes and letting the cleaning cabinet do its work, Van Hee uses a clean cloth to remove lingering solvent residues and any other traces of paint from his paint gun. Because he has consistently taken excellent care of this piece of equipment, it has remained in perfect operating condition through years of use. Note that other spray guns are hanging from a rack below the cabinet. You are advised to never lay paint guns on their sides, as drops of liquid residue could dry in passageways to cause future problems.

Once that has been completed, fill the cup about ¼ full with clean solvent and spray it through the unit. Then, thoroughly clean the cup. Once that's done, spray clean thinner through the gun head again to be sure nothing but clear solvent comes out. Use only those brushes designated for spray paint gun cleaning on housings, air caps and other parts. *Never* use sharp objects to clear clogged air caps or other ports. The slightest scratch damage to finely machined spray gun parts can ruin otherwise perfect fan sprays.

Use a clean cloth damp with the proper solvent to clean bulk paint drips or splotches from exterior surfaces. Satisfied that interior ports and passageways are clean, run plenty of clean, dry air through the unit to remove lingering deposits of solvent. Hang or place guns in a vertical position for storing after completely drying them with clean cloths.

Painting Plastic or Flexible Assemblies

A great many different kinds of plastics are in use today on all types of automobile parts and assemblies. They range from Acrylonitrile Butadiene Styrene (ABS) to Thermoplastic Olefin (TPO) and Sheet Molded Compounds (SMC) to Reaction Injection Molded Plastic (RIM). Each has its own place, from rigid grillework sections to flexible bumper covers.

In a sense, most flexible parts must be sprayed with paint containing a special additive which allows it to be flexible along with the part. Although this sounds like an easy choice, you may have to use special undercoats in addition to topcoat additives. The only way to be certain that the products you use are compatible and designed for painting the parts you intend to spray is to check with your autobody paint and supply specialist.

The same caution applies to rigid plastics. Some materials are compatible with normal painting systems. Others may require specific undercoats. By using the designed paint system and proper additives, along with the recommended preparation techniques, you will be assured that newly applied paint coats will not peel, crack or flake off. In rare cases, certain solvent-sensitive plastic or urethane parts cannot be repainted when factory primer seals have been broken. In those situations, you have to replace parts with new ones

8

After Paint Spraying

Once a vehicle has been satisfactorily spray painted, a number of other tasks are required to ensure the overall quality of the job. You cannot simply rip off masking materials, at that point, and call it good. Paint has to dry sufficiently, nibs must be wet sanded smooth, and masking tape must be carefully removed to prevent unnecessary paint edge peeling or other accidental finish damage.

Uncatalyzed enamels cannot withstand wet sanding or polishing. With this kind of paint system, what you see is what you get, unless you later decide to sand a blemished panel, that has completely cured, and repaint it to perfection. Certain lacquer and urethane paint finishes can be wet sanded and polished to remove nibs, flatten orange peel and otherwise smooth small blemishes. This work is normally done on clear coats, as opposed to

actual color coats, and may require additional light applications of clear. For this reason, professionals seldom remove masking material until they are pleased with the entire paint job and satisfied all imperfections have been remedied.

To remove evidence of wet sanding, finishes are rubbed out or buffed with fine compound. This work also brings out more shine and luster as well as flattening slight hints of orange peel. For spot painting or single-panel jobs, polishing adjacent body sections may be desperately needed to bring their lightly oxidized surfaces back to the point where they shine as brilliantly as the new paint.

As meticulous as you were while masking, there may be a few body parts that exhibit signs

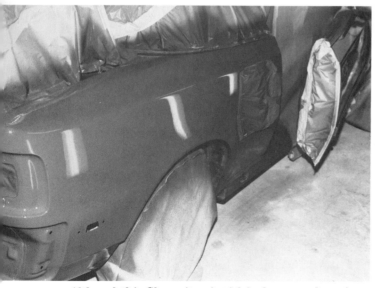

Although this Glasurit paint job looks great, the painter should not immediately begin ripping off masking paper or tape. Close inspection may reveal a minor imperfection which needs wet sanding and may even require another coat of clear. In addition, a certain amount of time must be allotted for adequate paint drying, as prescribed by label instructions and recommendations in information sheets or application guides. Be sure to take masking material off carefully, so as to not damage paint edges.

Surfaces that have been wet sanded will need to be buffed or rubbed out to remove the fine scratches left behind by coarse compounds. Here, a pneumatic buffing machine is used to polish a painted surface with a fine compound to remove any swirls or other minor finish imperfections. There is no need to use a lot of polishing compound when buffing. The amount shown here is sufficient for about a 2 sq. ft. area.

of overspray. Before putting all of the dismantled exterior body parts back on, you might consider removing obvious overspray and then repaint those affected areas with a proper color. In some cases, such as on fenderwells, you could get away with just new coats of black paint or undercoating material. A task of this nature would be easier to accomplish while masking is still in place on the vehicle.

After the last particle of paint has been sprayed on your car and you are content with the outcome of that phase, clean your spray equipment as recommended and then take a break. After that, carefully inspect the paint finish for flaws and formulate an organized plan to tackle whatever remaining chores are necessary to make the finish perfect.

Drying Times

Automotive paint has to dry. If not allowed to do so in a clean environment, dust, dirt or other debris could still penetrate wet surfaces. Professional painters always leave freshly sprayed vehicles in paint booths until enough time has elapsed for the material to completely cure. Specific time frames are determined by information on product labels and application guides.

For example, PPG recommends their Duracryl Acrylic Lacquer paint systems be allowed to dry overnight (sixteen hours) at 70 degrees Fahrenheit

or be forced dried for forty-five to sixty minutes at 140 degrees Fahrenheit. Force drying requires the use of portable infrared heaters or high-tech paint booths equipped with heating units. For their Deltron Basecoat and Clearcoat systems, PPG lists specific drying times for air drying, as well as force drying, for each of the products used in the system. This is critically important information, especially when base coat materials have already been sprayed and you need to determine exactly when the clear coat can be effectively applied.

Factory paint jobs with urethane paint products and those that are suitable for force drying, are baked on body surfaces at temperatures around 450 degrees Fahrenheit. This can be accomplished only while cars are in a stripped condition. Otherwise, plastic, rubber and vinyl parts would melt. For painting cars that are outfitted with all of their mechanical and accessory items, temperatures for force-drying cannot exceed 160 degrees Fahrenheit.

Other factors must also be considered when using heat lamps and other force dry methods. Of great importance are initial flash times. Most paint products must air dry for fifteen minutes, or longer, to let the bulk of solvent material evaporate on its own. In these cases, too much heat applied too soon will cause excessive solvent material to evaporate much too fast, resulting in blemishes to the paint finish. Likewise, too much heat could

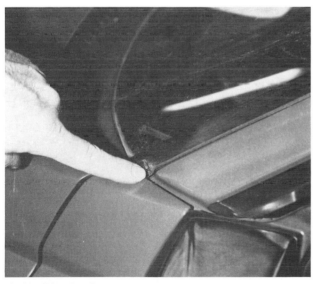

A tiny bit of paint overspray is detected along the windshield molding that runs up to the roof. The painted surface must be masked off and the overspray gently rubbed off with the proper solvent. This is a meticulous task that could have been avoided if masking work would have been more accurate. If this kind of overspray exists on your car from a previous paint job, remove such parts for repainting and clean them while they are off the vehicle so that they will be in crisp condition when you put them back on.

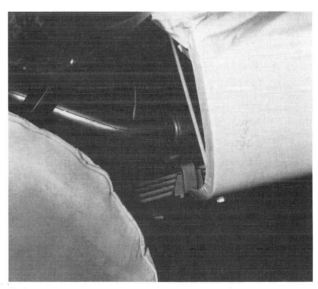

Paint overspray on the leaf springs of this pickup truck will have to be covered with black paint in order to make the paint job look clean and crisp. Items found under vehicle sides and through fenderwells are generally able to accept coats of black paint or undercoating with no problem as a means to cover overspray. However, special cars with painted fenderwells or undercarriages must be protected from overspray because efforts to remedy such problems would entail sanding and repainting in the proper color.

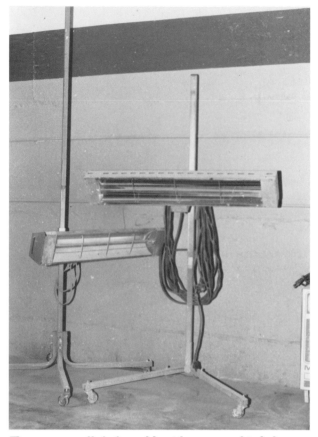

These are small, infrared heat lamps used to help cure areas of spot paint work. They can be adjusted up and down the support post. Most professional paint shops have a number of such lamps available to assist in speeding their work process. Novice painters seldom have to rely on such equipment, as most paint products will air dry overnight. For special jobs in extra cool or damp weather, though, you might confirm the use of a heat lamp with your local autobody paint and supply jobber and rent a unit from a rental yard.

cause damage to onboard computers, familiar assemblies on many newer automobiles.

All of the information you need to make determinations on how long to wait before wet sanding or buffing is supplied through information sheets and application guides provided by paint manufacturers. Along with recommendations on how long to wait before wet sanding or recoating, there are specific time frames related to how much time is allowed to elapse before these chores will not be effective. Waiting too long, in other words, may require some finishes be scuffed sanded and cleaned before application of touchup paint coats.

Before starting your paint project, you might highlight certain time frame recommendations and other important data so that you can quickly refer to them during your job. You could even write out a small outline including all of the painting and drying steps in sequential order and check each one off upon its completion. This could be a great help in reminding you what step comes next and how long you have to wait until effecting it.

Repairing Imperfections and Problem Solving

Perhaps one of the best explanations of common paint finish problems, their causes and remedies is included as part of PPG's *Refinish Manual*. With permission from PPG, it is included on the following pages:

Acid and Alkali Spotting
Appearance

Spotty discoloration of the surface (Various pigments react differently when in contact with acids or alkalies).

Cause

Chemical change of pigments resulting from atmospheric contamination, in the presence of moisture, due to industrial activity.

Remedy

a. Wash with detergent water and follow with vinegar bath.
b. Sand and refinish.
c. If contamination has reached the metal or subcoating, the spot must be sanded down to the metal before refinishing.

Prevention

a. Keep finish away from contaminated atmosphere.
b. Immediately following contamination, the surface should be vigorously flushed with cool water and detergent.

Bleeding
Appearance

Discoloration of the surface of refinish color.

Cause

Solvent penetration from fresh color material dissolves old finish, usually reds and maroons, releasing a dye that comes to the surface.

Remedy

a. Remove all color coats and recoat.
b. Or, allow surface to cure, then apply bleeder sealer and recoat.

Prevention

Apply bleeder sealer over suspected bleeder colors before spraying new color.

Blistering
Appearance

a. Small swelled areas like a water blister on human skin.
b. Lack of gloss if blisters are small.
c. Broken edged craters if the blisters have burst.

Cause

a. Rust under surface.
b. Painting over oil or grease.
c. Moisture in spray lines.

d. Trapped solvents.

e. Prolonged or repeated exposure of film to high humidity.

Remedy

Sand and refinish blistered areas.

Prevention

a. Thoroughly clean and treat metal.

b. Frequently drain air line of water.

c. Avoid use of overly fast thinners when temperature is high.

d. Allow proper dry time between coatings.

Blushing (Acrylics and Lacquer)

Appearance

The finish turns milky looking.

Cause

a. Fast thinners in high humidity.

b. Unbalanced thinners.

c. Condensation on old surface.

Remedy

a. Add retarder to thinner and respray.

b. Sand and refinish.

Prevention

a. Keep paint and surface to be painted at room temperature.

b. Select a good quality thinner.

c. Use a retarder or reflow solvent when spraying in high humidity and warm temperatures.

Chalking

Appearance

a. Lack of gloss.

b. Powdery surface.

Cause

a. Natural weathering of paint films.

b. Lack of thorough agitation of paint.

c. Use of poorly balanced thinners create earlier failures.

Remedy

Sand to remove soft surface material, clean and refinish.

Prevention

a. Agitate color coats thoroughly.

b. Use recommended PPG thinner for good balance.

Checking-Crazing-Cracking

Appearance

a. Crowfoot separation (check).

b. Formulation like shattered glass (crazing).

c. Irregular separation (cracking).

Cause

a. Insufficient drying of films prior to recoating.

b. Repeated extreme temperature changes.

c. Excessive heavy coats (cold checking).

d. Paint ingredients not thoroughly mixed.

e. Adding materials to a product not designed for it (incompatibility).

f. Recoating a previously checked finish.

g. Thinner attacking the strained surface of a cured acrylic lacquer (crazing).

Remedy

Remove finish down through checked paint film and refinish.

Prevention

a. Follow proper drying times between coats.

b. Avoid extreme temperature changes.

c. Spray uniform coats, avoiding excess particularly with lacquers.

d. Mix all ingredients thoroughly.

e. Use only recommended balanced materials, thinners, etc.

f. Remove a previously checked finish before recoating.

g. Use DURACRYL® Acrylic Lacquer Thinner (DTL 151) to help prevent crazing of acrylic lacquer.

h. Use Sealer 70 (DL 1970).

Dirt in Finish

Appearance

Foreign particles dried in paint film.

Cause

a. Improper cleaning, blowing off, and tack ragging of the surface to be painted.

b. Defective air regulator cleaning filter.

c. Dirty working area.

d. Defective or dirty air inlet filters.

e. Dirty spray gun.

Remedy

a. Rub out finish with Polishing Compound (DRX 25) (not for enamels).

b. If dirt is deep in finish, sand and compound to restore gloss. Metallic finishes may show mottling with this treatment and will then require additional color coats.

Prevention

a. Blow out all cracks and body joints.

b. Solvent clean and tack rag surface thoroughly.

c. Be sure equipment is clean.

d. Work in clean spray area.

e. Replace inlet air filters if dirty or defective.

f. Strain out foreign matter from paint.

g. Keep all containers closed when not in use to prevent contamination.

Dulled Finish

Appearance

Gloss retards as film dries.

Cause

a. Compounding before thinner evaporates.

b. Using poorly balanced thinner or reducer.

c. Poorly cleaned surface.

d. Top coats put on wet subcoats.

e. Washing with caustic cleaners.

f. Inferior polishes.

g. Inadequate flash time between coats.

h. Insufficient film build.

Remedy

Allow finish to dry hard and rub with a mild rubbing compound.

Prevention
a. Clean surface thoroughly.
b. Use recommended materials.
c. Allow all coatings sufficient drying time.

Fisheyes and Poor Wetting
Appearance
a. Separation of the wet film.
b. Previous finish can be seen in spots.
Cause
a. Improper cleaning of old surface.
b. Spraying over finishes that contain silicone.
Remedy
Wash off paint while still wet.
Prevention
a. Clean surface with ACRYLI-CLEAN™ (DX 330) Wax and Grease Remover.
b. Use FISHEYE PREVENTER (DX 77) in finish coats to be sprayed over old films containing silicone.

Lifting
Appearance
a. Raising and swelling of the wet film.
b. Peeling when surface is dry.
Cause
a. Improper drying of previous coating.
b. Sandwiching enamel between two lacquers or acrylics.
c. Recoating improperly cured enamel.
d. Spraying over unclean surfaces.
Remedy
Remove lifted surfaces and refinish.
Prevention
a. Clean old surfaces thoroughly.
b. Allow all subcoats full drying time.
c. Seal old finishes.

Mottling
Appearance
Streaking of the color. Generally associated with metallic finishes.
Cause
a. Excessive wetting of some areas.
b. Heavier film thickness in some areas.
Remedy
a. If color is freshly applied, back away and increase air pressure for final coat. Avoid over reduction.
b. On a dried finish, scuff down and apply additional color.
Prevention
a. Avoid excessive wetting or heavy film build-up in local areas.
b. Be careful not to over-reduce color.

Orange Peel
Appearance
a. Resembles ball peen hammer dents in paint.
b. Resembles the skin of an orange.

Cause
a. Under reduction.
b. Improper thinning solvent.
c. Lack of proper flow.
d. Surface drying too fast. Improper air pressure.
Remedy
a. Enamel: rub surface with a mild polishing compound. Lacquer: sand or use rubbing compound.
b. Sand and refinish.
Prevention
a. Proper air and gun adjustment.
b. Proper thinning solvents.

Peeling
Appearance
Separation of a paint film from the subsurface.
Cause
a. Improper surface preparation.
b. Incompatibility of one coat to another.
Remedy
Remove peeling paint completely, prepare metal properly and refinish with compatible materials.
Prevention
a. Thoroughly clean and treat old surface.
b. Use recommended primers for special metals.
c. Follow acceptable refinish practices using compatible materials.

Pin Holes or Blistering Over Plastic Filler
Appearance
a. Pin point holes in finish.
b. Air bubbles raising the film causing craters when erupted.
Cause
a. Excessive amounts of hardeners.
b. Excessive vigorous stirring or beating in of hardener.
Remedy
Sand thoroughly and recoat with a glaze coat of Body Filler or DFL Putty.
Prevention
a. Mix in recommended quantities of hardeners.
b. Stir mildly, the hardener goes in quickly.
c. Work out possible air traps when applying filler.

Pitting or Cratering
Appearance
a. Small craters.
b. Like dry spray or over spray.
Cause
Same as Blistering (except blisters have broken).
Remedy
Same as Blistering.
Prevention
Same as Blistering.

Plastic Bleed Thru
Appearance
Discoloration (normally yellowing) of the top-coat color.

Cause
a. Too much hardener.
b. Applying topcoat before plastic is cured.
Remedy
a. Remove patch.
b. Cure topcoat, sand and refinish.
Prevention
a. Use correct amount of hardener.
b. Allow adequate cure time before refinishing.

Plastic Filler Not Drying
Appearance
  Stays soft after applying.
Cause
a. Insufficient amount of hardener.
b. Hardener exposed to sunlight.
Remedy
  Scrape off plastic and re-apply.
Prevention
a. Add recommended amount of hardener.
b. Be sure hardener is fresh and avoid exposure to sunlight.

Rust Under Finish
Appearance
a. Peeling or blistering.
b. Raised surface spots.
Cause
a. Improper metal preparation.
b. Broken paint film allows moisture to creep under surrounding finish.
c. Water in air lines.
Remedy
a. Seal off entrance of moisture from inner part of panels.
b. Sand down to bare metal, prepare metal and treat with phosphate before refinishing.
Prevention
a. Apply DP Epoxy Primer directly to metal.
b. Locate source of moisture and seal off.
c. When replacing ornaments or moulding, be careful not to break paint film and allow dissimilar metals to come in contact. This contact can produce electrolysis that may cause a tearing away or loss of good bond with the film.

Runs
Appearance
a. Running of wet paint film in rivulets.
b. Mass slippage of total film.
Cause
a. Over reduction with low air pressure.
b. Extra slow thinners.
c. Painting on cold surface.
d. Improperly cleaned surface.
Remedy
  Wash off and refinish.
Prevention
a. Use recommended thinner at specified reduction and air pressure.
b. Do not paint over cold surface.

c. Clean surface thoroughly.

Sags
Appearance
  Partial slipping of paint in the form of curtains created by a film that is too heavy to support itself.
Cause
a. Under reduction.
b. Applying successive coats without allowing dry time between coats.
c. Low air pressure (lack of atomization).
d. Gun too close.
e. Gun out of adjustment.
Remedy
  Sand or wash off and refinish.
Prevention
a. Use proper thinner at recommended reduction.
b. Adjust air pressure and gun for correct atomization.
c. Keep gun at right distance from work.

Stone Bruises
Appearance
  Small chips of paint missing from an otherwise firm finish.
Cause
a. Flying stones from other vehicles.
b. Impact of other car doors in a parking lot.
Remedy
a. Thoroughly sand remaining film back several inches from damage point.
b. Properly treat metal and refinish.

Undercoat Show Thru
Appearance
  Variations in surface color.
Cause
a. Insufficient color coats.
b. Repeated compounding.
Remedy
  Sand and refinish.
Prevention
a. Apply good coverage of color.
b. Avoid excessive compounding.

Water Spotting
Appearance
a. Dulling of gloss in spots.
b. Mass of spots that appear as a large distortion of the film.
Cause
a. Spots of water drying on finish that is not thoroughly dry.
b. Washing finish in bright sunlight.
Remedy
  Sand and refinish.
Prevention
a. Keep fresh paint job out of rain.
b. Do not allow water to dry on new finish.

Wet Spots

Appearance

Discolored and/or slow drying spots of various sizes.

Cause

a. Improper cleaning.
b. Excessively heavy undercoats not properly dried.
c. Sanding with gasoline or other chemically contaminated solvent.

Remedy

Sand or wash off thoroughly and refinish.

Prevention

a. Clean surface with ACRYLI-CLEAN™ (DX 330) Wax and Grease Remover.
b. Allow undercoats to dry thoroughly.
c. Use only water as a sanding lubricant.

Wrinkling

Appearance

a. Puckering of enamel.
b. Prune skin effect.
c. Loss of gloss as it dries (minute wrinkling not visible to the naked eye).

Cause

a. Under reduction or air pressure too low causing excessive film thickness.
b. Excessive coats.
c. Fast reducers creating overloading.
d. Surface drying trapping solvents.
e. Fresh film subjected to heat too soon.

Remedy

Break open top surface by sanding and allow to dry thoroughly.

These are various grades of sandpaper sheets commonly available at autobody paint and supply stores. 3M brand Wetordry can be used with water, whereas regular production grade sandpaper cannot. Water helps Wetordry material to sand faster and smoother. Water also helps to keep sandpaper clean. The addition of a little liquid soap such as Ivory also helps to prevent sanding residue accumulations on sandpaper, as well as prolong the sandpaper's working life and smoothing ability.

Prevention

a. Reduce enamels according to directions.
b. Apply as recommended.
c. Do not force dry until solvents have flashed off.

Wet Sanding

Not every type of paint system can accept wet sanding. Enamels, for example, cure with a sort of film on their surface which will be damaged if broken by sandpaper or harsh polish. You have to wait about ninety days before polishing enamels.

Lacquers and some urethane products can be sanded with fine sandpaper soon after they have cured. Although it is not recommended you wet sand color coats, you might be able to lightly sand off nibs providing you are prepared to touch up the spots with a light color coat. Best results are found when their clear coat finishes are wet sanded and then polished.

Lacquer paint systems generally call for a number of color coats and then clear coats. Especially with candy finishes, sanding directly on the color surface will distort the tint to cause a visible blemish. Wet sanding for them is done on clear coats only. The same principle holds true for urethanes. Your wet sanding efforts should be concentrated on clear coats in order not to disturb the underlying color coats. Wet sanding clear coats will bring out a much deeper shine and gloss when followed by controlled buffing or polishing.

Painters use very fine 1000 to 1500 grit sandpaper with water to smooth or remove minor blemishes on cured paint finishes designed to allow wet sanding. Only sandpaper designated wet-or-dry must be used, however. Those kinds not waterproof will fall apart and be useless.

As with all other sanding tasks, you have to use a sanding block. Since nibs of dirt or dust are small, fold sandpaper around a wooden paint stir stick instead of using a large hand block. The size is great for smoothing small spots and since the width of ordinary wood stir sticks is only about an inch, the area covered is limited to just what is needed. Only a small amount of pressure is required for this type of delicate sanding. Be sure to dip sandpaper in a bucket of water frequently to keep the paint surface wet and reduce the amount of material build-up on the sandpaper.

If a lot of sanding was needed on certain blemished areas, new coats of clear may have to be applied. This is why you should leave masking material in place while accomplishing wet sanding chores. Should clear coat touchup be needed, the vehicle will already be masked, saving extra masking work.

You must confirm ahead of time that the paint system you use is compatible with light wet-sanding repair efforts. Your autobody paint and supply jobber can do this while you are discussing your paint needs at time of purchase. Each auto-

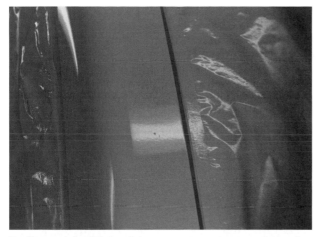

In the center of this picture, you can see a rectangular light reflection. In the center of that reflection is a nib, an imperfection in the paint. Very light wet sanding will remove the nib and render the paint flawless, with the exception of some sanding swirls which are removed with polish. Should nibs be so defined that wet sanding goes through actual color coats, you will have to repaint the spot and blend new coats in with the existing paint. Information sheets and application guides list specific time frames in which chores like this can be accomplished without having to treat new paint like an older surface finish.

motive paint manufacturer has its own set of recommended guidelines it advises painters to follow. What may be good for PPG's Deltron system may not be so good for a BASF or DuPont system. In fact, you might even be advised to completely disregard wet sanding and opt instead for polishing to guarantee a perfect finish with the type of product you have chosen to use.

In some cases such as lacquer paint jobs on show cars, the entire car body may be wet sanded to bring out the richest, deepest and most lustrous shine possible. Because they anticipate extensive wet sanding and polishing operations, painters of these cars make sure they have applied plenty of clear coats. If they didn't, wet sanding would surely remove all of the thin clear coat material to eventually reach actual color coats and destroy an otherwise fine paint job.

Removing Masking Material

To many enthusiastic automobile painters, removing masking paper and tape to reveal a new paint job or quality spot paint repair is like opening Christmas presents. It is always a pleasure to see a finished product, especially after viewing it in primer for any length of time. However, unlike the wrapping paper on presents, masking materials must be removed in a controlled manner to prevent unnecessary finish damage.

By now, you should fully understand that paint products have solids in them that build up on

While wet sanding the roof of Roy Dunn's 1935 Chevrolet Sedan Delivery, Mycon sprays on a mixture of water and mild liquid dish soap. This helps Wetordry sandpaper to cut quicker, last longer and resist clogging. Here, he is using a wooden paint stir stick as a sanding block while sanding the rounded edge of the roof. You can apply water through a squirt bottle like this, instead of using a bucket, when sanding areas other than vehicle sides. It makes the sanding job easier.

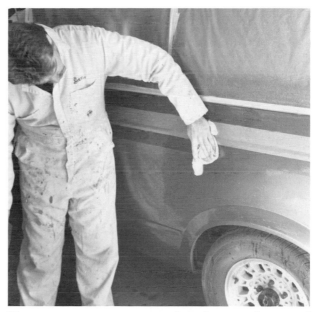

Mycon uses a water-saturated cloth to wet down and wash off a spot where a nib needs sanding. The custom graphic painted on Kathryn Mycon's van sports four different colors, three of which are over a white base coat, part of a three-step paint system. All of them have been covered with clear to allow wet sanding. After this, he will buff the entire car with a soft pad and fine polish to bring out a beautiful, swirl-free shine.

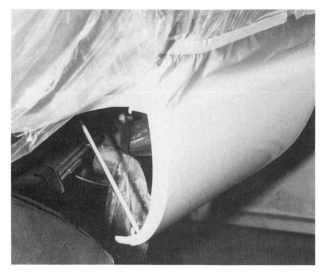

Because white paint covers the lowest strip of masking tape, and because this is a black-and-white picture, it is difficult to determine where the paint stops and masking tape starts. Especially when custom lacquer paint jobs require several light coats, paint build-up along masking tape can be quite thick. For that reason, removing masking tape must be a delicate and exact procedure. Always pull tape away from the body surface at an acute angle to cut paint as the tape is pulled back.

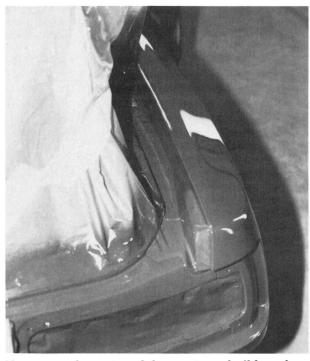

Numerous color coats and clear coats can build up along masked edges to cause flaking problems when tape is pulled. In extreme cases, paint has been known to bridge the lip between its car body surface finish and the top of tape. In those cases, meticulous painters have used a sharp razor blade to actually cut paint films as tape is pulled away at an acute angle away from the body surface.

car bodies. Especially on jobs where numerous color and clear coats were applied, the thickness of the paint can bridge the lips along masking tape edges. What will occur, in some situations, is the formation of a paint film on a car body that continues over to include the top of tape. Therefore, if tape is pulled straight up, it could take with it flakes of paint from the body surface.

To prevent paint flaking or peeling along the edge of masking tape strips, painters pull tape in a direction away from the newly painted body and back upon itself to create a sharp angle at the point tape leaves the surface. In a sense, this sharp angle can cut extra-thin paint films instead of pulling them away to cause flakes or cracks on the finish.

When several color and clear coats have been applied to a body surface, meticulous painters often use a sharp razor blade to physically cut paint films between body surfaces and tape edges.

This is a rack of 3M brand polishing compounds located at Wesco Autobody Supply. Each different material contains a specific amount of grit which is designed to polish to a certain degree. The coarser grit contained in any compound, the more strength it has to remove deeply embedded paint problems. For new paint, very fine grades of compound are all that is needed. Be sure to read labels to determine which brand is best suited for your needs and which products are suitable for machine use or recommended to be used by hand only.

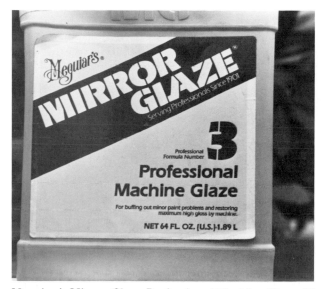

Meguiar's Mirror Glaze Professional Machine Glaze #3 is designed for use with a buffing machine. The grit contained in this product is not so coarse that machine buffing will easily damage paint. Conversely, it can be used to buff out minor paint problems to restore maximum high gloss. After it is used, you might consider buffing the surface again with a finishing pad and liquid wax to remove all traces of swirls and spider webbing. Be sure to read the label before using.

You might consider this for lacquer jobs which can require as many as six color coats and four clear coats, or more. Should edges be damaged during masking material removal, you will have to sand them and repaint as needed.

Rubbing out and Polishing

As with wet sanding, not every type of paint system can stand up to vigorous polishing or rubbing out. You must confirm the compatibility and need for extensive polishing with your autobody paint and supply jobber before starting the procedure. In cases of uncatalyzed enamel, buffing new paint with a gritty compound will only dull the surface and ruin the finish. In contrast, polishing a catalyzed urethane or cured lacquer might make their finishes much more brilliant, lustrous and deep shining.

A wide variety of polishing compounds are available for use on new paint finishes. Autobody paint and supply stores carry the biggest selection. Some are designed to be used by hand, others can safely be polished with buffing machines. Foam pads work best with prescribed compounds and buffing machines limited to slower rpm, while pads made with cloth material are better suited for other compounds and machine speeds. For a complete breakdown of all the different compounds, pads and buffing machines, visit an autobody paint and supply store.

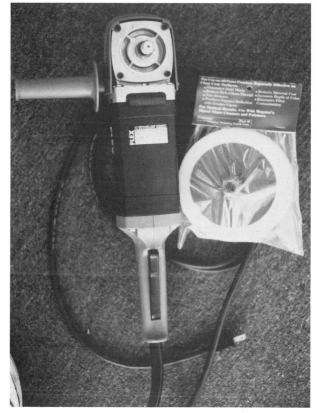

This is a brand-new electric-powered buffing machine with a new-style foam buffing pad next to it. Most buffers require the use of cloth pads and you must be sure that the polishing product you use is suited for a foam pad application. 3M manufactures products designed to be used with foam pads, and you will have to check with your autobody paint and supply professional to see if he or she carries other brands with similar applications.

PPG manufactures their own brand of rubbing and polishing compounds designed to be compatible with their paint system products. You should never go wrong using them with PPG paints. In addition, companies like 3M and Mequiar's produce several varieties of polishing products, all of which carry labels with specific instructions for their intended use and application.

Basically, rubbing compounds include relatively coarse polishing grit material. They are designed to quickly remove blemishes and flatten paint finishes. Because of compounds' coarse nature, light scratches, also called swirls, will be left behind on paint finishes. Therefore, after an application of compound to flatten orange peel or produce a higher surface luster, paint finishes need to be buffed or polished with a very fine grit material. In some situations, especially with dark colors, this is accomplished with exceptionally soft finish buffing pads and wax.

Although paint finishes may appear dry, especially those that included a hardening agent, they

These buffing pads are made of a soft cloth material. The one on the top is used for cutting, that is, polishing heavily oxidized or badly blemished paint finishes. The pad on the bottom is much softer and is used for finer polishing tasks, like removing swirls or spider webbing. Along with their intended uses, you must employ the correct polishing compound for the job. Using a coarse and abrasive polishing compound with a soft finishing pad will cause a lot of scratches, swirls and other finish problems.

may not be ready for buffing right away. You must allow sufficient time for all solvents to evaporate before smothering them with polishing compound. Application guides and information sheets will generally list the recommended time. The information sheet for PPG's Polyurethane clear, for example, states, "Allow 16 hours before polishing either air dried or force dried DCU 2001 [their product number for this clear]."

The very light scratches highlighted on the door panel and fender of this S–10 Blazer can be easily removed with a buffer and soft polish. These lines are essentially swirls, caused by extra-light wet sanding with 1200 grit sandpaper or polishing with an abrasive material. Use the mildest polishing compound first in attempts to remove swirls. If repeated tries do not result in satisfactory finishes, move up to a little coarser compound. It is better to start out with a mild product and work toward a more abrasive one than vice versa.

By hand, use a soft, clean cloth for rubbing out and polishing and follow directions on the product label. Many auto enthusiasts have discovered best polishing results by applying polish in straight back-and-forth movements from the front to back of vehicles, instead of circular patterns. They profess that by polishing panels in this manner, their chances for creating swirls are greatly reduced.

You need experience practicing with a buffing machine before using it on your car's new paint job. Buffers with maximum speeds of about 1450 rpm are best for novices. Machines with faster revolutions require more user experience to prevent the likelihood of paint burns—polishing through paint finishes down to primer or bare metal. Be aware, though, even the slower 1450 rpm buffers are quite capable of causing paint burns if users do not pay attention to what they are doing.

To use a buffer, first spread out a few strips of compound, each about 4 to 6 in. apart to cover an

Agressive buffing with a coarse polish will quickly burn through paint. A paint burn is an imperfection where color coats have been polished through to primer or bare metal. The light line next to the buffer's finger is an indication of a paint burn. You can burn paint with any buffer and any compound if the machine is not handled in a cautious manner. Here, too much pressure was applied, or, the buffer was allowed to sit for too long on top of the ridge until paint was finally worn through to primer.

Van Hee uses a pneumatic-powered buffer to bring out the shine on this Honda trunk lid after paint work has been applied and thoroughly cured. Be alert to the air hose or power cord attached to buffers, as they can mar surfaces they are dragged against. If need be, the power supply hose or cord could be draped over your shoulder to keep it out of your work space and prevent it from coming in contact with body edges.

Art Wentworth has applied just the right amount of polishing compound to the roof of this Pantera for buffing a 2 sq. ft. section. Notice that the fluffy buffing pad edge is raised toward the right, the direction in which the pad will be maneuvered. When going to the left, the left side of the pad will be raised. Back-and-forth movements will slowly work their way down until the entire area has been polished to a brilliant shine. Keep buffing pads moving at all times. Pads left to polish on one spot for any length of time will surely result in a paint burn.

Operating a buffing pad directly on top of an edge like this is just asking for trouble. Because paint applications might be slightly thinner on edges or ridges, and because there is only a minimal amount of surface area for the buffing pad to rest against, the possibility for paint burns in situations like this one are very great. Buff up to edges but not on top of them. If you have to polish an edge or ridge, do it by hand to prevent any possibility of paint burn blemishes.

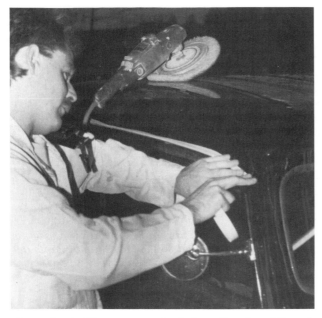

Extensive buffing was required along the edge of Dunn's Chevrolet. To be certain he doesn't buff through the paint, Mycon is placing a piece of masking tape along the drip-rail edge. This is an excellent idea for all novices who lack experience with buffers; novices should protect all ridges and corners with masking tape.

area no bigger than 2 sq. ft. Operate the buffing pad on top of a compound strip and work it over that strip's area, gradually moving down to pick up successive strips. The idea is to buff a 2 sq. ft. area while not allowing the pad to become dry of compound. Buffing continues on that body section until compound is gone and all that remains is shiny paint.

Buffing pads can be operated back and forth, as well as up and down. Always keep them moving. Just like with power sanders, if buffers are allowed to rest in one spot, the chances for paint burns greatly increase. Likewise, be exceptionally careful buffing near ridges, gaps and corners. The swift rotation of buffing pads will quickly burn paint on these areas. As opposed to operating buffing pads on top of ridges, run them just up to their edge and stop. Some painters prefer to mask edges, ridges and corners with strips of masking tape to protect them against accidental buffing burns. This might be a good idea for you, too.

If you have to buff in tight areas such as those near door handles, throttle the machine on and off to lower the rpm speed. This action will slow the pad and help to reduce the possibility of paint burns. Be sure plenty of compound is spread over the area. For extra-confined spaces, apply compound by hand with a soft, damp cloth.

Buffing next to side lights, emblems or any other body obstruction carries with it an element of possible part damage. The high-speed revolutions of buffing pads can quickly break off body parts. Many detailers and painters have been whipped in the face by radio antennas and have broken off plastic emblems, trim and body side moldings. Whenever buffing next to any object, slow the speed of the buffing machine by throttling it down or by turning it on and off with the trigger.

Another area where paint burns are easily made is along gaps between body panels. Here, Van Hee carefully buffs the trunk edge next to the quarterpanel. Pad speed is lessened as he works his way around the trunk lid gap. Too much pressure applied to the buffing machine, or prolonged buffing in one spot, will quickly produce paint burns along the gap edges. Keep the buffing pad moving at all times and buff up to gaps, not over them. Here, concentration is made along the top edge, as the side of the pad is off of the gap.

128

Power cords for electric buffers and air hoses for pneumatic models should not be dragged over painted finishes. A good way to keep them under control while buffing roofs, hoods and trunk lids is to drape them over your shoulder. Also, to make sure scratches do not occur on the sides of cars while you buff top panels, wear an apron or make sure the clothes you wear do not feature large belt buckles or rivets near pocket seams. A long sweat-shirt that hangs over the top parts of trousers might work well.

Power buffers will throw spots of compound all over your car, clothes and nearby surfaces. Be prepared for this kind of mess by covering adjacent cabinets or workbench items with tarps or drop cloths. As cloth buffing pads become covered with compound, use a pad spur or screwdriver to clean them. With the pad spinning, gently but securely push a spur or screwdriver tip into the pad's nap. This will break loose compound and force it out of

To buff the side of this vehicle, Wentworth reversed the position of his left hand so that his thumb points out instead of in toward the machine. This is a much more comfortable position for a right-handed person while buffing the lower side of any vehicle. It offers much better control and maneuverability. Be sure to slow the pad speed when buffing next to trim or body side molding pieces.

Power buffers will throw polishing compound in all directions. Be prepared for this by wearing coveralls and draping tarps over nearby shelves or workbench areas. Buffing the sides of vehicles is a bit awkward. You have to bend down in order to reach all areas and may have to change hand positions for maximum control. Be especially careful buffing up next to fender flairs, as the pad edge could be stout enough to cause paint burns if left in one spot too long.

To clean accumulations of polishing compound from buffing pads, use a pad spur or a dull screwdriver. Here, a dull screwdriver is gently inserted into the buffing pad as it spins. Be sure to secure the buffer against your knee and maintain a firm grip with your operating hand, as shown. Then, slowly insert the screwdriver tip into the outer perimeter and gradually move it toward the center to break loose compound and debris. This process will create a lot of dust, so be sure to do this away from your work area.

129

the pad. You will be surprised at how much material comes off of pads, so be sure to do your pad cleaning away from your car and anything else you do not want covered with compound or pad lint.

Overspray

Polishing and buffing efforts usually work well to remove very light traces of overspray from hoods, roofs and trunk lids. Extra-heavy overspray residue may require a strong polishing compound for complete removal. For severe problems, consult your autobody paint and supply jobber.

When meticulous masking has been accomplished, most overspray problems, if any, usually involve items like tailpipes, fenderwells, horn units and other items located around lower vehicle areas. You could spend a lot of time removing overspray from painted items, like fenderwells, or spend a lot less by simply covering overspray with black paint or undercoat. However, if yours is a special car and the fenderwells are intended to be painted the same color as the body, this quick fix will not work. In cases of special cars, make sure that masking is done in such a way that no overspray will mar painted surfaces. Repairs to them will require sanding and polishing, possibly even repainting.

Overspray on chrome might be easily removed with a chrome polish, like Simichrome. Heavy concentrations may require the extra strength of #0000 steel wool with polish. Some chrome items commonly prone to overspray might be tailpipes, wheels, bumpers, grille pieces and trim. Once again, the best way to avoid overspray problems on these accessories is to mask them properly with plenty of tape to secure paper edges so puffs of paint spray cannot infiltrate the masked space.

Paint overspray on glass is cleaned off using the proper solvent that matches the type of paint system used on the car body. Dab some solvent on a clean cloth and rub off overspray. If that does not work, try using #0000 or finer steel wool and solvent. In extreme cases, you might have to delicately use a razor blade to scrape overspray off glass.

Caution: If your car is a newer model, the windshield and some other glass might be scratched by use of any steel wool on its surface. Some newer windshields are made with acrylic ingredients that will not stand up to fine steel wool as well as regular glass. If you are not sure whether your car's wind-

Buffing any automobile brings with it a lot of compound debris. You must be prepared to spend an adequate amount of time wiping compound off of door, hood and trunk lid edges, like this. Accumulations of polishing compound will infiltrate all body gaps and adhere to door edge undersides, as well as hoods, trunk lids and around trim. Use a soft cloth to remove compound, enlisting the help of a soft paintbrush as necessary to remove residue from confined spaces.

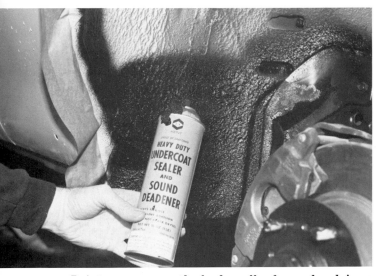

Paint overspray on the fenderwells of everyday drivers can be covered with black paint or undercoating material, as shown here. Undercoating is not a rustproofing material, rather, it helps to reduce road noise and protects metal fenderwells from rock chips and other collision debris damage. This material is especially good for fiberglass fenderwells, as it cushions impacts from rocks to reduce the chances of stars or other damage from appearing on the tops of fender and quarterpanel sections.

shield is solid glass or an acrylic, check with a dealership service department, auto glass business or your autobody paint and supply jobber.

Overview

Taking care of the tasks described in this chapter are easier before installing parts back on your vehicle. Not only will buffing throw compound all over trim, bumpers and the like, the rapid revolution of buffing pads can quickly break off emblems, badges and trim sections. If just a corner of a fast-spinning pad catches on an object, that item can easily be whipped off the car body and thrown against nearby objects to shatter not only itself, but anything it smashes into.

Take your time to effectively smooth nibs with fine 1200 grit sandpaper. Use a sanding block with plenty of water. Be prepared too, in those wet sanding instances, to buff out or polish the spots smoothed with sandpaper. Polish will remove sanding scratches to leave the surface blemish-free and looking crisp.

By all means, take your time removing masking paper and tape. Be certain to pull tape at an angle away from the newly painted surface and also at a sharp angle over itself. This should alleviate problems associated with flakes peeling off along with tape. In extreme cases where paint coats are numerous and consequently thick, have a sharp razor blade handy to cut paint that may look like it is ready to peel off with tape. Consider masking-material removal an important chore and treat it with the same respect and attention you gave to its application.

Your efforts during this phase of an auto paint operation should result in your car or truck's finish being as close to perfect as possible. With masking paper still in place, you can add light coats of clear as necessary, or, touch up spots that need that kind of attention. It is at this time that you essentially have your last chance to fix mistakes or repair blemishes.

The next phase of your paint project consists of installing those body parts removed and stored during the body preparation and painting processes. Once all those parts are put back on the car body, repainting efforts would be hindered, possibly to the point of requiring the removal of those parts soon after they were put back on.

Urelastic Black Bumper Coating is a product designed to make urethane bumper parts look new. According to directions, products like this can be applied to urethane bumper faces. You should consider this type of detail work to help your bumper faces look as good as the paint job you just completed on your car. Be sure that appropriate masking is in place, and that all repairs have been adequately completed before spraying this material.

To make any paint job stand out and look its best, other body parts must also look clean and crisp. Jerry McKee realized that, after Mycon painted his 1970 Jaguar XKE V-12 Roadster, the muffler and exhaust pipes looked a bit old and rusty. McKee applied high-temperature silver paint to these items and made them look a lot better. This is an important concern, especially for automobiles like this and Corvettes where exhaust system components are clearly visible. Polished tailpipes and a silver muffler complement Mycon's paint job and helped McKee take first place in a Concours d'Elegance competition.

9

Part Replacement

By now, your car or truck's body should look great. It has been painted and all blemishes wet sanded, polished or touched up. Overspray problems have been corrected and masking removed. The last phase of your job is now at hand, part replacement and detailing.

Part replacement and detailing go hand in hand. Unless dismantled parts were cleaned and shined at the time of their removal, they will have to be detailed before you put them back on your vehicle's pristine body. After that, you will need to spend some time in the engine compartment, interior and trunk space to vacuum sanding dust and generally clean everything so it looks as good as the body.

This part of any overall auto paint job will greatly help to make the vehicle stand out and look crisp. Windows that are clean on both sides, a dust-free dashboard, spotless doorjambs, scrubbed tires, polished chrome, a well-groomed interior, grease-free engine compartment and a tidy trunk space all work together to complement new body paint and make the automobile look, feel and smell like new.

Installing various parts on car bodies must be done systematically, similar to the way they were dismantled. Certain trim sections are designed to be put on first with part of their edge covered by the next section. Failure to follow an intended sequence the first time will require you to take off those out-of-order sections and put them back on correctly. This not only creates extra work, it also increases the chances for scratching or nicking the vehicle's new paint.

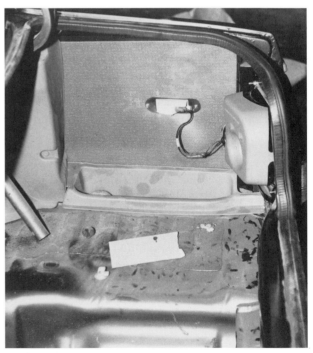

The taillight and side light have been installed on this import car. The cardboard quarterpanel liner has also been released from its folded position. Be sure that all parts are put back together the way they were designed. Sometimes certain parts have to be fastened before others, so that an entire unit is assembled structurally and visually acceptable. As needed, use the appropriate adhesive to secure those parts that were loosened during dismantling.

Always use a clean cloth for wiping off painted body surfaces. Folding cloths into quarters works well. As one side becomes soiled, you can unfold to another and continue the cleaning process. Wipe finishes in a straight back-and-forth pattern from front to back to eliminate the possibility of swirls or other minor imperfections. Soft cotton cloths work best, like baby diapers or soft flannel.

There is no immediacy surrounding the detailing or replacement of dismantled parts—except the excitement of enjoying your totally finished project. You should take your time to carefully detail and assemble body parts so that they go on right the first time and look good once in place. This might be the last time you have the opportunity to thoroughly clean and detail dismantled parts completely. And, since they will be off of the vehicle body, the jobs of cleaning, polishing and waxing will not be hindered by their attachment to body panels or locations in confined spaces.

Glass

Although windows are not generally removed for just the purpose of accomplishing new paint jobs, complete restorations and project vehicles may have called for their removal for any number of reasons. Depending upon individual circumstances, glass could have been installed prior to paint, or purposely left off until all exterior and interior restoration projects were complete. Regardless of the reasons, installing glass after a vehicle body has been painted must be done with care in order to avoid scratches or nicks along window frame edges.

Since paint should be cured by the time you begin installing glass, consider laying strips of wide masking tape along window frame edges to guard against accidental bumps that could otherwise cause paint scratches or nicks. Be sure to use automotive masking tape, because generic tape might leave adhesive residue on surfaces.

To avoid any future problems with galvanic corrosion, make sure that metal clips used to hold glass panels in place are mounted correctly and do not come in contact with sheet-metal body panels. Also, use caution during their installation to prevent accidental paint chips which could lead to corrosion problems down the road. Even the smallest paint chip could allow an oxidation process to begin. Once started, especially on areas hidden by trim, oxidation will spread under layers of paint and not be noticed until severe metal rust damage causes paint finishes to bubble, crack or otherwise present obvious problems. Should that occur, repair efforts could require extensive metal work and, of course, new paint.

Along with recognizing the importance of preventing paint chips while installing glass, you should be concerned about watertight seals all around window perimeters. Not only are water leaks annoying, their puddling accumulations can lead to corrosion damage on metal panels and rot or mildew in upholstery and carpeting.

Fixed-glass panels, like windshields, rear and some side windows, are held in place by different means. Not all makes and models utilize identical attachment methods. Some may feature clips, others might rely on thick rubber moldings and many

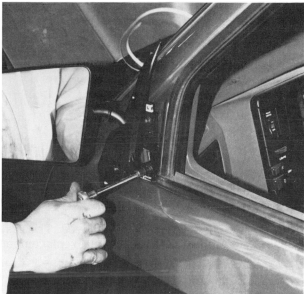

Parts that are put back on freshly painted automobiles should be clean and detailed. This will help to complement the entire job. Be sure to use the correct tools while installing parts. A slip of any kind could result in paint chips or scratches. Here, a mirror is replaced using the correct socket size, and an extension with the ratchet to prevent scraping against the new paint finish.

call for strips of butyl- or urethane-based sealers to hold panels safely in place. If you are not familiar with auto glass installations, seriously consider hiring a professional to complete the work for you. Most auto glass businesses offer mobile service, allowing specialists to complete glass installations, or removals, at your working location.

Rear window glass on pickup trucks and hatchbacks oftentimes is set inside grooves along the inside perimeter of heavy rubber moldings. Another groove is around the outer molding perimeter. Once the molding is fitted around glass, a cord is inserted into the outer perimeter groove and pulled taut. While one person holds the glass and molding unit in place from outside a vehicle, another person starts pulling the cord from the vehicle's interior.

The combination of outside force being put on the glass or molding unit against a window opening and a person on the inside pulling out the cord, causes the inside portion of the molding's outer perimeter to fold over a sheet-metal body lip around the center of the vehicle's window opening. Both installers have to communicate and work together in order to complete the task. Easiest results have been found when the bottom sections of molding units are placed first, followed by alternately inching along the sides and finally completing the top by pulling from each outer end toward the middle.

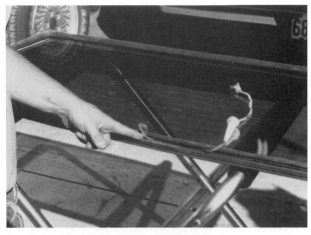

A rope has been inserted into the outer groove on this window molding. A person on the outside will push against the window and molding unit while another pulls the rope from the molding on the inside. Gradually, the innermost flap of the window molding will be pulled over the window opening lip to secure the unit in place. This is the easiest and most effective way to install those glass units secured with rubber moldings.

Jeff Lund, owner of Jeff's Quality Auto Glass in Bellevue, Washington, says that the installation of fixed-glass units with urethane sealer actually adds a degree of structural strength to some automobiles. Windshields and side-mounted fixed-glass units on newer cars and vans are commonly secured in place by continuous beads of a urethane sealer. In some cases, a bead of butyl material is used instead of urethane. According to Lund, butyl has a strength of about 5 psi, where urethane boasts adhesion strength approaching 500 psi.

Instances that call for butyl beads alone are usually those where extensive bodywork was completed at or near window openings. Concerns over possible imperfect body window openings and resultant water leaks may lead to the need for glass removal so body sheet-metal adjustments can be made. Since butyl is not nearly as strong as urethane, the removal of such glass units is much easier.

About the only way to remove fixed-glass units secured by butyl or urethane beads is to actually cut through the beads with a special tool. Essentially, the tool consists of a piece of strong wire with handles at each end and requires two people to

In the passenger compartment, rope is being pulled from inside the outer perimeter groove of the rear window molding; it is located just a couple of inches up from the lower left corner of the glass. As the rope is pulled out, the inner flap from the molding is forced over a designed metal lip located in the center of the window opening. Best results are found by securing the bottom molding section first and then carefully pulling rope from the sides. The top is last, as both ends are pulled from the corners at the same time.

The black material located inside the window groove opening is old butyl and urethane sealer material. It has to be cleaned out before the window can be put back in place. Fixed-glass assemblies, like this section located above the quarterpanel area on a Bronco II, are actually designed as structurally supportive units for many automobiles. This is why super-strength urethane sealers are used to hold them in place and why their installations must be done according to recommended practices.

A glass installer from Jeff's Quality Auto Glass applies a strip of butyl tape to the perimeter of a Bronco II fixed side window assembly. Because extensive bodywork was done to the quarterpanel on this vehicle, butyl alone will be used to affix glass, instead of a urethane sealer. This way, the window unit can be quickly and easily removed in case of water leaks and the need to adjust some of the sheet-metal work completed around the window unit.

A butyl strip is located in the center of the trim surrounding this window section, as indicated by the blackest area. If a urethane sealer was also planned for the installation, this strip would be applied at a forty-five-degree angle. However, since butyl alone will hold the window in place, a solid strip has been installed. Pressure from the outside will force this material against the window groove to form a tight seal which will hold the unit in place and prevent water from leaking in.

operate. An opening is made in the urethane bead and the wire inserted through it. With handles then attached at both ends, a person on the inside and another on the outside maneuver the wire around fixed glass to cut through the urethane bead. Afterward, a special solvent is used to loosen old bead material for its removal.

The installation of fixed-glass units requires their supportive body opening be clean from all contaminants. Then, a bead of butyl material is laid around the window opening perimeter. For butyl-only installations, the bead is solidly shaped. If urethane will also be used, the butyl bead's side that touches the vehicle body will be angled at about forty-five degrees. Along that angle, urethane material will be placed to fill in the triangular void left open by the butyl bead's forty-five-degree angle.

For either kind of installation, butyl actually holds glass in place. This is an important factor for

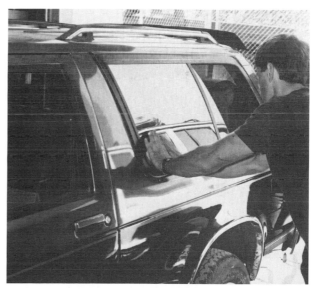

Jeff Lund presses against the Bronco II fixed side window to force butyl sealer in place; his assistant is also pressing against the opposite corner. Installing large sections of fixed glass is not always a simple process; neither is the process involved with removing them. Plan to have a helper assist you for chores like this, or pay the nominal fee to have a professional complete the work for you.

Lund uses a special cleaner solvent to remove excess butyl material that has oozed out of the window frame as pressure was applied to it. He makes this kind of work look easy because he has done it so many times. Using an inappropriate solvent next to fresh paint could result in damage to the freshly sprayed body surface finish. Therefore, whenever tackling a project like this, be sure the materials used are compatible with paint and other materials.

Older cars seem to feature more paintable trim strips than newer cars. This is a kick plate located over the rocker panel area on a 1960s vintage automobile. If the doorjamb areas were painted, this unit had to be removed. In that case, it should be cleaned and re-painted. Nicks and paint chips can be repaired with the proper paint and an artist's fine paintbrush. Taking care of detail items like this will help to make any paint job look crisp and pristine.

urethane jobs, as it takes some time for that material to fully cure. While it is curing, butyl holds glass in a fixed position. The end result should be a near-perfect and leak-free installation. Lund says that urethane works great, as he almost never has any returns or customer complaints of leaks.

The tools and material needed to remove and install fixed-glass units are available at autobody paint and supply stores. Be sure you fully understand all installation instructions for the products you use. In addition, have a helper available to assist you in removing or replacing glass units as they can be quite heavy and cumbersome. If for any reason you are hesitant to tackle such a job, consider the services of a professional auto glass installer. Compared to the cost of replacing broken glass units (from $100 to well over $1,000), a professional auto glass installer's fee is minimal.

Trim

Along with detailing trim pieces before their installation, you might consider using an artist's fine paintbrush and compatible paint to fill in chips, scratches or peeled sections in paint lines. Older cars generally feature metal trim pieces with painted lines that run lengthwise along grooved indentations.

Many emblems and trim pieces are secured to newer cars with double-backed tape. Be sure that the body surface and the backsides of emblems are completely clean before the installation of double-backed tape. Contaminants and dirt debris will weaken the adhesive's strength and may allow parts to fall off while vehicles are driven at highway speeds.

This is a small assortment of 3M emblem and trim adhesive products. Manufacturers develop various adhesive strengths for specific applications. It would be nice if one "super glue" type product was satisfactory for all adhesive needs, but that is not the case. You must read labels to determine which product is best suited for your needs. Be sure to follow instructions and provide clean surfaces for all adhesive-secured parts.

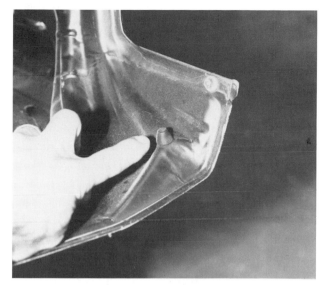

This small bumper part plays an important role in the rattle-free position of its Honda trunk lid. Failure to retrieve this part from a damaged trunk lid will necessitate the purchase of a new one. Be alert to small items, like this, while dismantling parts or transferring salvaged items from an old part to a new one. Besides the monetary savings, this kind of missing part hassle can be frustrating.

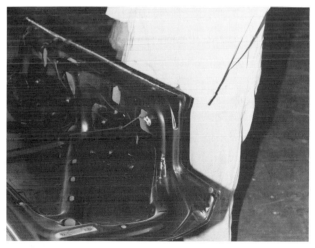

Brand-new doors, trunk lids and other assemblies are stripped of all accessory parts. You have to salvage items like linkages, bumpers, fasteners and the like from old parts. In this picture, Burrous is removing the linkage assembly to a Honda remote trunk lid opener so that it can be installed on the new trunk lid put on the repaired vehicle. Until you carefully inspect body assemblies, you will be amazed at how many accessory parts are featured on them.

This mirror housing is secured with Allen head screws. Operation of an Allen wrench next to a freshly painted door must be done carefully, to prevent accidental scratches or paint nicks. If part replacement procedures need to be undertaken next to freshly painted body panels, consider laying strips of masking tape down to protect those panel areas in the most vulnerable areas.

MOUNTING PADS continued...

Years	Stock #	Price	Description
BENTLEY			

NOTE: Please send tracing of your metal base with all Bentley orders.

Years	Stock #	Price	Description
'30	MP 112-E	5.90/ea.	Parklight pad.
'33-'39	MP 112-L	7.30/ea.	Headlight bracket pad.
	MP 112-M	7.10/ea.	Front fender side light pad.
'38	MP 112-A	8.75/ea.	Headlight pad.
	MP 112-B	4.35/ea.	Door handle pad.
	MP 112-C	7.60/ea.	Windshield post pad.
'46-'52	MP 112-F	7.60/ea.	Standard body tail-light pad.
'52-'53	MP 112-H	11.10/ea.	License light pad.
'54-'55	MP 112-G	7.60/ea.	Tail-light pad.
—	MP 112-J	7.60/ea.	License bracket pad.
—	MP 112-K	11.10/ea.	**Bentley, 74.9 & 74.10 models only.** Tail-light pad.
—	MP 112-N	11.80/ea.	Tail-light pad. Same as MP 112-K (see above), but has bottom flange.

BMW

Years	Stock #	Price	Description
'37	MP 116-A	6.35/ea.	**BMW, model 328.** Tail-light pad.
'58	MP 116	5.90/ea.	**BMW, 300-600.** Turn signal pad.

BRITISH CARS

Years	Stock #	Price	Description
'35	MP 1053	4.25/ea.	**Morris Minor.** Headlight pad.
—	MP 111-W	1.65/ea.	**Austin Healey, Jaguar, MG, Sunbeam, etc.** Windshield wiper transmission pad.

BUICK

Years	Stock #	Price	Description
'27-'29	MP 120-A	3.80/ea.	Sunvisor pad.
	MP 142-B	7.60/ea.	Rumble seat step-plate pad.
	MP 334-B	3.25/ea.	Door handle pad.
'28	MP 120-C	5.00/ea.	Headlight bar pad.
'29	MP 121	5.00/ea.	Headlight bar pad.
'32-'34	MP 131-A	5.15/ea.	Headlight (upper) pad.
	MP 131-B	5.15/ea.	Headlight (lower) pad.
	MP 134-C	2.70/ea.	Windshield wiper transmission pad.
	MP 134-D	2.80/ea.	Wiper arm pad.
	MP 160-B	3.25/ea.	Headlight body pad.
	MP 336-C	11.60/4 pc.set	Trunk lock pads.
'32-'33	MP 120	4.40/ea.	Parklight pad.

Years	Stock #	Price	Description
(BUICK, cont.)			
'32	MP 130	4.40/ea.	Tail-light pad.
'33	MP 132	5.90/ea.	Tail-light pad.
	MP 133	4.40/ea.	Headlight bar pad.
	MP 139	2.85/ea.	Headlight pad for between upper bracket and radiator.
	MP 140	2.85/ea.	Headlight bracket pad.
	MP 150	5.15/ea.	Headlight pad.
	MP 160	3.50/ea.	Parklight pad.
'34	MP 170	6.35/ea.	Headlight pad.
	MP 180	5.90/ea.	Tail-light pad.
'35-'37	MP 136	7.30/ea.	Parklight pad. Fits 1-1/16" wide metal.
	MP 137	7.30/ea.	Parklight pad. Fits 7/8" metal.
	MP 143	7.30/ea.	Parklight pad. Fits 1-1/8" metal.
'35-'36	MP 135	5.75/ea.	Tail-light pad.
'35	MP 336	5.75/ea.	Headlight pad.
'36-'37	MP 546-Y	2.70/ea.	**Buick. '36:** all. **'37:** series 80 & 90, except convertibles.
'36	MP 135-B	3.80/ea.	License light pad.
	MP 190	6.95/ea.	Headlight pad.
	MP 200	5.75/ea.	Tail-light pad.
	MP 311	5.90/ea.	Rumble seat step-plate pad.
	MP 336-D	11.45/4 pc.set	**Buick Victoria Coupe.** Trunk hinge pads.
'37-'38	MP 335-B	11.55/4 pc.set	Trunk hinge pad.
	MP 210	7.10/ea.	Tail-light pad.
	MP 280-A	3.00/ea.	**Buick, 40 & 60 series.** Windshield wiper transmission pad.
'37	MP 220	12.50/ea.	Trunklight pad.
	MP 230	12.50/ea.	**Buick Slant-Back.** Trunklight pad.
'38-'40	MP 300	7.60/ea.	Trunk handle pad.
	MP 280	3.10/ea.	**Buick, 80-90 series.** Windshield wiper transmission pad.
'38	MP 181	6.35/ea.	Trunk emblem pad.

All kinds of exterior body accessories must be installed over designed mounting pads. In addition to cushioning parts from vibration against sheet-metal bodies, they form a barrier between incompatible metals which could cause severe galvanic corrosion problems if allowed to rub against each other. Newer car owners should be able to find replacement pads at a dealership. Auto restorers might have to locate specialty auto parts companies, like Metro Molded Parts, Inc., to find the exact pads needed for their unique automobiles. Metro Molded Parts, Inc.

Vinyl or rubber trim sections might be treated to a solid scrubbing with an all-purpose cleaner such as Simple Green and a soft brush. This kind of in-depth cleaning might expose painted body panels to scratch hazards if pieces were installed first and then cleaned. When they are dry, apply a satisfactory coat of vinyl dressing. Rub the treatment in with a cloth or very soft brush. Be sure to wipe off all excess. If you do not want to use a silicone-based dressing product, check with the autobody paint and supply store to see if they carry vinyl and rubber rejuvenation products that do not include silicone ingredients.

Make sure that all of the clips and retainers are on hand before attaching trim pieces. Make sure you fully understand how they are intended to work before forcing them on in an inappropriate manner, breaking them in the process. As you did for their removal, have a helper assist you in replacing extra-long pieces. This will not only help to prevent bends or wrinkles on the trim, but also adds more control to the installation to prevent accidental scratches on paint finishes.

When installing belt moldings around windows, do not use a screwdriver or other hard object to flip rubber edges over on top of painted frame openings. Instead, use a plastic tool designed for this procedure. They are available at autobody paint and supply stores and some auto glass shops. Shaped somewhat like a doctor's tongue depressor, these plastic tools will not scratch paint while being used to position rubber or vinyl molding and trim edges.

Since door handles and key locks attach directly to painted body panels, you must install them with care so as not to accidentally cause scratches, chips or nicks to the finish. In many cases, gaskets or seals are designed for placement between hardware and body skin. If the old gasket is worn, cracked or otherwise damaged, do not use it. Wait to install that handle or exterior door item until a new gasket is acquired.

If a defective gasket is used, the chance for the handle to come in direct contact with the sheet-metal body panel increases. Should the metallic makeup of the handle be incompatible with the sheet-metal body, their direct contact offers a perfect situation for the start of galvanic corrosion. This is an oxidizing process where dissimilar metals make contact, react adversely to each other and result in the weaker material oxidizing (rusting).

The screws, nuts or bolts used to secure door handles are normally accessed through openings on the interior sides of doors. You have to reach through with your hand to tighten the fasteners. Be sure to use wrenches or sockets of the correct size to make this awkward job as easy as possible. After handles and key locks are secured, you must attach linkages or cables that run to the actual latch mechanisms.

Grille

Most grille sections are secured by screws of some type. A lot of them are tightened into metal clips, as opposed to nuts. These clips have to be positioned correctly in order to securely support grille pieces. Pay attention to the way you place clips, as they can slide around to cause scratches along the metal supports they fasten to. Likewise, screws must line up with the center of these clips in order to work properly.

Your experience dismantling a vehicle will be of great help when it comes time to put it all back together again. Some grille assemblies require certain pieces be put in position first, followed in order by other sections. Failure to install them in their proper order will result in one or more pieces not fitting together smoothly, or not at all.

Headlight buckets, housing or trim rings are generally separate from grilles. This is so burned-out headlights can be changed without a need to dismantle the entire grille. Remember, there are

Not all grille assemblies are put together the same. With some automobiles, you actually have to search for the mechanisms that hold parts in place. Many grilles are composed of a number of pieces held together by special clips. Be sure to clearly understand how these units are removed and installed before haphazardly removing or tightening screws, nuts or bolts.

normally two screws next to headlights which tighten down over springs. These are used to position headlights only; adjusting them up or down, left to right. If they were taken off for paint work, you must put them back on, of course, but will need to have them accurately adjusted by someone with headlight leveling equipment.

As with other exterior trim pieces and accessories, you should take this opportunity to clean, polish and detail grille assemblies while they are off of your car. Touch up paint nicks, clean tiny nooks and crannies and wax metallic parts as necessary. Use a soft toothbrush and cotton swabs to reach into tight spaces. Should painted parts look old and worn, consider sanding and repainting them. Tiny chips or nicks can be touched up with the proper paint using a fine artist's paintbrush.

Bumpers

Older cars and trucks feature bumpers that are relatively easy to take off and put on. The bolts attaching them are generally in clear view and plenty of room is provided for adequate maneuverability. Newer cars, on the other hand, can require some rather intricate dismantling and installation procedures.

Once the bumper was tightly snugged into place, it was determined that the headlight and grille section on the driver's side nose area could not be fitted into place. Therefore, the bumper had to be loosened so the headlight assembly could be installed. There is a method and sequence for the installation of all body parts. While dismantling, take notes, photographs or video movies of your progress so that you will have a chronological guide to follow when putting all of them back later.

Many newer bumpers are actually combinations of a number of different parts. A basic frame assembly bolts onto supports that are mounted to structural members under the front or rear ends. To that frame, urethane faces, rock shields, guards and other items may snap into place or be held on by a number of screws. Each part must be installed correctly or the entire unit may not be able to sit flush with ground effects or other body designs.

If you are not the person who originally removed the bumpers from your vehicle, or if you have simply forgotten how they are supposed to go back on, take your time during installation and do not cinch bolts or nuts down until you are sure the entire unit is assembled correctly. In some cases, shields or faces must be put on first before the bumper is secured to mounts. Otherwise, they will not be able to fit into place. If that happens, simply loosen the bumper, pull it out and insert the shield. Then, slip the unit back in and tighten it up.

Some front bumper assemblies are quite large, more or less encompassing the entire nose of some vehicles. Because of their size and weight, plan to have someone help you install them. In addition, most of these units feature a lot of screws and bolts which work somewhat in unison to adjust the bumper from a number of different points. In other words, do not tightly cinch up any fastener until all of them have been snugged up and the entire unit is positioned perfectly. If this is not done, one side may stick out farther than the other and certain gaps might not line up evenly spaced with other ones. Again, this is where a helper can prove valuable by lifting, pushing or pulling parts of the bumper into their proper position and holding them there while fasteners are tightened.

Emblems and Badges

A thorough cleaning with a soft toothbrush and mild cleaner should work well to remove accumulations of polish, wax or dirt from tiny corners and designed impressions to make these items look new. Be sure their fastening mechanisms are intact. Plastic emblems are not always easy to remove, and many times their plastic pins or supports are cracked during dismantling. If yours are damaged, you may have to replace them with new ones.

Chipped paint on emblems and badges does not necessarily mean they have to be replaced. You can use an artist's paintbrush, or lettering brush, to repaint delicate emblem designs. Check with your autobody paint and supply jobber to determine the correct color. Unless your vehicle is a concours contender or other special classic, you might be able to match emblem colors closely with vials of autobody touchup paint. However, for those vintage, classic or concours needs, you may have to special order the perfect type and color

SPECIAL PURPOSE GROMMETS CONTINUED...

GM	Buick	Buick	GM	Chevrolet	Corvette	Chevrolet & Corvette	GM	GM	GM
SM 47	SM 50	SM 51	SM 52	SM 53	SM 54	SM 55	SM 56	SM 57	SM 58

Chevrolet	Chevrolet	GM	GM	GM Convertibles	GM	Mercury	GM	Chevrolet & Corvette	Rolls Royce & Bentley
SM 59	SM 60	SM 61	SM 62	SM 63	SM 65-A	SM 67	SM 68	SM 69	SM 70

Rolls Royce & Bentley	Ford	Ford	GM	Buick	Ford Products	Mercedes	Chevrolet	Ford & Mercury	Chevrolet
SM 70-A	SM 71	SM 78	SM 80-A	SM 82	SM 83	SM 84	SM 85	SM 87	SM 88

Cord	Cord	Oldsmobile	Corvette	Cadillac	Ford & Mercury	Ford	Corvette	Chevrolet	Mercedes
SM 89	SM 90	SM 91	SM 92	SM 94	SM 96	SM 97	SM 98	SM 99-A	SM 99-Z

Mercedes	Hudson	Metropolitan	GM	Metropolitan	Oldsmobile	Oldsmobile	Chevrolet	Chevrolet	METRO...
SM 100	SM 100-A	SM 100-B	SM 101	SM 102	SM 103	SM 104	NEW SM 105	NEW SM 106	Quality Rubber Products since 1918.

Make/Year	Stock #	Price	Description
CHEVROLET			
'28-'53	SM 69	2.40/ea.	**Chevrolet, most models.** Pressure Ring Washer for interior door handles and window regulators. Fits between escutcheon plates and door panel. Made of sponge rubber. 1-7/8" O.D., 3/4" I.D., 3/8" thick.
'32-'46	SM 88	5.60/ea.	**Chevrolet. '32-'39:** Passenger models. **'32-'46:** Trucks. Wire Grommet for throttle, choke, oil and temperature lines. Held by steel retainers.
'33-'35	SM 43-A	11.65/ea.	**Chevrolet.** Floorboard Grommet. For accelerator rod through floorboard. Steel sleeve like original.
'35-'40	SM 43	12.00/ea.	**Chevrolet, most models, including Commercial.** Floorboard Grommet. For accelerator rod through toeboard. Steel core like original.
'36-'54	RP 2-A	9.35/ea.	**Chevrolet. '36-'54:** Passenger models. **'36-'53:** Commercial. Brake Cover for inspection hole
'36-'40	SM 34	2.20/ea.	**Chevrolet.** Firewall Grommet. For headlight and tail-light wires.
'37-'52	SM 3	3.25/ea.	**Chevrolet, some models.** Wire Harness Grommet.
'37-'48	SM 68	2.00/ea.	**Chevrolet.** For headlight wire loom through body.
'37-'38	SM 38	6.00/ea.	**Chevrolet.** Wire Harness Grommet. For speedometer cable through toeboard. Replaces OEM #594341.
'39-'50	SM 36	4.65/ea.	**Chevrolet.** Wire Harness Grommet.
'39-'48	SM 17	0.45/ea.	**Chevrolet, some models.** Speedometer / Cable Firewall Grommet. Fits 1-7/8" long hole. NOTE: Not used when car was factory-equipped with windshield washers.
'39-'42	SM 37	4.05/ea.	**Chevrolet.** Rubber Seal Grommet. For hand brake pull-rod through firewall.
	3M 44	2.10/ea.	**Chevrolet.** Fender Grommet, For headlight wires. Fine reproduction.
'40-'60	SM 4	1.90/ea.	**Chevrolet, all models.** For firewall, fuel gauge wire, horn wire, hood latch cable and fresh air cable. Fits 1/2" hole. 1/8" center hole.
	SM 8	2.20/ea.	**Chevrolet.** Firewall / Utility Grommet. Fits 3/4" hole. 3/16" center hole.
'40-'58	3M 2	2.40/ea.	**Chevrolet.** Speedometer Cable Grommet.
'40-'48	SM 60	3.35/ea.	**Chevrolet, Passenger models.** Firewall Grommet. For temperature gauge. 1-5/8" O.D.
	SM 56	2.90/ea.	**Chevrolet, Passenger models.** Windshield Washer Grommet. Fits 1" hole.
	SM 62	2.70/ea.	**Chevrolet.** Choke Cable Grommet. Fits 5/8" hole. 1/8" center hole.
'40-'41	SM 63	2.70/ea.	**Chevrolet.** Firewall Grommet. For top vacuum hose. Fits 7/8" hole. 3/4" center hole.
	SM 61	2.25/ea.	**Chevrolet.** Hood Cable Grommet. Fits a 7/16" to 1/2" hole. 3/16" center hole.
'40	SB 63	1.85/ea.	**Chevrolet.** Floor Plug. Fits 9/16" hole.
	SB 28	1.70/ea.	**Chevrolet.** Floor Plug.
'41-'48	SM 65-A	9.35/ea.	**Chevrolet, all models.** Radio Fuse Boot and Wire Harness. For original radio only.
'46-'52	SM 6	1.45/ea.	**Chevrolet.** Wiper Pivot Grommet.
'49-'58	SM 52	1.75/ea.	**Chevrolet.** Cowl Bumper. Fits 1/2" to 9/16" hole.

Make/Year (Chevrolet, cont.)	Stock #	Price	Description
'49-'55	SM 55	6.65/ea.	**Chevrolet.** Firewall Grommet. For throttle rod tube, oil pressure gauge pipe, heat indicator tube and choke rod.
'49-'54	SM 106	3.50/ea.	NEW **Chevrolet.** Wire Harness Grommet. Fits through left end (radiator core) support. Fits 15/16" hole in sheet metal. 5/8" center hole.
'49-'52	SM 53	3.45/ea.	**Chevrolet.** Firewall Grommet. For tachometer, speedometer and emergency brake cable. Fits 7/8" hole. 1-3/16" O.D. 1/4" I.D.
	SM 105	1.80/ea.	NEW **Chevrolet, all models.** Vent Cable Firewall Brace Grommet. Fits 7/16" hole in sheet metal. 1/4" center hole.
'52-'57	SM 57	4.35/ea.	**Chevrolet.** Headlight Wire Grommet. Used with square clip (not included). Fits 7/8" hole. 7/16" center hole.
'53-'56	SM 30-A	4.65/ea.	**Chevrolet, all V-8 engines.** Ignition Wire Holder.
'53-'54	SM 54	3.45/ea.	**Chevrolet.** Firewall Grommet. For headlight and parklight harnesses. Fits 7/8" hole. 1-3/16" O.D. 9/16" I.D.
'54-'56	SM 38-A	11.00/ea.	**Chevrolet, some models.** Wire Harness Grommet to Firewall. Finely detailed.
'56-'58	SM 3	3.25/ea.	**Chevrolet, some models.** Wire Harness.
'57	SM 85	2.85/ea.	**Chevrolet.** Firewall Grommet.
'61-'62	3M 99-A	4.05/ea.	**Chevrolet, all Full-Size Passenger models.** Heater and Defrost Cable Grommet.
'64-'72	SM 80-A	1.70/ea.	**Chevrolet, all models.** Firewall Insulation Fastener.
'64-'67	RP 9	3.20/ea.	**Chevrolet.** Positive Crankcase Ventilation Grommet.
'67-'72	SM 101	2.25/ea.	**Chevrolet, including Trucks.** Dash and Firewall Grommet. Single-hole type (SM 101) is for one wire. Double-hole type (RP 1-G) is for two wires. Used for heater motor and accessory wires. Many applications.
	RP 1 G	2.25/ea.	
	3M 30-C	2.35/ea.	**Chevrolet.** Spark Plug Wire Retainer and Organizer. Self-locking type Made of black plastic.
—	SM 59	3.45/ea.	**Chevrolet, all with 6-cylinder engines.** Timing Hole Plug.

CHEVROLET CORVETTE

Make/Year	Stock #	Price	Description
'53-'55	SM 56	2.90/ea.	**Corvette.** Windshield Washer Grommet. Fits 1" hole.
	SM 57	4.35/ea.	**Corvette.** Headlight Wire Grommet. Used with square clip (not included). Fits 7/8" hole. 7/16" center hole.
	SM 58	3.65/ea.	**Corvette.** Trunk Wire Harness Grommet. Two used per car. Fits 7/8" hole. Flexible 3/16" center hole.
'53-'54	SM 55	6.65/ea.	**Corvette.** Firewall Grommet. For throttle rod tube, oil pressure gauge pipe, heat indicator tube and choke rod.
	SM 69	2.40/ea.	**Corvette.** Heater Hose Washer at firewall. Made of sponge 1-7/8" O.D. 3/4" I.D. 3/8" thick.
	SM 54	3.45/ea.	**Corvette.** Firewall Grommet. For headlight and parklight harnesses. Fits 7/8" hole. 1-3/16" O.D. 9/16" I.D.
'56-'62	SM 92	2.10/ea.	**Corvette.** Firewall Grommet. Fits 1-3/8" hole. Replaces OEM #3708181.
'57-'58	SM 98	3.25/ea.	**Corvette, fits through early '58.** For High-Performance Cars ONLY (2 & 4 barrel carbs and fuel injections). Tachometer Drive Grommet to firewall. Used on firewall behind distributor . 1-3/4" O.D. 7/16" I.D. Angled hole. Replaces OEM #3751551. *Continued on next page...*

Many times, during the complete dismantling of an automobile for paint work, one will notice that wiring harness grommets or other rubber parts are dried out, cracked or worn. Plan to replace these damaged items while installing parts after a complete paint job. If yours is an older car, consult companies like Metro Molded Parts, Inc. to locate replacements for those grommets or other rubber items that are beyond repair. Metro Molded Parts, Inc.

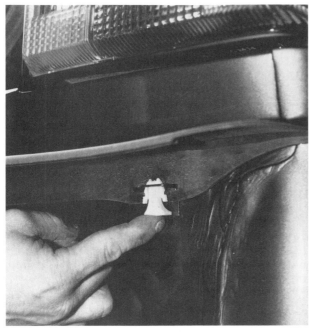

Newer cars have many special clips, like this one, that support or secure assemblies. This one is designed to hold a bumper in place. During dismantling, be sure to note such special clips so that installation can progress smoothly. Also, should any clips be broken during removal, try to have replacement parts on hand before installing assemblies after paint work has been completed.

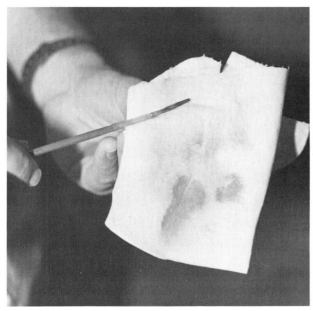

An artist's fine paintbrush, like this one, is perfect for applying touchup paint to emblems, badges and trim. You may need to have an autobody paint and supply store mix a special paint color to match the tint currently existing on such parts, or to keep those items authentic for Concours competitions. For ordinary cars, bottles of touchup paint may provide the right shade for your needs.

Roy Dunn is using an artist's paintbrush to paint the Chevrolet emblem a custom color. Work like this calls for brushes the exact width of emblem letters or slightly smaller. For the most part, slow-drying enamel paint works well for work like this. It can be found at artist and sign painter supply stores.

paint to keep emblem and badge equipment in original condition.

New emblems, badges and other decorative body items are normally available through dealership parts departments, even those for a lot of older cars and trucks. For those parts that are not stocked at dealerships, you may have to look elsewhere for replacements. One of the best sources for locating companies that specialize in hard-to-find automobile parts is *Hemmings Motor News*.

This monthly publication is packed full of company-sponsored and individually supported advertisements that list just about every kind of automotive-related part, accessory and service any auto enthusiast could ask for. Since its hundreds of pages are broken down into a number of separate categories, you should be able to quickly find a source for the parts you need. Along with this publication, there are also a lot of other magazines dedicated to auto enthusiasts, restorers and do-it-yourself customizers. Their pages also include sources for older car and truck parts.

Vinyl Stripes and Decals

Unless a spot paint job enabled you to carefully mask along the edge of a vinyl stripe or decal, chances are the entire piece on that section of the car's body had to be removed. For complete paint jobs, all stripes and decals should have been taken off. Replacement vinyl stripes in all sorts of colors and widths, as well as decals, are available through dealership parts departments and autobody paint and supply stores.

If only one panel on your car was painted, leaving all of the rest of a vinyl stripe design intact, you might be able to purchase only that piece needed, as opposed to an entire stripe set. Factory-installed stripes come in sections, whereas individual packets of custom striping just come in certain length rolls. Therefore, especially for newer cars, check with dealership parts departments when you need to buy a certain section of vinyl stripe tape. This can save you money over the purchase of an entire roll of matching, yet generic, stripe tape at the autobody paint and supply store.

Before attaching vinyl stripes or decals to vehicle bodies, make sure fresh paint has cured according to label recommendations. Then, use a clean cloth dampened with wax and grease remover to clean those areas where you expect to attach them. Read any instructions provided with the vinyl material.

This is the end section from a piece of factory vinyl stripe tape for a Jeep Cherokee. Notice how there is a bend just a few inches in from the end of the strip. This is designed into the strip to account for a corner that it has to go around. Normal rolls of generic stripe tape will not have this bend. Because the length of this factory stripe is exact, there is no room for error in its installation. You must take your time while adjusting items like this to make sure they are attached correctly on the first attempt.

Autobody paint and supply stores and auto parts outlets carry supplies of automotive vinyl stripe tape. Many different colors and widths are available, which should make matching an existing stripe design quite easy. In addition, dealerships carry specific stripe schemes that match factory-installed graphics and other vinyl tape designs. Be sure to mention the year, make and model vehicle to parts personnel to receive the correct stripe part.

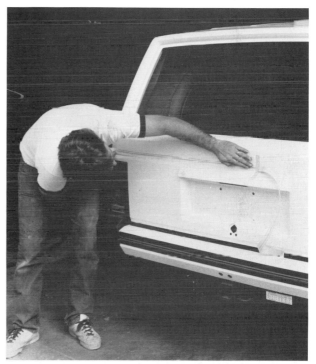

Van Hee has secured the piece of factory stripe tape with a section of masking tape. This way, he can adjust the stripe as many times as necessary until it is positioned perfectly. If the stripe is off a little, all he has to do is loosen the masking tape strip. This work will continue until both ends of the stripe tape are lined up perfectly with their edges. In addition, the angled part of the tape has to be situated just right on the corners of the tailgate assembly.

Vinyl tape stripe has two protective coverings: one protects the top of stripes while the other provides a backing for the adhesive. In this picture, Van Hee is sighting down the stripe to make sure it is perfectly centered and positioned because the backing paper has already been pulled off. With stripe material out from the body by an inch, or so, he can carefully guide it toward the body surface for attachment as long as it is lined up along body ridges. Previous alignment work guaranteed that the end would attach at the gap between the rear body panel and the quarterpanel.

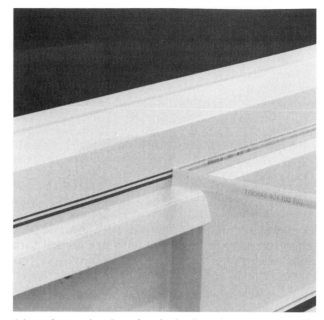

After the entire length of vinyl stripe was securely placed, Van Hee removed the outer protective film to expose brand-new vinyl stripes. This film is mandatory in this case, in order to keep both stripes equally spaced apart. If it would have been taken off too soon, there would have been a good possibility that they might not be positioned exactly even.

This side of the vinyl stripe has been attached. The color is lighter than the stripe color to the right because a protective film is still in place over the stripes. Van Hee uses his hand to apply pressure against the stripe to make sure it is securely attached.

For those pieces that are already cut to size, you have to carefully position them before peeling off any of the backing paper. This is so you can match both ends an equal distance from body panel edges and make adjustments to height as needed. Van Hee does this by securing vinyl tape sections with a piece of masking tape. As the vinyl's position indicates, the tape is loosened and position changed. After all of the proper adjustments have been made and the vinyl stripe or decal satisfactorily placed, backing paper is carefully peeled away from one edge and the vinyl unit attached to the body surface.

With thin stripes, you might be able to lightly lay a section down and lift it up again for repositioning. However, wide stripes and decals are not so forgiving. Once their extra-strength adhesive makes contact with a body surface, they cannot generally be pulled off without suffering some sort of damage. So, take your time, have patience and ask someone to help you when working with large projects.

Painted pinstripes can be matched using the proper kind of pinstripe paintbrush and slow-drying enamel paint. Unless you have done this before, you will have to practice on an old hood or door before trying your hand at it on your favorite car. The Eastwood Company offers a full range of pinstripe and lettering paintbrushes for all kinds of uses. They also sell a variety of slow-drying lettering enamel most commonly used by professional pinstripers. Autobody paint and supply stores also sell these supplies.

Although practice with a pinstripe brush may help you learn how to put stripes on straight and symmetrically, trouble may be found when you attempt to match the exact color of those pinstripes already in place on your car. A lot of times, professional pinstripers mix different colors to arrive at new and exciting tints. Through trial and error, and some advice from a color expert at your autobody paint and supply store, you can match existing colors by following color charts and mixing drops of one color with drops of another.

In order to paint perfectly symmetrical and evenly spaced pinstripes, once the right color has been mixed, you might want to use stencil tape. Finesse Stencil Tape looks like pinstripe tape except that all of the different sizes and designs are the same color. It is placed like vinyl pinstripe tape, but instead of staying on the car body as a design, pinstripe paint is brushed over it. Paint attaches to the car body between tape sections in perfectly straight and even widths. Once the paint has been applied, tape is pulled off to reveal perfectly painted pinstripes. Finesse Stencil Tape is available at autobody paint and supply stores and artist supply houses.

Miscellaneous

When you stop to analyze the exterior of almost any motor vehicle, you are likely to observe

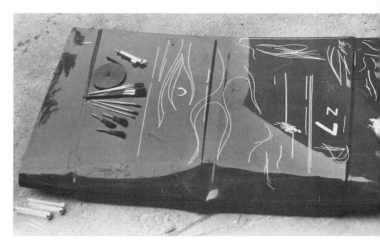

Painting on pinstripes takes a lot more practice than positioning vinyl stripes. Before you tackle that kind of job, find an old hood or trunk lid to practice on. This hood worked out great for practice sessions with pinstriping brushes, lettering brushes and the Beugler Pinstriping Tool. Brushes and tool courtesy of The Eastwood Company

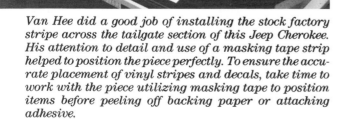

Van Hee did a good job of installing the stock factory stripe across the tailgate section of this Jeep Cherokee. His attention to detail and use of a masking tape strip helped to position the piece perfectly. To ensure the accurate placement of vinyl stripes and decals, take time to work with the piece utilizing masking tape to position items before peeling off backing paper or attaching adhesive.

Roy Dunn is a professional pinstriper and sign painter. He is also a talented artist. Here, he is applying a painted pinstripe along the fender of a new pickup truck. Practice with pinstripe brushes will help you learn how to put them on straight. However, you will need to learn how colors are mixed and matched in order to develop the ability to produce custom colors, so familiar with pinstripe designs.

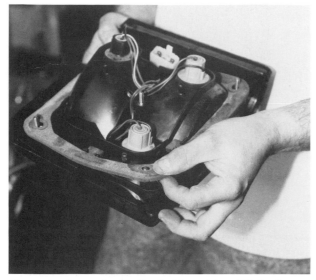

The gasket located on the backside of this taillight fixture must be in good shape or it will leak water to possibly ruin the light fixture. Such attention to detail makes the difference between a good paint job and restoration and a great one. If worn-out parts are put back on body assemblies, their need for replacement will be noticed soon enough. Why not replace them now, while your car or truck is dismantled and ready for restoration?

Burrous is replacing a Honda taillight that was removed for painting purposes. The entire unit is put into place from the outside. Protruding screw mounts are then secured with nuts from the inside. When installing taillight assemblies, be certain the gasket between the housing and the vehicle body is in excellent condition. In addition, you must attach electrical wires correctly, or the stop light, turn signal and back-up light will not operate properly.

that there are a lot of parts and accessories attached to them. So far, many of the major items have been described. In reality, there are a lot more. Definitive instructions for the replacement of every kind of exterior body part found on every make and model automobile on the road today could literally fill volumes and volumes of books. In fact, they do! Just check out the number of parts catalogs displayed at any auto parts house or dealership parts department, and these only list the parts themselves, much less the instructions on how to dismantle or replace them.

So, with any kind of automotive-related project, even painting, you have to exercise some common sense, at times, to figure out just how some parts are removed and then put back on. The best advice for these situations is not to be in a hurry. Take your time, study the part and carefully inspect the area around it for clues as how it is supposed to come off or go back on. When in doubt,

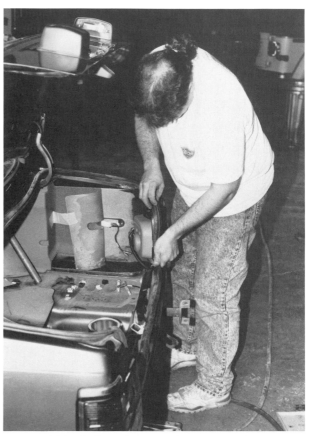

Along with light fixtures and other accessories, molding strips have to be installed according to their design. Some simply snap in place, others are secured by clips and many are held tight with adhesive. The molding around this trunk opening can only be installed one way. Take your time to figure out just where each curve is supposed to be positioned before securing any portion. Do this by loosely maneuvering the piece in position first and then starting the installation at a corner.

ask a dealership service manager, autobody technician, fellow car club member or neighborhood auto enthusiast.

Along with those parts already mentioned, you might have to install windshield wipers, license plates, side reflectors, trunk locks, radio antennas, luggage racks, door edge guards, mud flaps, running boards, ground effects, spoilers, weatherstripping, hood bumpers and so on. If you took them off in preparation for your car or truck's paint job, you should at least have an idea of how to put them back on.

Use strips of masking tape to protect painted body areas against accidental paint chips when located adjacent to sites of part installation. Large cotton towels work well under newly painted doors to prevent scratches or chips as they are supported by crates or other means while you work to secure hinges. Think of new paint as your car's skin, and treat it as you would your own. Plan ahead while replacing parts and try to anticipate potential scratch or chip hazards. Use masking tape, towels, cardboard or whatever to maximize the degree of protection offered newly painted parts so they do not incur scratches, chips, nicks, scrapes, gouges or blemishes of any kind.

Detailing

After spending considerable hours, and maybe even days, cleaning, polishing, painting and even waxing exterior body parts, you may think that your car is detailed to the highest degree. But, have you looked at the vents on your car's dashboard? Are they dusty? If you spent any time at all sanding the body of your car or truck, chances are good that more sanding dust than you had imagined has infiltrated the interior, trunk and engine compartment. That stuff is amazing. It seems to find its way into just about every nook and cranny possible.

Since the outside of your automobile looks so good, why not spend a little time on the interior? Your vacuum cleaner with a soft brush attachment will work well to remove large accumulations of dust on and around the dashboard. Use a soft cloth, toothbrush or cotton swab to clean corners and confined spaces. The vacuum cleaner's crevice attachment fits into tight spaces around seats and center consoles to remove dust and debris.

Mix a small amount of a cleaner, like Simple Green, into a bucket and dip cleaning cloths into it periodically to help clean sticky steering wheels, stained sun visors, dirty door panels and vinyl seats. You will be amazed at how much dirt accumulation gathers on your cleaning cloth.

Next, vacuum the trunk thoroughly. If yours is an older American car that features an open metal space with no cardboard or carpet siding and it has been neglected for far too long, detail it. Remove scale, rust deposits and other debris with a wire brush. Use a vacuum to remove residue. Then, con-

This Honda has yet to be detailed, as sanding dust is visible on the bumper and rear window. However, all of the exterior parts have been installed correctly. To ensure that all accessories are correctly aligned and wires connected to the proper plugs, all the lights were tested and trunk lock operated, as indicated by the key in the key lock just to the right of the license plate.

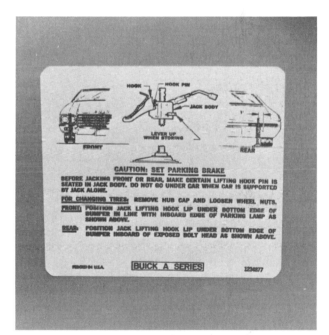

This is a stock, jacking equipment operating instruction decal for the trunk lid on Art Wentworth's 1970 Buick GS 455 Convertible. Factory items like this can be located at dealerships for newer cars and some older models. For classic and vintage automobiles, you may have to rely on specialty auto parts outlets or catalog sales companies to find original equipment like decals, emblems and the like. An excellent source for locating companies that sell older car parts is Hemmings Motor News. Other auto-related magazines may also carry similar advertisements.

Sanding dust is so fine, it will infiltrate almost every nook and cranny on your car. An easy way to remove much of this residue from vent openings on dashboards is with a soft brush attachment on a vacuum cleaner. More meticulous cleaning could involve use of cotton swabs or paintbrushes. Now that your car sports a new paint job on the exterior, why not spend a little extra time detailing the interior and other areas so they look equally as nice?

sider applying a couple of coats of a rust-inhibiting paint, like Rustoleum, as a sealer. To really make the trunk space look new and original, apply a quality coat of trunk splatter paint. Two cans are generally enough for normal-sized, 1950 to 1970 vintage American car trunks.

Trunk splatter paint comes in a few different colors. The unique part about splatter paint is that three colors are generally spit out. The base color might be gray and it will be highlighted by spots of white and black, just like an original finish. Do not apply this material to the backsides of rear seats, and make sure the entire space is clean before application.

Engine compartments can present detailers with more than just sanding dust. Years of accumulated grease and oil may make cleaning it seem like an impossible chore. But, the use of an engine cleaner, like Gunk, and pressure from the wand of a self-serve car wash can easily remove the bulk of those accumulations. Be sure to cover newly painted fenders with large towels or other soft material, and keep the water wand away from the distributor and carburetor.

After that, some time with a stiff paintbrush and a cleaner such as Simple Green can make the engine compartment on your automobile look almost as good as the new paint job. You can take more time to make the engine compartment look better, by painting the engine block and polishing all of those items that need it. The more you do, the better it will look.

After a complete paint job, Wentworth was dismayed by the appearance of this neglected trunk space. With some elbow grease, a couple of cans of rust-inhibiting paint and two cans of trunk splatter paint, this trunk can be made to look like new. If the trunk space on your car looks this bad, consider cleaning and painting it so it will blend with the freshly painted and new-looking exterior. The timing should be perfect, as you have been working on this car for a while and all of your tools and necessary equipment will be right at hand.

Initially, rust and scale had to be scraped off of the floor in the trunk space on Wentworth's Buick. A putty knife worked well for this chore. Residue was quickly and easily picked up with a shop vacuum unit. Applying any kind of paint product over flaking material like this is fruitless. Before long, the new paint will also flake off and in no time, the trunk space will look just as bad as it does now.

After the big stuff was scraped off with a putty knife, a more thorough cleaning was accomplished with Scotch Brite pads and sandpaper. The goal was to remove all loose debris and also sand away visible surface rust deposits. Depending upon the condition of your trunk's floor, more intense cleaning may require the use of a wire brush. The object is to get the space as clean and rust-free as possible in preparation for paint.

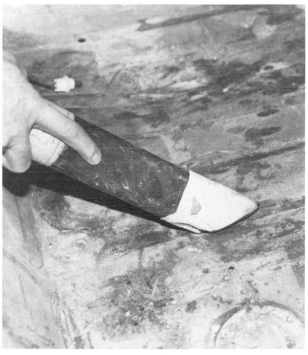

A crevice tool attached to the end of a shop vacuum hose works great for removing accumulations of rust and scale flakes, as well as sanding dust and other debris. If all you have is a household vacuum cleaner, remove large debris accumulations with a dust pan and whisk broom or piece of thin cardboard and paintbrush. Use the vacuum cleaner to pick up dust and other small accumulations of debris. Be sure to vacuum inside crevices and other featured grooves, nooks and crannies.

When the trunk space has been completely cleaned to your satisfaction, apply two good coats of a rust-inhibiting paint, like Rust Magic or Rustoleum. This will serve as an excellent base for splatter paint and also help to reduce the amount of rust and corrosion prevalent. Read the directions on labels to be sure application is made correctly. To help aerosol paint cans perform their best, warm cans in a sink of lukewarm water before spraying; water should not be too hot for your hand. Spray paints like these seem to work much better at 70 or 80 degrees Fahrenheit than at cooler temperatures.

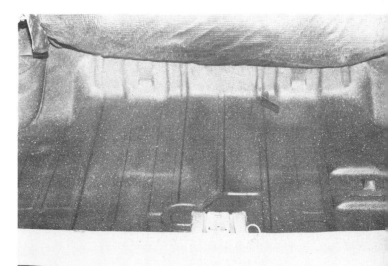

After the application of two cans of rust-inhibiting black paint and two cans of trunk splatter paint, the trunk on Wentworth's Buick looks great. The entire project only took about two hours. Trunk splatter paint is available in different colors, all of which are available at auto-body paint and supply stores and some auto parts houses. Now, doesn't this look more like a trunk that belongs with a freshly painted automobile?

The engine compartment on Wentworth's Buick looks equally as bad as the trunk did. Because the car was subjected to a lot of sanding both before and after painting, accumulation of sanding dust in the engine compartment was quite severe. The area could have been sealed off with plastic, but paint work was needed on the aprons. Depending upon the degree of paint work needed on your car, its engine compartment could easily be this dirty once the project is completed.

A little work with Simple Green cleaner, a paintbursh, scrub brush, some gloss black paint and polish made the engine compartment on Wentworth's Buick look new. Along with a new-looking trunk, clean interior, scrubbed tires and polished wheels, the detailed engine compartment really helps this automobile to stand out, and look crisp and pristine. All of the extra detail work blended together to make the overall paint job look super.

Overview

Painting automobiles is not a procedure that is simply limited to the spraying of paint. There are preparation chores, chemical mixing tasks, masking, painting and follow-up work that has to be done. Across the country, there are thousands, possibly tens of thousands of professional and do-it-yourself autobody painters. In a sense, they all try to do the best they can. However, many are limited by time constraints, hassled by shop managers that expect jobs to be done quickly and those who are simply in too much of a hurry to take the time necessary to accomplish a first-class paint job.

The difference between a mediocre job and a professional one relies on end results. At Newlook, Mycon could easily tell his employees to fix and paint cars as fast as they can in a way that looks good for the moment and the heck with what they look like six months down the road. He could collect his customers' money and worry about the future later. But, instead of looking for the quick buck, he gives his customers a good deal, from the start through final delivery.

Not only does he insist his autobody technicians and painters provide the best possible work for the buck, he makes sure every car is detailed before delivery. When his customers arrive to pick up their repaired automobile, not only do they see previous damage repaired professionally, they immediately realize that their car looks better at that moment than it has for years! No wonder he continues to attract new customers.

As long as you have your automobile torn down for paint work, why not spend some extra time detailing the extras? Not only will the effort make your paint job look its best, it will also do a lot to prolong the life of many accessory parts. Besides, everyone knows an automobile runs better when the windows are clean.

10

Long-Term Paint Care

Although newer catalyzed paint products are much more durable and long lasting than the materials used before them, you cannot expect their finish to shine forever without a minimal amount of routine maintenance. Basically, this entails washing, some polishing as needed and scheduled waxing.

Even though some paint products may be advertised as never having to be waxed, many auto enthusiasts and professionals believe that good coats of wax not only help provide greater paint longevity, but also make washing car bodies a lot easier. It almost seems like dirt and road debris simply float off waxed surfaces instead of having to be rubbed off.

Unless yours is a show car that will seldom, if ever, be driven, you have to face the fact that sooner or later nicks or small chips will appear. Along with regular maintenance, you must also repair these kinds of minor paint problems as soon as possible. If not, exposed metal will oxidize and that corrosion will spread under paint to affect adjacent metal areas.

Because a lot of time, effort and money has gone into the beautiful new paint job on your car, make sure you keep it looking that good for years to come with just some simple, but consistent, maintenance.

Washing, Polishing and Waxing Products

For years, farmers washed their tractors with kerosene. Not only did it do a good job of cleaning, it also afforded a measure of rust protection by forming a film over the tractor body. This procedure might be good for farmer's tractors, but is certainly not the way you should take care of your newly painted car or truck.

Auto parts stores, some variety outlets and even a few supermarkets sell car wash soap products. For the most part, almost any brand of car wash soap should be well suited for the finish on your vehicle. Many auto enthusiasts prefer to use liquids, as opposed to granular types, because they believe just one undissolved granule on a wash mitt could cause scratches. Be sure to follow the mixing directions on labels of any product you use.

The best way to prevent minute scratches or other blemishes on paint is to wash the car in

sections. Wash the dirtiest parts first, like rocker panels, fenderwell lips and lower front and rear-end locations. Then, thoroughly rinse your soft cotton wash mitt and wash soap bucket. Mix up a new batch of wash soap to clean the vehicle sides. If their condition was relatively clean to start with, you can continue with that bucket of sudsy water to wash the hood, roof and trunk areas.

This process rids your wash mitt and bucket of dirt and other scratch hazards, like sand and road grit. If you were to wash your entire car with just one bucket of sudsy water, you increase the chances of your wash mitt picking up debris from the bucket where it will then be rubbed against the vehicle's lustrous finish. Likewise, anytime you notice that your wash mitt is dirty or if it should fall to the ground, always rinse it off with clear water before dipping it into the wash bucket. This helps to keep the wash water clean and free of debris.

Many detailers and avid auto enthusiasts have found Simple Green to be an effective and safe cleaning product. Here, it is being used to loosen up and remove some minor dirt and grease accumulations on McKee's 1970 Jaguar XKE V-12 Roadster engine compartment. You can use this product straight from the jug or dilute it in water. Perhaps the most economical means to acquire Simple Green is to purchase it in gallon containers.

To clean inside tight spaces, like window molding edges, cowling louvers and the like, use a soft, natural-hair floppy paintbrush. Do not use synthetic-bristled paintbrushes because they could cause minute scratches on paint surfaces. In addition, wrap a thick layer of heavy duct tape over the metal band on paintbrushes. This will help to guard against paint scratches or nicks as you vigorously agitate the paintbrush in tight spaces, possibly knocking the brush into painted body parts such as those around headlights and grilles.

One of the most confusing areas surrounding automotive finish maintenance for novice auto enthusiasts seems to focus on polish and wax products. Although both are designed as paint-finish maintenance materials, each has its own separate purpose. Polishes clean paint finishes and remove accumulations of oxidation and other contaminants. On the other hand, wax does no cleaning or shining. It does, however, protect those paint finishes that have already been cleaned and polished. Simply stated, polish cleans—wax protects.

Autobody paint and supply stores generally carry the biggest selection of auto polishes and waxes, although many auto parts stores stock good assortments. Every polish product should include a definitive label which explains what kind of paint finish it is designed for; for example, heavily oxi-

dized, mildly oxidized and new finish glaze. Those designed for heavy oxidation problems contain much coarser grit than those for new car finishes.

Along with descriptions of just which kind of paint finish particular polishes are designed for, labels will also note which products are intended for machine (buffer) use. Those with heavy concentrations of coarse grit are not recommended for machine use. Their polishing strength, combined with the power of a buffer, could cause large-scale paint burning problems.

Carnauba wax is perhaps the best product to use for protecting automobile paint finishes. Meguiar's, Eagle 1 and other cosmetic car-care product manufacturers offer auto enthusiasts an assortment of carnauba-based auto wax products. There are other paint protection products available that profess to work like wax but contain different chemical bases which you must clearly understand before applying them to your new paint job.

Some of these (typically, they have poly or polimer in the product name) are loaded with silicone materials. Although they may protect your car's finish for a long time, professional auto painters advise against their use because the silicone content is so high and saturating that repaint efforts down the road are difficult to achieve without facing severe fisheye problems. In some cases, silicones have been known to penetrate paint finishes to eventually become embedded in sheet-metal panels.

If you find yourself in a quandary when it comes time to select a polish or wax product, seek advice from a knowledgeable autobody paint and supply jobber. This person should be up to date on the latest product information from manufacturers and user satisfaction from professional painters and detailers in the field.

When to Wash New Paint Finishes

Plenty of time should be allotted for paint solvents to evaporate or chemically react before newly sprayed car bodies are washed. For uncatalyzed enamels, this may entail a few days or a week. Newer paints with hardener additives can generally be safely washed after one or two days, as long as mild automotive paint finish soap products are used and gentle washing efforts practiced.

Because auto painters have such a wide selection of paint products to choose from and since each brand or system may react differently than others, it is always best to confirm appropriate paint drying times with a professional autobody paint and supply jobber before washing, polishing or waxing any new finish.

Once an automobile has been repaired and painted at Newlook Autobody, Mycon insists his detailer thoroughly clean each customer's car before delivery, including an exterior wash. Some-

To keep the paint finish on your car or truck looking great for a long time, you should wax it at least four times a year. Once a year, many auto enthusiasts prefer to use a mild polish to clean off wax build-up before applying a new coat. This is a rack of Meguiar's polish and wax products as displayed at an auto parts store. Be sure to read the labels in order to choose the right product for your needs. New paint should not be waxed for 90 to 120 days, and you must confirm appropriate polishing time frames with the information sheet or application guide for the paint used.

In order to reduce the chances for swirls on paint finishes, many professional painters, detailers and auto enthusiasts prefer to rub on their car's surface in straight back-and-forth patterns from front to back, as opposed to washing or polishing in circular patterns.

Here, a soft cotton wash mitt is used with a sudsy car-wash soap mixture in this manner. It might be best to insert your hand into a wash mitt in order to protect it from accidental scrapes or cuts on sharp corners or trim pieces.

times, washing takes place quite soon after paint work was accomplished. The detailer can wash those cars that soon because their paint jobs were helped to cure more quickly by the careful use of infrared heat.

According to manufacturer instructions, paint jobs are allowed to air dry for a specific amount of time, generally fifteen to thirty minutes, before external heat is applied. Then, according to label instructions, new paint is subjected to temperatures around 140 degrees Fahrenheit for up to forty minutes. Unless you have the means to apply external heat, plan to wait at least two days before washing any new *catalyzed* paint finish, longer for uncatalyzed products.

How Long before Waxing?

The rule of thumb is to wait 90 to 120 days before waxing your freshly painted vehicle. This length of time varies according to weather conditions. During summer months, while temperatures are warm and humidity low, 90 days should allow plenty of time for paint solvents to completely evaporate. Cool, wet weather reduces solvent evaporation activity and therefore will require longer waiting periods before waxing.

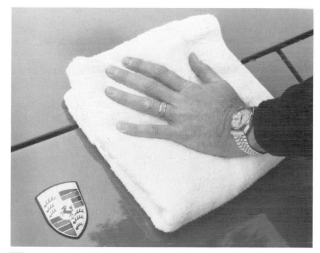

Whenever working on or near the paint finish on your car, always remove rings, watches and other jewelry that could cause potential scratch hazards. If Wentworth's hand was to slip off of this towel, his ring or watch could easily scratch the paint finish on Clint Worthington's beautiful Porsche 944. In addition, be sure that you wear proper attire while working on your car. Metal belt buckles and rivets on denim jeans are potential scratch hazards, especially while you lean over a fender or against a body side to reach the hood or roof.

Finding nice soft cloths for removing dry polish or wax is not always easy. Many enthusiasts use only old cloth baby diapers, assuming that they have never been subjected to any kind of abrasive substance. Wentworth has had good luck with soft cotton flannel material purchased at a fabric store for these chores. He cuts sections of the material into about 2 sq. ft. pieces which are easily folded into manageable working sections. After using them for a polish and wax job, he cleans them in a washing machine. When they come out of the clothes dryer, they are soft and ready for the next wax or polish job.

Light coats of quality auto wax actually form protective seals on top of paint finishes. Even though they are quite thin and by no means permanent, these wax seals will prevent solvent evaporation. Should that occur, those vapors which need to exit paint would be trapped. Consequently, as confined vapors continue their evaporation activity and persistence in reaching the open atmosphere, minute amounts of pressure are built up which eventually cause damage to paint finishes, frequently in the form of blistering.

So, instead of protecting a paint surface, waxing too soon after new paint applications can actually cause unexpected damage. Remember, this is wax, not polish. Polish does not normally carry with it any long-lasting protective additives. Its main function is to clean and shine. However, be aware that a lot of new cosmetic paint finish products are now available that are advertised as

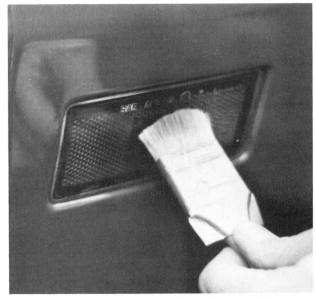

Although careful polishing and waxing should prevent material build-up in seams, emblems or light lenses, there are times when this situation occurs. To gently remove such build-ups, use a small, soft paintbrush with the bristles cut to about ¾ in. The stout nature of these bristles works great for breaking loose and dislodging accumulations of polish, wax and dirt. The strip of duct tape wrapped around the metal band on this paintbrush protects paint finishes from accidental scratches or nicks as the brush is used in confined spaces.

Using the clean end of a paper matchstick, Mycon applies leftover paint to a chip on a Chevrolet Crew Cab. Paint is lightly dabbed into place to effect the repair. You can also use an artist's paintbrush to accomplish the task. Be sure to repair nicks as soon as you find them; deep chips could expose bare metal to oxidation and rust problems. Once rust gets a hold on metal, it travels under paint and will eventually cause extensive paint blistering, flaking and peeling.

cleaner-waxes. In essence, they *do* combine polish and wax ingredients.

Do not use combination polish-wax products until paint has been allowed to cure for at least 90 to 120 days because the wax ingredients in these products will form light seals over surfaces and trap solvents, just like dedicated wax-only products. If you need to effect polish work on a new catalyzed or lacquer paint job, be absolutely certain the polish used contains no wax ingredients. Read labels to be sure, and do not be afraid to consult with an autobody paint and supply store jobber.

Repairing Small Nicks

No matter how hard you try to guard against them, it seems small nicks or paint chips are prone to occur on new paint finishes much sooner than expected. For those vehicles driven on a daily basis, this dilemma is simply unavoidable. Along with rock chips that occur in traffic, parking lot door slammers are merciless. Add to that a long list of other accidental and careless mishaps and sooner or later, your new paint job will suffer some degree of minor damage.

As disheartening as it may seem, small nicks on the paint finish of your car do not have to linger as permanent eyesores. You can repair them with a minimal amount of work, providing they are small and the affected paint job is not exotic. You will need some touchup paint, a small artist's or lettering paintbrush and masking tape.

Clean the damaged area with wax and grease remover and then closely mask off the nick, or nicks. Stir or shake paint as needed. Now, simply dab your small artist's paintbrush into paint and retrieve just a very small amount of paint on the tip of the bristles. Apply that drop of paint to the nick. Do not attempt to fill in the entire nick depth with the first paint dab. Wait for a while to let the first dab set up and then apply a second small dab.

Continue the dabbing and setting up until paint has filled the nick to just over the surface. It should be obvious that too much paint was applied to the spot as work continued. Once this has been achieved, let the new paint cure. Do not touch it for about a week to ten days.

After a lengthy drying period, mask the nick again. This time, though, mask a wider area. Then, use 1200 grit sandpaper with water to gently smooth the nick area and bring the surface of new paint down to the surrounding finish. The application of masking tape will prevent unnecessary sanding on the surface surrounding the repair area.

When you have determined that the newly applied dabs of paint have been smoothed to within the same level as the rest of the finish, remove masking tape. Then, use polish to further

Very fine, 1200 grit Wetordry sandpaper is used to smooth a paint chip application. If the chip had been masked, sanding marks surrounding the chip would be nonexistent. This sanding maneuver must be done carefully, in order to avoid sanding completely through paint down to undercoat materials. Just as important, you must wait a week to ten days before sanding, to let the new paint dry completely so it will sand smooth.

blend the repair into its surroundings. If polishing scratches appear, graduate to a finer polish. Let the repair cure for a few weeks before waxing.

Overview

Automotive paint jobs can last for years as long as their finishes are maintained, protected and not abused. Frequent washing, maintenance of effective wax protection and limited exposure to ultraviolet sun rays will add greatly to almost any paint job's longevity. Although the new catalyzed paint systems are more durable than most paint products employed before them, gross neglect will cause their shine and luster to fade and oxidize over time. It is up to you to maintain them in clean condition and prevent the penetration of lingering dirt, tree sap, bird droppings, airborne pollution, mildew and so on.

The use of soft wash mitts, soft cotton towels and soft waxing applicators and cloths go a long

Worthington always keeps his Porsche 944 under a quality car cover that breathes. This one is from Beverly Hills Motoring Accessories. In addition to protecting the paint finish from insect and bird droppings, it guards against ultraviolet sun rays to prolong the paint's life. If your freshly painted automobile must be kept outdoors, seriously consider the use of such a car cover. Be sure the type you buy is made of a material that breathes. Plastic tarps will trap air and moisture inside their covered areas, which is not recommended.

The preparation work, actual paint application and the tasks that follow will combine to make your car or truck look new, stand out and be a pleasure to admire and drive. To keep it in its pristine condition, you must maintain a consistent schedule of cosmetic and mechanical preventive maintenance. Worthington believes in such a system of automotive upkeep, which is why his Porsche 944 looks, feels and smells like new.

way toward keeping paint finishes in pristine condition. Operating any mitt or cloth on your car's surface in a straight back-and-forth movement will also help to greatly reduce the formation of swirls or spider webbing. Always read the labels of any car wash soap, polish or wax product to determine just exactly what it is intended to do. If you still don't understand, ask for help.

Quality car covers made of materials that breathe provide an excellent means for overall paint protection, especially when your car has to sit out in the sun for days on end. You must realize that the sun is your paint finish's enemy. The more you can do to prevent it from suffering through endless days of baking under harsh sunlight, the longer its shine will last. If a quality car cover is not within your budget now, try parking in the shadow of a building. Or, park head first in the parking lot on one day and then back in the next to alternate sunlight exposure between your car's body sides.

From beginning to end, automobile painting can be interesting, illuminating, fun and rewarding. By the time you have completed your project, a lot of time will have been devoted to sanding, masking, spraying, cleaning and polishing. You will have spent a lot of time reading product information sheets and application guides, as well as conferring with your local autobody paint and supply jobber. You will have spent hundreds of dollars on materials, chemicals, tools and equipment. But, you will have saved a lot more by doing the job yourself and will have also gained a lot more personal satisfaction than you would ever have by simply dropping your favorite car off at the local paint shop.

With the advances in chemical applications and the compatible relationships thereof, automobile painting has become a high-tech profession. The multitude of material choices and their ability to blend or bond with similar, yet unlike substances, has added a great deal of responsibility and caution related to the purchase of any paint system and its application. In this arena, you have to read labels and confirm product usage with your autobody paint and supply jobber. And, you

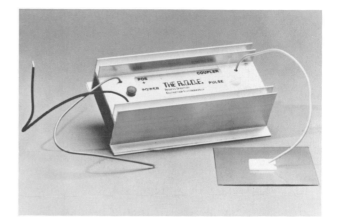

A high-tech new way to protect your paint job from rust damage is the R.O.D.E. The R.O.D.E. (Reduces Oxidation Destruction Electronically) unit runs off the twelve-volt system of your vehicle by a patented method called Capacitive Coupling. A DC voltage is pulsated through all metal surfaces of the vehicle. The voltage electrostatically forms an excess field fluid of ions. This protective field inhibits the formation of rust and oxidation. Custom Trim of Akron

absolutely must acknowledge, accept, understand and incorporate all of the available safety recommendations set forth by paint manufacturers and the regulatory agencies responsible for overall worker safety.

After your job is complete, tools wiped off and put away, materials carefully sealed and stored, your work place squared away and hands clean, stop and take a good long look at your achievement. Although it takes years of experience to become a professional automobile painter, conscientious auto enthusiasts with a keen do it yourself desire to learn can accomplish professional results if they understand the basics and are not afraid to ask for help. By no means is this book intended to be the last word in auto painting, but I hope it has given you the information needed and self-confidence required to at least go out and give it a try.

Sources

Unless a person had decades of professional automotive painting experience, it would be foolish to expect anyone to amass enough information about painting, in all its varied contexts, to write a complete book about it without seeking assistance from a number of sources. Therefore, listed here are names of companies from which I obtained valuable information and material. Included also are addresses where they can be contacted, should you have any questions or comments.

Information or material received from these sources was not necessarily limited to quotes. In many cases, questions were raised by reviewing this information and then answered by professionals like Mycon, Van Hee, Laursen, Murdock and Shrewsbury. So, even though you may not have seen actual quotes from some of these companies or individuals, they were very helpful nonetheless.

The Eastwood Company
Auto Restoration News
Jim Poluch, Christine Collins
Eastwood Advertising
580 Lancaster Ave.
Box 296
Malvern, PA 19355

PPG Industries, Inc.
Linda Toncray, Advertising Manager
19699 Progress Dr.
Strongsville, OH 44136

E. I. DuPont De Nemours & Company
Tom Speakman, Marketing Development
and Services
Wilmington, DE 19898

BASF Corporation, R-M, Glasurit
George P. Auel, Manager
Marketing Communications
19855 W Outer Dr., Suite 401 E
Dearborn, MI 48124

Metalflake Corporation
PO Box 165
Amesbury, MA 01913

Jon Kosmoski's House of Kolor
2521 27th Ave. S
Minneapolis, MN 55406

Hemmings Motor News
Box 100
Bennington, VT 05201

3M Automotive Trades Division
Bldg. 223-6NW 3M Center
St. Paul, MN 55144

Northwest Vintage Tin Magazine
Bill Buxton, Editor
Dick Page, Feature Writer
PO Box 5546
Bellevue, WA 98006

Mitchell International
Collision Estimating Guide References
9889 Willow Creek Rd.
San Diego, CA 92126

Metro Molded Parts, Inc.
PO Box 33130
Minneapolis, MN 55433

Pro Motorcar Products, Inc.
22025 US 19 N
Clearwater, FL 34625

Finesse Pinstriping, Inc.
PO Box 1428
Linden Hill Station
Flushing, NY 11354

Classic Auto Restorer
PO Box 6050
Mission Viejo, CA 92690

Custom Trim of Akron
916 E Buchtel Ave.
Akron, OH 44305

Index